New Voices

New Voices
Student Activism in the '80s and '90s

Tony Vellela

South End Press   Boston, MA

Front cover photos:

Barbara Ransby addressing University of Michigan president Harold Shapiro at racism hearings: Scott Lituchy, *Michigan Daily*.

Chip Mitchell doing telephone organizing at the University of Wisconsin: Mary Martin

Student contingent at the April 25 march in Washington, DC: Linda Miller.

Text Photos:

Columbia students blockade building: Ed Keating; Madison divestment march: Mary Martin; Dartmouth shanties (before): Steve Young; Dartmouth shanties (after): *The Dartmouth;* Take Back the Night: Mary Martin; Back of truck: Doug Calvin; Chicano Student Conference: Sonia Pena; Pouring Coors beer: Frontlash; CIA on Trial project: Elizabeth A. Osder; Marchers in San Francisco: Eric Rasmussen; April 25, Washington, DC: Christopher Noble; American and El Salvadoran students: Doug Calvin; Gay and Lesbian march: Richard Schimpf; National Student Convention: Anthony Ching.

Back cover photos:

Collage by Ed Keating

Manufactured in the United States

Typset, layout and design by the South End Press Collective

Cover design by Tony Vellela and Sheila Walsh

Library of Congress Cataloging-in-Publication Data

Vellela, Tony.
New voices.

1. College students--United States--Political activity. 2. Student movements--United States. I. Title.
LA229.V45   1988   378'.1981'0973   88-4453
ISBN 0-89608-342-X
ISBN 0-89608-341-1 (pbk.)

South End Press, 116 St. Botolph Street, Boston, MA 02115
98 97 96 95 94 93 92 91 90 89 88   1 2 3 4 5 6 7 8 9 10

This book is dedicated to Howard Fink and Sidney Hirth. Each in their own way provided me with the space and time I needed to do my work.

TONY VELLELA is a New York-based journalist and author. He has written for the *Christian Science Monitor,* the Pacific News Service, *Saturday Review, Rolling Stone, Crawdaddy, Campus Voice, Rodale Press,* the Bell-McClure Newspaper Syndicate and dozens of other publications. His first book, *Food Co-ops For Small Groups,* was chosen to be included in the *Whole Earth Catalog.* He has served as a consultant to the New York State Consumer Protection Board and the Harlem Consumer Education Council, and a guest lecturer at the New School for Social Research and Syracuse University. He is a past president of the Consumer Cooperative Alliance, and a member of the National Writers' Union.

Table of Contents

Preface

The vitality of student political activism on today's college and university campuses attracted me to the idea of writing this book. This is not a work of history or sociology or political analysis; instead, my intention has been to capture glimpses of what is happening now, to record the voices of the men and women who are making it happen.

Political activism on campus has an impact that goes beyond students and beyond the university. Many of today's politicians, bureaucrats, labor leaders, organizers and public servants were campus activists, and honed both their skills and their ideologies during their undergraduate days and nights. And every candidate for every office welcomes the eager assistance of politically savvy college volunteers looking for campaign experience. Today's activists appear ready to challenge the existing systems and to assault the institutionalized roadblocks to substantive change.

Campus political activism adds bodies and energies to anti-corporate campaigns, consumer boycotts and drives for safety and environmental legislation. Organized religion also feels the impact of this activity as students organize for equal rights for women and for homosexuals, clashing with some established doctrines, while others look to the church to become more active in issues that concern them.

University administrations have stepped up their efforts to develop a position in relation to political activism. Some have reached out, creating mechanisms that allow students to share in decision-making processes; most, however, regard activism as something to keep in check, and have redesigned their disciplinary procedures, security measures and even, some charge, admissions policies accordingly. The idea of student empowerment has not been welcomed in most university board rooms, even as students continue to chart ways for their influence to be increased and institutionalized.

Between November 1986 and July 1987, I conducted more than 100 interviews with undergraduate and graduate students, as well as others connected to the emerging campus political scene, and travelled to 23 campuses around the country. My colleagues Michael Herman and Miles Pomper, both students, also interviewed people for the book. In addition, with the assistance of Columbia professor Dr. Richard Christie, I drew up a survey that was distributed at the annual conferences of three different national student organizations. This was in no way a scientific review, but it did offer an opportunity to gather comments from students at more than 100 different schools who consider themselves activists. (See the Appendix for the details of the survey and its results.)

To coordinate the information necessary for this project, and assess the direction it might take, I was fortunate to have the capable, reliable assistance of Miles Pomper and Michael Herman, who served as assistants to me. I am grateful too for the participation of Cynthia Peters and John Oakes, who provided valuable editorial guidance. Contributing to the extensive research were Amy Bayer, Mario DiGangi, Allan Freedman, Soterios Johnson, Tom Judson, Jason Myers and Mitchell Orenstein. And the following people were also very helpful: Yosef Abramowitz, John Adamson, Matthew Alexander, Jay Allain, Bruce Allen, Peter Anderson, John Atwell, Philip Ault, Jeff Aurich, Chris Babiarz, Dean Baker, Jeff Bankoff, Michael Barr, Joy Barrett, DeWaine Beard, Chris Benner, Nadine Bent, Michael Berry, Jean Besanceney, Kim Bobo, Josh Boorstein, Carolyn Breen, Gale Brewer, Darryl Brown, Kevin Brown, Harry Browne, Purvette Bryant, Elizabeth Burpee, Sara Buttenwieser, Chris Cabaldan, Mark Caldiera, Doug Calvin, Steve Cancian, Steve Carlin, Amy Carter, Dina Cherin, John Chiaia, Richard Christie, Bill Clay, Doug Coates, Nora Cody, Debi Cohen, Matthew Countryman, Michael Cowan, Bill Cruices, Bob Cutter, Brian D'Agostino, Dennis Dalton, Michael Deacon, Aaron Delwiche, Duchesne Paul Drew, Francisco Duarte, Semyon Dukach, David Edquist, Daniel Ellsberg, Phyllis Englebert, Connie Esberg, Erica Etelson, Ann Evans, Patty Fado, Jerry Farelli, Ed Farmer, Danny Fass, Ethan Felson, Donald Gallegos, Steve Ganz, Joey Garcia, Kevin Geiger, Mark Giaimo, Todd Gitlin, Gus Glaser, Jared Goldstein, John Gorley, Peter Premarajah Granarajah, Doris Green, Matt Greene, Steven Greene, Chris Gunderson, David Gwinn, Rick Harbaugh, Michael Harrington, Kevin Harris, Matt Hayes, Carolyn Helmke, Terry Hillman, Eric Hirsch, Abbie Hoffman, Nicole Hollander, David Hughes, Joe Iosbacker, Sarah Jackson, Cheryl Johnson, Jennifer Johnston, Rob Jones, Jeremy Karpatkin, Emily Katz, Kanani Kauka, Ed Keating, Erwin Keller, Steve Keller, Peter Kiang, Steve King, Ethel Klein, Kirsten af Klinteberg, Rachel Kolman, Nick Komar, Tom Landry, David Lawrence, Bob Lekachman, Jack Lester, Howard Levine, Phil Levy, Gary Lucek, Mark Lurie, Mary Maloney, Jon Mandle, Julianne Marley, Ginnie Martin, John Martin, Steve Max, Jane McAlevey, Elissa McBride, Michael McClatchy, Mary Jean McGrath, Joe McLaughlin, Neil McLauglin, Eduardo Mendicta, David Modesbach, Jose Morales, Roger Morey, Karen Moulding, Kristi Nelson, Billy Nessen, Josh Nessen, Bruce Nestor, Chris Noble, Patricia Noguera, Pedro Noguera, Tim O'Connor, Terry Oechsner, Steve O'Halloran, Dan Orenstein, Bitsy Osder, Lindsay Pahs, Kim Paulis, Mary Pepper, Brain Perkins, Sonia Pena, Miriam Peskowitz, John Peterson, Frances Fox Piven, David Plotke, Jason Pramas, Anna Rabkin, Marty

Rabkin, Heidi Rand, Barbara Ransby, Eric Rasmussen, Chad Reisbach, Michael Reissman, Ted Riko, John Ritter, Jacqueline Ross, Joe Rubin, Mark Rudd, Chris Ruge, Kirkpatrick Sale, Ann Scaritt, Peter Dale Scott, John Scheinen, Mary Scholl, Murray Sexton, Hilary Shadroni, Lisa Sheehy, Bridgette Sheridan, Jim Shoch, Malina Silverstein, Kristine Smock, Peter Soloman, Bill Sonn, Bill Spenser, Jonathan Stein, Jack Steinberg, Tom Swann, Robin Sweeney, Tarek, Amy Thesing, Tony Thesing, David Thompson, Rita Toll, Sophia Taurog, Eric Utne, Maria Varela, Ricardo Velasquez, Carrie Vellela, Jackie Victor, Val Wagner, Joy Wallin, Rodney Ward, Stephanie Weiner, Leonard Weinglass, Lamoine Werlein-Jaen, Dave West, Rick White, Gary Wilkes, Winston Willis, David Wong, Scott Zachary and Howard Zinn.

CHAPTER ONE

Assessing the Situation

It never went away.

It may have subsided, and it certainly changed, reflecting changing times and circumstances, but progressive student political activism never really stopped after the much-heralded anti-Vietnam War era.

College students of the late 1980s live in a different universe than their older brothers and sisters (or parents). How they view the world, and how they choose to act in it, stems from factors and influences college students a generation ago did not encounter. Those who dismiss today's politically active college students as "throwbacks" or "nostalgia freaks" or "escapists from reality" would do well to acquaint themselves with these differences.

Social relationships between men and women, between students of different racial, ethnic, economic and geographic backgrounds, between heterosexual and homosexual students, between students and not-students—all these interactions both complicate the atmosphere on the campus, and make that campus a test area for future encounters.[1] Co-ed living arrangements place students of all kinds in close proximity with one another, forcing them to confront hidden prejudices and feelings of superiority or inferiority, often with dramatic results. Students understand that the personal is political.

Colleges today teach more and more "non-traditional" students—those older than 22; those who are married or divorced, have children, have a full-time job, are seeking to change careers; those who are not able-bodied, those for whom English is a second language.[2] And women students play a larger role in the political life of

5

a campus than ever before. This remarkable diversity provides a demanding political mix as well.

This generation does not face the prospect of being drafted into the armed services, and has grown up with the idea that 18-year-olds have the right to vote (but not to consume alcohol). "Transfer students" are now more common:[3] in 1987, an estimated 20-25% of students graduated from a school other than the one they first entered as freshmen. And taking five years to complete an undergraduate degree also has become an accepted route, to ease financial pressures, or to allow time off for work experience or travel, or to reassess college choices before it's too late to change to another major.

Students organizing on campuses now find progressive faculty members willing to work with them. They experiment with non-hierarchical governing structures and shared decision-making. They enjoy the considerable advantages of computers, and inexpensive printing, all new in the last two decades.

Obtaining an undergraduate degree can easily leave a student heavily in debt,[4] forcing choices designed to satisfy their creditors rather than their ideals, and increasing the pressure to do well academically. Students particularly fear suspension or expulsion and university administrators use those fears to limit political activism—disciplinary measures now routinely stay on campus rather than being turned over to local police.

More studying, plus the likelihood of a part-time job, leave little "free time" for non-academic activities such as political work, but many students are making that choice. On campuses large and small, public and private, rural, suburban and urban, students are working to make their views count. Rallies may draw the spotlight of popular attention, but the organizing needed for such events, for educational campaigns, lobbying or joining with others, especially non-students, to support a particular cause, are the measure of campus activism. And all these activities are taking place, everywhere. To get a general idea of who these students are and what they represent, an informal survey was conducted. Details are in the appendix.

This book considers the issues students are working on: South Africa, Central America, the role of the CIA, the War Machine, the Economy, Racism, Women's Issues, Gay, Lesbian and Bisexual Rights, and Student Empowerment.

Students tend to be drawn by a specific issue: women to women's issues, students of color to groups fighting racism and apartheid, etc. Because our society continues to label people, these features continue to play a part in student involvement. But students rarely fit neatly into one or another of these groupings. There are definite cross-overs in substance, influences and the individuals involved. Some other issues, such as drug testing or the rights of the disabled, are gathering momentum and may soon take their place on this list.

Opposition to their universities' financial ties to South Africa sparked large-scale campus protest in 1985 and 1986. Press coverage of the sit-ins, demonstrations and confrontations led to more protests. Because opposition to South Africa's system of separating races and denying basic rights to non-whites presented a clear-cut moral issue to many students, it was no surprise that the movement found support on campus. What did surprise many was that there was progressive activism going on at all—thousands of students pressuring their administrations to divest and translating these victories into springboards for other political work.

Opposition to American policies in Central America grew slowly, partly as a response to news about the murder of civilians. But an important vehicle for reaching students on these questions has been the firsthand testimony of hundreds of friends and classmates who have gone to see the region for themselves. Tied to that movement is growing opposition to the Central Intelligence Agency's role. Most often these protests have taken the form of efforts to prevent the agency from recruiting employees on campuses.

The War Machine manufactures not only weapons, but information. Students active in this category range from those who oppose nuclear testing to those who favor complete disarmament. On campus, the target is often the use of federal money to conduct war-related research.

Students have reacted to several consequences of the changing economy: some organize to oppose cutbacks in federal money for higher education; others mobilize around broader issues, including the environment. A sizeable number work with those who are hungry and homeless. Coalitions with striking workers, with boycott organizers, with farmers, all link students to political actions on and off their campuses.

For women, many serious issues remain unresolved: access to birth control and abortions, rape prevention and the treatment of rape victims, adequate health care and economic equality.

Students who are gay, lesbian or bisexual have emerged in the last few years with a strong political consciousness and a fierce determination to end the discrimination and homphobia that has often turned to violence.

Student empowerment encompasses every attempt by students to take more control over decision-making within their universities—students seek a voice in curriculum design, admissions, use of student funds, granting tenure to faculty, working conditions for university employees, tuition costs and the role their university plays in society.

Eight national organizations serve the needs of politically active progressive students. The American Committee on Africa (ACOA) has been a leader in raising awareness about political and economic conditions in Africa for decades. When students escalated their attention to the injustices of apartheid, ACOA provided most of the hard information to university groups and to the press at a time when press coverage played a key role in building that movement.

As Central American concerns rose sharply at the beginning of the Reagan era, with a stepped-up effort to intervene in the the region, the Committee in Solidarity with the People of El Salvador (CISPES) started chapters around the country, including many on college campuses, to alert the American public.

The Democratic Socialists of America (DSA), the country's largest socialist organization with chapters in more than 80 cities, maintains a Youth Section organization that keeps an identity and agenda of its own. Chapters on college campuses have been growing in recent years.

The National Chicano Students Association (formerly MECHA) reflects the increased political consciousness of students from Mexican, Central American, Puerto Rican, native American and other backgrounds. Chapters, already common in the west and southwest, are cropping up in other parts of the country, and address ethnic studies, racism, college and foreign policy issues.

The National Student Action Center serves as a clearinghouse for student political activism. A newsletter supplies a rundown of news and upcoming events; the Center also sponsors or coordinates a few events of its own.

The Progressive Student Network (PSN), launched in 1980 in Iowa, is a multi-issue group that believes in strong autonomy for campus chapters, with its newspaper serving as a link among the diverse, somewhat independent affiliates.

Addressing anti-nuclear and anti-military concerns, the United Campuses to Prevent Nuclear War (UCAM) combines education and lobbying to construct its political agenda. The sole campus-only anti-military organization, it is based in Washington, DC.

Through nearly four decades, the United States Student Association (USSA) has been an organization of students involved in student governments on their campuses. While addressing a cross-section of major issues, it emphasizes the impact of federal budgeting on higher education, and on the student's role in formulating university policies.

These national organizations have come to play a prominent role in today's campus organizing. For more information on these and other national organizations, see the appendix.

Other national organizations lend support and materials to campus activists, and some regional organizations, such as the Asian Pacific Students Union or the Northeast Lesbian and Gay Students Union (NELGSU), are a strong presence, as are many state-based Public Interest Research Groups (PIRGs).

Today's student political activism derives from centuries of political upheaval. Students may not have emerged as a fully identifiable political segment of society until the 1960s, but they did participate in many previous movements, lending their bodies to picket lines and marches, and their time to the organizing that created them.

During the Depression era, US college students, like the rest of society, looked to other systems in other countries. "Liberal Clubs" or "Social Problems Clubs" examined the alternatives, which included the American Communist Party. As the decade went on, the threat of a foreign war engrossed many students. "American campuses seethed with politics during the late thirties. Every day there would be some kind of rally or speaker at Sather Gate at the University of California at Berkeley or on the steps of Low Library at Columbia"[5]—though most students and teachers, as in every era before or since, kept themselves separate from the activity. "At the same time, thousands of students all over the country signed the Oxford Pledge, a pacifist import from Great Britain that stated, 'We pledge not to support the United States government in any war it may conduct.' "[6] The threat of war, and falling career expectations, engaged many students in political involvement. The Hitler-Stalin Pact of August 1939, and Russia's annexation of the Baltic states and invasion of Finland, startled young American Communists, and many left the party in disgust.

After World War II, the McCarthy Era brought serious breaches of academic freedom and destroyed many careers. The universities were cowed into accepting their place as havens for apolitical intellectual pursuit. As the 1950s went on, a few journals like *Dissent* demonstrated that progressive, liberal thinking had not been eradicated. Young people opposed to the country's consumerist ethos, like bohemians of earlier generations, gathered in New York's Greenwich Village, in San Francisco's North Beach and in Venice near Los Angeles, to advertise their opposition. The burgeoning civil rights movement and the early anti-nuclear movement were both born in the late fifties, and by the early sixties found curious, politically inexperienced and energetic listeners on college campuses.

A few fledgling independent liberal student groups appeared, such as SLATE at Berkeley, VOICE at Michigan and POLIT at Chicago. US efforts to topple Fidel Castro were greeted by a rash of student "Fair Play for Cuba" committees. National organizations interested in peace, like the American Friends Service Committee and the War Resisters' League, began to extend themselves to students. In 1960, both Students for a Democratic Society (SDS) and the Student Non-Violent Coordinating Committee (SNCC) began to build their respective agendas. Michael Harrington's *The Other America*, published in 1962, opened the eyes of students to hidden poverty within their own country.

In 1964, the issue of student empowerment enjoyed its greatest victory to date—the Berkeley Free Speech Movement. "The actual spark that ignited the Berkeley campus was the question of whether student political activities and recruiting for off-campus issues should be permitted on a strip of university property... This small area had been the marshaling yard for student activists for many months without serious protest from university authorities." Then, on September 15, 1964, Dean of Students, Katherine Towle, notified all student organizations that they could no longer distribute literature on university property if it concerned off-campus issues.[7] A series of meetings, petitions and sit-ins followed, the final one ending in hundreds of arrests and charges of police brutality. On the night of October 1, a milestone in student activism history, one protestor was arrested and placed in a police car; students who were present surrounded the car, then thousands of others joined them, and for the next 30 hours, they held the car and its occupants hostage on Sproul Plaza. Still, almost four more months passed before the university regents acceded to most of the demands presented by the FSM organizers.

Most of today's student activists have at least some familiarity with the history of activism in the 1960s because they feel it has some relevance to their lives and politics. The two most influential organizations of that era are SNCC and SDS.

In January 1960, four black students walked into a ten-cent store and sat down at its lunch counter in the area designated "for whites only." The arrests, confrontations and nationwide headlines that followed showed that black students had opened a new chapter in the civil rights movement. Combining the non-violent principles of Ghandi with Southern Baptist dedication to the "beloved community," the group first met at Shaw University under the auspices of the Southern Christian

Leadership Conference, and heeding veteran activist Ella Baker's advice, remained an independent movement.[8]

SDS evolved from the student arm of the League for Industrial Democracy, a weak coalition of liberals, socialists and some radicals. The students opted for a more radical agenda. Their 1962 "Port Huron Statement" declared that students were willing to fight for a society based on the values of humanism, individualism and community. In 1960, C. Wright Mills, an inspiration to its authors, wrote that students were "possible, immediate, radical agency of change."[9]

Organizationally, SNCC started out as a coalition of already-established campus groups seeking to coordinate their work. SDS, on the other hand, was a tightly controlled hierarchy that attracted loosely-run new groups which identified with its general purposes. Within the next few years, SNCC staff members consolidated their power by voting themselves in as the group's coordinating committee. SDS, on the other hand, feared that it would be accused of creating its own bureaucratic system when it tried to introduce formal ways of conducting its business.

Through the middle sixties, both groups struggled with the issue of what to act on, when, how and where. Both favored grassroots community organizing, but this proved complicated, less clear-cut than some earlier efforts. Young whites were not always welcome or trusted in poor black neighborhoods. Some young black organizers were murdered. SNCC eventually closed its membership to whites. SDS marched through phase after phase, moving finally into more radical activity, as some of its leaders came to believe that this would align them with the struggles of third world peoples.

By the late 1960s, both groups had fallen into disarray, though their influence continued, more through their reputations than their actions. At the 1968 Democratic convention in Chicago, young demonstrators came not only from SDS and SNCC, but also from the Yippies, from the Mobe (Mobilization Committee to End the War in Vietnam), from the Black Panthers, or from no organized group at all. By that time, the movement against the Vietnam War was pulling in larger and larger numbers of students, its appeal to students more compelling than efforts to eradicate economic injustice and discrimination. And while black students had been killed doing political organizing work, no event radicalized students more than the killing of four white students by National Guardsmen on the Ohio campus of Kent State University.

On April 30, 1970, President Richard Nixon announced the invasion of Cambodia. On dozens of campuses the next day, students staged protests—including Kent State, where demonstrators focused on the building that housed the campus ROTC. According to Alan Canfora, a student there at the time, students unsuccessfully tried to set fire to the building.[10] On May 3, Ohio Governor James Rhodes visited the campus and delivered a highly provocative law and order speech. He then called in the National Guard. On May 4, as students assembled, the Guard shot off tear gas. The skirmish escalated. The Guard fired into the crowd, killing four students.

Within the next few days, hundreds of campuses had been shut down, and hundreds of thousands, perhaps millions of students were on strike. Vandalism, riots, building occupations and destruction of ROTC headquarters hit dozens of schools. In numbers far greater than ever before, students proclaimed the country's failure to deal with a flawed foreign policy, and its inability to tolerate dissent at home.

While SDS and SNCC deteriorated as organizations, their contributions toward awakening a student conscience cannot be overlooked. They drew attention to a tragic war and forced Americans to see the truth about it; the black liberation movement was an inspiration to women and gay people to take a stand for their own liberation, protests against corporate immorality led to a more aggressive environmental movement, new civil rights legislation was enacted. And the idea that students could not or should not openly challenge the system was erased.

Campuses did quiet down, especially following America's retreat from Vietnam. The late 1970s were spent institutionalizing the movement gains of the preceding decade: women's centers and black student unions found permanent homes on many campuses; gay and lesbian students began to create formal organizations; student governments sought a greater role in university operations.

By the early 1980s, campuses witnessed new rumblings. US incursions into Central America, the worsening situation in South Africa, a widening gap between whites and people of color, all nurtured a progressive political consciousness that had not been fully exercised in a decade. And the rekindling of activism was not confined to this country. In 1986 and 1987 alone, student protests in a dozen countries catapulted their political establishments into a stark realization that serious problems needed to be faced.

In June 1987, when South Korean president Chun Doo Hwan announced that his successor would be another former general, and that democratic reforms would be postponed, students in that country reacted by taking to the streets. In less than a week, 60,000 students at 45 colleges in six cities rioted over the government's failure to open the selection process. The students succeeded in bringing out deep-seated resentment against the government, and attracted hundreds of thousands of civilians from all segments of South Korean society. In Seoul, students led a sit-in at the plaza of the Roman Catholic Cathedral; soon after, Cardinal Kim Sou Hwan called on the government to reverse its decision. Students stepped up their action, until the government began negotiations with opposition leaders long held under house arrest.[11] In the same week, Chinese students resumed protests calling for more democratization within their country.[12]

In Mexico, Spain and France, millions of students were mobilized during 1986, protesting government plans to narrow access to higher education. When students took to the streets, and insisted on having their voices heard, the threatened policies were reconsidered.[13]

In many countries, students, like working people, belong to a union, linking them to all students in the country. When the position or welfare of students is threatened, union leaders can call for a mass action and be assured of support. Most are part of the International Union of Students (IUS), founded by students from 40 countries in 1946 in Prague. The United States has no national union of students, and is not a member of the IUS, but USSA does send delegates to observe. At the most recent session, held in Prague, according to Dave Edquist of USSA, "There were about 300 or 350 students from 125 countries. It was basically a forum of ideas, how education is a part of a society in each of the countries, and what kind of role it plays. Also, student rights at the universities. Is there some financial aid? Is it free? There were panels and exchange of ideas on peace issues, drug and alcohol abuse among students. Really, workshops on just about everything."[15]

Dave noticed that "on the IUS Secretariat, there was only one woman out of 32 members,"[14] and he talked with two women from New Zealand "who were very upset about the sexism shown to them by students from other countries." There was a lot of third world representation, but no openly gay or lesbian students in leadership positions. "The leaders went out of their way to make us feel more comfortable, because of course there was a lot of anti-US rhetoric—anti-imperialism, from many countries—Africa, Central America. Especially in the peace forum, a lot of people had things to say about US military policies."[16]

In this country, the USSA has often discussed forming a national union of students as a long-term goal. For now, students group themselves by issue, by region or by personal background.

Today's student activism is unique. If any historical parallels are to be drawn, they are usually made with the early 1960s, when the country was also shaking off the influence of a conservative, materialistic period, entering an era of addressing problems left hidden or unattended. But comparisons tend to devalue the legitimacy of these students, to marginalize their lives, and to avoid dealing with the true range of commitments, issues and actions they represent.

CHAPTER TWO

Examining the Strategies

"For me, it's perfect, because I work with a computer all day. I have a computer at home. I deal with information through my computer. I don't want a book. I want something on my computer, because that's where I am all the time."[1]

When the University of Pennsylvania's Rick Harbaugh made a serious commitment to the struggle to end apartheid, he applied his particular talents to a general problem—access to information. His work added a new strategy to the student activists' arsenal of tactics. When Columbia students began building their pro-divestment blockade or when anti-CIA recruitment action heated up at Boulder, student leaders tapped into computer lines to communicate with others around the country, even as the actions were unfolding.

Rick created the "Divestment Disk," which allows users to investigate ties between individuals or institutions (for instance, members of boards of trustees, or universities) and their South African investments. It also helps with mass mailings, coordinates phone trees to mobilize large numbers of people and generally enhances networking functions. The Divestment Disk, which has been made available to progressive student groups for a few dollars, symbolizes the growing prominence of computers in student political organizing, and how their use underscores a basic strategy: know your facts, and know when and how to use them.

Computers are used most often for mailing and membership lists. But increased access to networks, interactive exchange of information and ideas, specialized disks and quick links to others connected to the same issue all spark political creativity among students and compliment other strategies a group may devise. The ability to compose leaflets and newsletters on a word processor and print them out instantly also speeds up the transition from plan to action.

When a hot topic sweeps a campus, dialogue within an internal electronic bulletin board serves as a barometer of the political climate. It also provides one method of identifying and reaching like-minded students who may then gather and form an organization or a support group. In the informal survey, half the DSA and NELGSU students and two-thirds of the USSA students said they use computers in their organizing.[2]

The University of California Student Association (UCSA) inaugurated its Grapevine computer network in early 1987, linking student government leaders throughout the state. UCSA President Michael Berry proclaimed: "The Grapevine is awesome. Our effectiveness has increased ten-fold because of it. I can now walk into meetings with UC administrators armed with data and documents sent from our staff in Sacramento. Previously, it took three days to communicate through the mail, and now it happens instantaneously."[3] The link-up feeds information inexpensively to student government leaders working on their own campuses and also provides system-wide information to those active in lobbying the state legislature. According to UCSA executive director Jim Lofgren, "our next step is the national campaign to link campuses outside California into the system."[4] Already, USSA has placed this objective high on its organizational agenda.

Building coalitions with other sympathetic organizations takes on a new wrinkle with computers. For instance, the DSA Youth Section is one of more than 100 peace-oriented groups around the world connected through PeaceNet.[5] A global computer network, it offers not only information, but the potential for teleconferencing among members. Other networks, such as Civitex, specialize in community development and alternative political problem-solving.

For the Divestment Disk, Rick created "Byteing Back Software." "I think there's a lot of potential. Before I finally got this out the door, I always had the fear that some right-wing organization would beat me to the punch with some similar political software, but this is the first of its kind, not just being a divestment program, but it's political software. It's nice to have the technological edge on the opponents."[6]

Whether it's 20 students in Portland, Oregon, staging a protest against laser weapons, or 20,000 marching down Pennsylvania Avenue past the White House to protest US policy on South Africa and Central America, public actions still occupy a solid place on the list of political strategies, providing an opportunity to speak out in public, explain the cause, and show the depth of their support. These also offer a chance to attract new supporters, students who might be reluctant to attend a meeting, but are willing to stand and listen. More than a few leaders were first moved to take a political position at a lunchtime rally.

Civil disobedience, the act of defying a law and risking arrest, remains controversial, but widely used. Arrests can draw attention to the issue; they can lead to a trial which further spotlights the cause though at times the arrests and those arrested become the focus of attention. Groups planning to engage in civil disobedience have an obligation to inform participants, to alert those not wishing to be involved. When that does not occur, students who support the cause but do not want to be arrested may find themselves in a compromised, even threatening position, and drop away from supporting the group.

Other methods—a panel discussion, forum, speaker or film—give the curious student the opportunity to sample the ideas without making a formal commitment. These events can come out of student government programs, political organizations, community groups or chapters of national organizations.

"Tabling," putting up a table on campus, and stocking it with literature and a volunteer during school hours, gives students a one-to-one contact, less intimidating than meeting "the group." School regulations govern such activities, but location and time of day play a role as well. At the University of Illinois Circle Campus in Chicago, a commuter school, all tabling is done in the Circle Center, its Student Union. Stephanie Weiner explains, "There is one part of that student union where people have to go by. I call it 'the strategic four feet.' Since everybody goes there, students literally walk down the escalator, like they're coming from a press conference, saying to us at the tables 'no, no, no, no,' shooing us away. They put up their collars and get ready to make a run for it to the revolving door!"[7] Many universities restrict tabling sites, hours and who or what has the right to set up a table. Some activists challenge these restrictions, others openly defy them or work through student governments to change the rules.

Postering, or distributing flyers or leaflets is also restricted on many campuses. And while walking around and handing out loose materials requires little planning, it can waste money if copies are discarded unread. Again, local conditions may present specific problems: the University of California at Santa Cruz is divided into eight separate residential colleges spread out through 2000 acres of hills, forests and meadowlands, stitched together by roadways. Organizers board an intercampus bus, give short talks about upcoming events, hand out leaflets, jump off the bus and on to another one. And in some universities, students do "chalking," writing messages about events onto sidewalks, walls or parking lots with chalk, to spread a message.

Teach-ins are still a popular device though full-scale teach-ins, with an auditorium and detailed lengthy presentations, are less common than the smaller version—a circle of people sitting in a public area or an empty classroom, hearing one speaker talk for half an hour and answer questions.

Using the education process itself to change a situation has often been a preferred route: women's groups, civil rights activists and the gay and lesbian rights movement have all worked to introduce courses that will help educate students about discrimination these groups face. In some places, the administration has been persuaded to create a new curriculum or field of study.

On many campuses, students who understand the political potential of a boycott connect their buying power to the pressure it can exert. In the informal survey of student activists, boycotts of Coca-Cola, Coors Beer, Shell, Hormel, General Electric, Campbell's products, Wonder, IBM, Hewlitt-Packard, Sara Lee and table grapes, among others, have been conducted on their campuses.[8] Students have also supported striking workers on and off campus, especially those negotiating with their own administrations.

To aid those affected by US policies in Central America, students have raised money, collected medical supplies, food, agricultural implements and books and other educational materials. Hundreds have decided their most effective contribution is to travel personally to Central America, to provide skills and labor. Similarly, in this country, volunteer activists have applied their energies to help the homeless and alleviate the suffering of the hungry.

Longer-range approaches to change take many forms. The most dramatic, a public trial, may lead to a heightened awareness of the issues under contention. More quietly, students are learning the intricacies of the legal system in their efforts to influence decision-making. When questionable policies flow from a board of trustees or board of regents, they may undertake an education campaign aimed at the board's members; with allocation of state funds to higher education, students are becoming increasingly sophisticated in the lobbying process at the state legislature.

In the broadest sense, political pressure at the ballot box still attracts students who choose to work for or against particular politicians. Always a source of free labor, students now can offer both organizing skills and access to a potentially large voting bloc: candidates routinely include a student organizer while savvy students in turn organize themselves to make sure potential office-holders understand their positions.

On campus, student concerns often parallel those of faculty and staff—questions about the degree of openness from the administration often affect students, faculty and staff alike and these groups are forming coalitions around such issues as military research on campus, the introduction of new courses or non-white representation among all sectors on the campus.

The emergence of politically-active faculty members openly proclaiming their views represents a resource to students. Organizations like Faculty for Human Rights in El Salvador and Central America (FACHRES) coalesce the energies of progressive faculty members across the country.[9] And politically sophisticated professors lend their time as well as their support to student organizing efforts. Faculty members often have access to more comprehensive sources on subjects such as military research, and contribute knowledgeable assistance to protest work. Many were students themselves during the anti-Vietnam War upheavals on campuses.

Howard Zinn, political scientist and historian, and himself an activist faculty member at Boston University, observes "Faculty are almost never initiators of these movements. But I think faculty support is important for the morale of students. And when I go around—every week I speak at one or two college campuses somewhere—and whenever I go around, I see on every campus a little group of young faculty who are right out of the sixties, and are teaching courses which reflect values that are important to students, and I think their presence encourages students, and supports students in what they do. In the '60s, we didn't have that."[10]

The drive for student coalitions, however, is not new. In the past, the failure to find common ground resulted in the demise of many organizations. Today, some of the national student organizations are based on a multi-issue doctrine, and students on particular campuses routinely form coalition groups to pool resources and strengthen political power on campus.[11]

Many campus political organizations still operate in a traditional style, with elected officers, parliamentary procedure and strict majority rule. But that method is rarely adhered to fully. Many groups have officers, but sharply restrict their activities; others delegate specific responsibilities, such as finances, to a committee rather than one person. Operating decisions and the formulation of group policy grow out of discussions where some form of consensus applies. Some groups only turn to voting when no consensus decision emerges, and use of facilitators rather than chairpersons to run meetings has grown—though these methods can block progress if they are not well understood or well executed.

Differences of opinion pepper every meeting about strategies: the correct strategy can enhance an issue or even make it explode on campus; the wrong one may discredit or even kill it. Because students face serious pressures on their academic time, the strategy chosen can be crucial on an individual level. Finally, in choosing among the possibilities, the group must decide whether it is seeking quick, dramatic impact, or building a slow, steady campaign. Few strategies can be labelled "student strategies" alone. And what may be effective for one movement on campus may not work for another on the same campus; a strategy used successfully at one school may misfire at another. The political climate, general awareness about the issue on campus, the resources available and the energy and competence of those involved all color the chances of success for a particular strategy.

CHAPTER THREE

Divestment

The issue which brought a spark to the student movement has been smoldering on and off campus for 25 years. And its history stretches back to the early part of the 20th century.

Ruled for centuries by various combinations of colonialist governments from Germany, Holland and Great Britain, the black population of South Africa made its first attempt at organized non-violent resistance with the creation of the African National Congress (ANC), in 1912. For the next half-century, non-whites fought through legal channels to establish political power. Then, in 1960, police at Sharpeville massacred 69 protestors demonstrating for equal rights. Soon after, non-white political party activity was outlawed.

Since that time, blacks have been systematically removed from white areas and resettled in bantustans, all-black areas with poor social and municipal services, and restricted in their freedom of movement. Of South Africa's 29 million people, only the 4.5 million whites have full political rights and social freedoms. In 1964, ANC leaders Nelson Mandela and Walter Sisulu were arrested and sentenced to life imprisonment for their efforts to reverse the political situation in the country.

In the United States, Reverend Martin Luther King frequently spoke out against the South African government throughout the 1960s, urging Americans to end trade and investments in that country, and some scattered references to apartheid did appear during the Vietnam era on American campuses. But it was not until the late 1970s that any appreciable activity took place. A social action group called Catalyst sponsored travelling speakers to campuses in 1976 and 1977.

19

Because institutions rather than individuals are the largest investors in South Africa, with holdings of $14 billion by 1982, strategies for change targeted university investments connected to that country. College portfolios routinely held stocks in companies deeply involved in South Africa, including Johnson & Johnson, General Motors and IBM. Actions at Hampshire College prompted its board to become the first American college to divest in 1977. Campaigns on campuses moved beyond the northeast. In Kansas, for example, the Kansas University Committee on South Africa, founded in 1978, dedicated itself to winning complete divestment.

When political activity by South Africa's blacks increased in 1985, the government declared a state of emergency. Americans responded with frequent demonstrations at the South African embassy in Washington, including a blockade that February involving nearly 400 students. Years of education on campuses paid off as students mobilized to react to the increase in state repression. Sit-ins and rallies cropped up around the country that spring.

The explosion of protests was ignited by the prolonged and volatile blockade at Columbia University in New York City. As early as 1983, the college's university senate had gone on record in support of divestment, but efforts over the next two years, including petition drives and small protests, had failed to move the university's board. Columbia's Coalition for a Free Southern Africa (CFSA), formed in 1982, continued to push for divestment, with regular campus protests. On March 25, 1985, seven CFSA members began fasting to show their commitment to the issue. When fasters confronted several trustees and asked what it would take for the board to meet with CFSA, they were told, "Keep on fasting."

On the anniversary of the assassination of Martin Luther King, April 4, about 300 students rallied at the campus Sundial, focal point for many political demonstrations. After hearing speeches, the crowd was urged to march through campus to show support for divestment. When they arrived at Hamilton Hall, they found rally organizers had chained shut the doors to the building. They were invited to sit down on the steps and blockade the entrance as a further indication of their commitment. Hundreds did so.

Because of Columbia's history—during the late 1960s student action closed down the university—and its New York City setting, this dramatic action immediately attracted national media attention. Within days, students eager to force their universities to divest staged protests of their own from Boston to Berkeley and at dozens of places in between. During the next year, sit-ins, blockades, rallies, confrontations with trustees and, most dramatically, the construction of makeshift cardboard and wooden shanties spread the message of divestment. When right-wing students at Dartmouth College sledgehammered the shantytown there, the resulting press coverage showed students that introducing this visible symbol could bring further attention.

Through the efforts of the ACOA's student organizing project, as well as the PSN and DSA, word spread on how to conduct various styles of protest. By February 1987, student political action had brought 128 schools to pledge to fully or partially divest holdings connected to South Africa. Schools ranged from Ivy League giants such as Yale and Harvard, and large state systems such as California and Wyoming, to Berea College in Kentucky, Spelman College in Georgia, Saint Augustine's in North Carolina, Ohio Wesleyan and Grinnell College in Iowa. Nearly $4 billion in investments have been affected.[1]

When the United Nations Special Committee Against Apartheid held hearings in June 1986, student representatives from 25 American unversities were the star witnesses.[2] From schools as diverse as Texas Christian, the University of Washington at Seattle, Vanderbilt and Purdue, reports of increased activism filled the special session.

Joshua Nessen, ACOA's national student coordinator, told participants: "Even while moving towards more direct action, organizers have recognized the critical importance of ongoing educational work and non-confrontational forms of protest, such as rallies and pickets. However, while these forms of protest help to build campus support, they have a limited effect given the undemocratic governance of the university by absentee, corporate-dominated boards of trustees. Especially on an issue like divestment—involving university finances—the formal channels are not subject to student or faculty control. In addition, while years of rallying set the basis for escalation, without direct action tactics there was limited coverage and public awareness of student organizing."[3]

And one after the other, students told of increased divestment action on their campuses during the previous school year. Darin Dockstader, University of Utah: "The most significant show of student support came on the 26th of March with a student march to the administration building to present a petition with some 3,000 signatures to university president Chase Peterson."[4] And Irene Furuyama, University of Hawaii: "Our last activity was a demonstration on June 16 in observance of the Soweto uprising. Every demonstration we organized grew larger in the number of individuals and groups who came and joined us in supporting the fight for freedom in South Africa."[5] And from Keith Jennings, Atlanta University: "The demonstrations, the construction of on-campus shanties, the sit-ins and take-overs reflect growing dissension against administration policies and lay the foundation for a new student movement."[6]

In New York, February 6-8, 1987, a regional conference to discuss the future of divestment organizing opened with remarks from representatives of the Southern Africa Liberation Committee, the Namibian liberation movement, SWAPO, and the Patrice Lumumba Coalition, all urging students to stay with the struggle. In workshops, delegates gave examples of the actions on their campuses, learned of the regional aspect of US intervention in southern Africa, the corporate and bank strategies, and discussed the role of American racism in the development of the US anti-apartheid movement. Rick Harbaugh introduced the "Divestment Disk" and offered to give copies to anyone who believed they could use it. The project, Byteing Back Software, now overseen by Jon Mandle, continues to work on the use of computers in divestment activities.

Campaigns continue at schools where divestment has not been achieved. During the annual Weeks of Action, called by ACOA in the spring of 1987, students held educational programs, conducted teach-ins, observed moments of silence, wore black armbands, and raised support money. Some targeted recruiters from South

Africa-invested corporations coming to their campus to find potential employees. At schools where divestment has been won, attention is shifting to corporate investors in South Africa, and to the issue of domestic racism.

The huge march on Washington on April 25, 1987 (discussed in more detail below), called "Mobilization for Justice and Peace in Central America and Southern Africa," attracted about 150,000 people, including an estimated 20,000 students. A smaller version of the same march took place in San Francisco.

Student-to-student sympathetic support has also included fundraising to sponsor the Solomon Mahlangu Freedom College in Tanzania for the many South African students forced into exile. Working through their national organizations, students have urged support for a series of bills introduced in Congress to send aid to the nine independent nations of southern Africa, grouped together in 1979 as the Southern African Development Coordination Conference (SADCC). Students have continued to push for more stringent and more inclusive sanctions by the federal government, a total ban on trade with South Africa and on intelligence-sharing with its government.

The regional scope of the situation in southern Africa is increasingly the subject of discussion on campuses as students learn that the strength of the South African regime rests on its political and economic domination of southern Africa. ACOA literature and personal testimony from refugees have informed students about refugee camps in Angola and arrests and torture in Namibia.

And the call for economic pullout has moved to a larger arena as students target corporations and banks directly. The April 13, 1987 edition of *Banking Week* reported student protests at the New York headquarters of Citicorp, the only US banking company to maintain a physical presence in South Africa, with simultaneous protests at Citicorp subsidiaries in Chicago, Baltimore, Syracuse and Tucson.[7] Sovran Financial Corporation, Shell Oil Company and Johnson & Johnson also saw student protestors at their premises.

One of the most successful campaigns unfolded at Johns Hopkins University in Baltimore. Using the Divestment Disk, the JHU Coalition for a Free South Africa identified seven trustees who were also directors of the Maryland National Bank which had extensive financial ties to South Africa. The students orchestrated a serious, longterm effort, picketing the bank's Baltimore headquarters for a month and a half, interrupting recruiting attempts by the bank at Hopkins, and constructing a shanty outside the bank headquarters.

When Maryland National attempted to merge with another bank, students blocked consideration of the request, invoking the Community Reinvestment Act and citing the bank's practice of "redlining," denying mortgage loans on the basis of geographical location. Johns Hopkins students fashioned a citywide grassroots coalition involving citizen and housing groups, the local NAACP, union representatives, and others. The results:

- Maryland National ended all financial ties to South Africa

- Maryland National agreed to commit $50 million over a five-year period to low-income Baltimore neighborhood development

- Maryland National agreed to offer free checking account service to low-income customers, including college students[8]

The new coalition is now pressing Johns Hopkins to accelerate its rate of divestment and to release university-owned housing to low-income and homeless community people.

In San Francisco, the Interfaith Center on Corporate Responsibility, has recommended ending the rescheduling of the South African foreign debt and trade financing as tactics for weakening the apartheid state of South Africa. A leaflet advises: "It is easy to find out if your bank is providing financial services such as trade financing to South Africa. Just call and ask:

- (to the international currency teller) I need to make a wire transfer to Johannesburg, South Africa. Do you have correspondent bank facilities at any bank there?

- (to the international loan officer) I own a local business and I need to arrange financing for some sales I'm making to a company in Johannesburg, South Africa. Can you provide a 30-day letter of credit?

If the answer to either question is yes, begin a campaign against that bank."[9]

Recently, students have been called upon to scrutinize past victories. ACOA has warned students of the need to track the actual progress of their university's divestment plan, especially since some companies which have announced that they are divesting are in fact simply switching titles—a paper shuffle. An ACOA newsletter to students reported: "In response to the divestment movement and political\economic unrest in South Africa, major US corporations have announced plans to 'disinvest' from South Africa. These disinvestments fall into two categories: 1) Genuine corporate withdrawal: as in the case of Kodak which will sell its assets and halt all sales of its products in South Africa. 2) Corporate shell games in which formal ownership changes but provision of products and technology continues—as in the cases of IBM, GM, and Coca-Cola following the lead of GE, GTE, Motorola and Navistar."[10]

The newsletter concludes that "in the face of these corporate moves anti-apartheid groups have explicitly stated that companies which have licenses and franchises in South Africa will remain divestment targets."[11] These "sham divestments," the newsletter notes, permit universities to interpret the promise to divest in a way that allows them to hold on to those corporations that have successfully shuffled papers. In California, where activists proclaimed victory when plans were announced to divest the University's $3.1 billion in holdings, the question is especially crucial. Many campuses have announced their intention to monitor closely of their trustees' actions.

SCENE

The Divestment Blockade, April 1985

Strolling along Upper Broadway, I could hear a distant rumbling of chants coming from the Columbia University campus. Passing through the large wrought-iron archway gates, I could hear bullhorn speeches, the words not distinguishable, the mood very clear.

Hamilton Hall, seat of the offices of the deans, was once again, as in 1968, the center of it all. Its entranceway, marked by three double doors and seven granite steps, stretches some 40 feet, but the area was covered with sitting, sprawling, hunkering students, maybe two hundred of them, debating, laughing, reading, conferring and establishing a presence. Armchairs and sofas dragged out from a nearby dormitory offered some comfort. Tarps were rigged up to provide shelter; blankets covered some who slept. The Columbia blockade was in its ninth day.

Justice Bruce Wright had issued a restraining order blocking the university from bringing police onto the campus to break up the blockade. Students passed along tattered copies of articles from the city's newspapers. From the sidelines, two dark-haired young women in bulky quilted coats offered the protestors bags of fruit, bottles of juice and cookies.

The group was racially mixed, with equal numbers of women and men. Spirits seemed remarkably high, given the disagreeable mid-April weather and the continuing uncertainty of the situation: leaders of the action received letters threatening them with expulsion within 48 hours of the start of the protest; disciplinary notices were issued to 30 more students within the next three days.

Cheers greet messages of solidarity from the African National Congress, rousing those few who had dropped off to sleep. Students drifted in and out, asking the blockaders what they hoped to achieve. Replies generally expressed unequivocal moral conviction, an inability to ignore their school's complicity, using student tuition money, in the worsening situation for black South Africans.

Later that day, a contingent of 150 Harlem neighbors marched to the blockade site to show support and bring food. Within a few days, 2,000 people were drawn to hear Jesse Jackson offer his support on a rainy, dreary afternoon. And the following week, the leaders would appear on the Phil Donahue Show, spreading the word about the blockade, the issues and their level of commitment. For most of America, the action was legitimized—something was happening on college campuses. Again.

INTERVIEW

Rob Jones, Columbia University   *June 4, 1987*

Rob Jones was present at the beginning of the divestment movement at Columbia University, and was a principal player in the campaign and the eventual blockade of Hamilton Hall. He now works with ACOA, lobbying legislators to pass laws divesting state government holdings in South Africa.

TV—*When was the Columbia steering committee put together?*

RJ—In the fall of '83. The history is that in '81 a bunch of the people in the Black Students Organization, myself included, sat down and said, look, there's been all this stuff going on around South Africa. We need to do something. We contacted ACOA, got some information, did some tables and a couple of forums, brought up a speaker from the ANC, brought up a speaker from ACOA. In '82, when I was away, Barbara Ransby who was in the student senate, brought the issue up there and the senate passed a resolution unanimously that the school should divest. When I came back, things were coalescing so that there were regular meetings and it was time to regularize the leadership. The organization by that time was called the Coalition for a Free South Africa. We sat down and figured out we needed a leadership body that was (a) mostly black, (b) mostly political and (c) able to answer to the needs of the campus and make links between the campus and the community and be political.

TV—*Was it still an internal project of the Black Students Organization?*

RJ—No. By '82, the Coalition formed. Barbara Ransby and Danny Armstrong were clearly the leadership, to the extent that they were the spokespeople. In '83 the decision was made to set up a steering committee to take responsibility for getting work done, because Barbara and Danny were getting burned out—Barbara did most of the writing, Danny did most of the speaking. If you've got a movement, you have to make sure there are enough people willing to work on an ongoing basis to support it. The steering committee functioned very well. It met, at minimum, once a week, and usually twice a week. At that point the coalition was meeting every other week, and doing a tremendous amount of work—demonstrations, forums, information tables, going through a whole process in the university senate a second time. When the steering committee was formed, it already had a mandate: it said, "Look, the senate said this is what has to happen, but the administration has done absolutely nothing." And it worked very, very well. By that time, we were pulling 500 people regularly any time we had a demonstration, and 100 or 150 any time we had a forum. The steering committee was mostly black but there were always one or two white people because we wanted to make it absolutely clear that it was not all black.

TV—*This was a committee of how many people?*

RJ—It fluctuated; usually around nine or ten. At the end of the year, some people would always be leaving, and so as a group we would sit down, figure out the number of slots there were, and, based on the activity of the people during the year, we would approach them and say, "Are you willing to take on this responsibility?" not "Are you willing to get this honor?" We never looked at it as, "We're leaders, and we're so important"—no, "We have a lot of work to do, and if you're willing to work really hard, we want you." It was absolutely imperative to have at least seven or eight people working on a regular basis, to get the posters out, do the phone calls, draft the resolutions. So that was always the conception of the steering committee in our minds.

TV—*Were you in touch with people at other schools?*

RJ—At that point, not really. We were very Columbia-centric, but we were also very conscious of making links to the Harlem community. We had speakers come up all the time, and always were trying to make links to Columbia's housing policy. During that period, there was a struggle for union recognition for the clerical workers, and we did a lot of good work together. When they did demonstrations, we spoke; when we did demonstrations; they spoke. We did joint leaflets.

TV—*What happened between then and the spring of '85?*

RJ—We went through a series of university processes. We went back to the senate and tried to get them to put forth a resolution condemning the university for not having followed through. We tried a number of things—one was a senate resolution calling on the university to put together a commission to study the issue of divestment and take recommendations back to the senate.

TV—*That sounds like something they'd go for.*

RJ—They loved it. We were excluded from that process. We fought very, very hard and won the right to have a representative on that commission. And learned by a year's wasted time, basically, that that's exactly what the commission was set up for: to try and dilute the movement and make sure we spent all our time lobbying these folks, writing documents and trying to convince them, as opposed to saying, "Look, we don't care how you do it, this is what you need to do and until you do that, we're going to keep messin' with you." As we all look back on it now, it was a complete waste of a year's time. We tried to name somebody to the commission who wouldn't be biased, and made a tremendous mistake, because we were trying to have a spy, someone who could seem on the up-and-up, but really (a) be reporting back to us, and (b) taking direction. And he agreed, and everything was all set. But as time went on, we found ourselves fighting with both the commission and with this person, because he was being co-opted. The report came out, and said, basically, that South Africa's bad but we should continue the policy of not investing in banks, and investing in the Sullivan Principles,[12] because we don't want to cut and run. The person we named didn't sign it, but it was clear his opposition was half-hearted. We had a whole dissenting opinion for him, and he wrote one page and tacked it on, and didn't fight to see that it was included. When he was interviewed in the press, he said we pressured him, and that he was afraid of us, that we were going to physically assault him—it was terrible, terrible, terrible. But we came through that process, and realized that's just nonsense. It had been set up to try and make the university look as if it was "bargaining in good faith." That was the spring of '84. We were fighting internally, in terms of whether to deal with the report, what it meant to participate in that process. But it didn't do what it was designed to, which was (a) split us up, and (b) render us ineffective. The deans would approach individuals in our group, and say, "If you sit down and talk, we can get some more language in." They were constantly trying to pit folks against each other. At the end of the 1984 school year we didn't have our normal huge protests and stuff like that—we were still effective, getting information out, having meetings, and people were still interested in the issue, but the report came out three days before graduation. That fall, we again had turnover on the steering committee, but it was a smooth transition. There was always dissension, different positions on how to move forward. But one thing we do that has served us tremendously well ever since: we never were undisciplined in public. If we had a problem, we would sit in a room for six hours if we had to, until we hashed out a consensus. And people were very good at maintaining that consensus sometimes saying to themselves, "Well, I don't agree with this, I think this is a really stupid thing to do, but most of you do, and I'm a part of this, so that's where I'll put my energy and time."

TV—*Did you feel you needed to move to another step, but maybe did not know exactly what it should be?*

RJ—Exactly. That fall was a very difficult time. People had spent a tremendous amount of time the year before on this whole university-senate-commission process, and so they were in academic trouble, had papers to finish and incompletes to do. The year before we had tried to set up an alternative investment fund, but it didn't work very well. We were thinking, should we put a lot of energy into that? We continued doing what we normally did, protesting at trustees' meetings, and that year we took it to the opening football game. But everything was in flux, it was very difficult. We tried to protest alumni support, and got about 15 people to come out; then we did something else and got one or two hundred—it was kind of back and forth. People were looking to us for direction, and we weren't really able to provide it in a concrete way. By the end of the semester we decided we had to do something. We went into the spring with a lot of energy. We did a lot of mobilization. The steering committee at that point was about eight folks. We were getting 40 people to meetings. There had been times when we were getting 75. So when we thought about doing a blockade, we really didn't have any idea whether it would be successful or not. But we knew there just had to be an escalation or things would die right down. Even if they kept going at the same level, the university would have won.

TV—*How much real planning was there?*

RJ—A lot. A lot. We had to figure out what the implications were, how we were going to do it, how we would handle being arrested, and how we would handle violence and verbal assaults, and how we would get into the buildings—which doors closed which ways. Despite whatever personal differences there may have been, that group worked as a unit. Outside the steering committee, there were probably eight people who knew. But those people knew they were not to tell their lovers, their friends; they were not to tell their mothers. The only reason they knew was because we needed them to do X, Y and Z on the day of the blockade.

TV—*The actual blockade took place on...*

RJ—April 4. We started the planning about two months in advance. By that time we had had so many demonstrations that we didn't ask for permits any more. That was part of the political statement. We just said, "Look, fuck it, you guys have messed with us so badly." They wouldn't give us office space, they wouldn't give us any funding, half the time they would deny us a permit, or put us off in a corner of campus, or say we had to do it at a time when nobody would come. When we wanted to demonstrate, we'd demonstrate, wherever we wanted to. Most of the steering committee wasn't at that demonstration. They were carrying out plans. There's a whole system of tunnels under Hamilton Hall and other buildings and we had figured out ways to get into Hamilton Hall, and get out, via the tunnels. There were three of us inside the building already, when the demonstration was happening. We had a system of signals to let people know, because there were two sets of doors, and I was on the inside; there were people on the outside. When we heard the signal, we went to work chaining the inside doors. Our people on the outside came out from behind the bushes they were behind and chained the other doors, just as the people from the rally, who had started to march around campus, were arriving.

TV—*What was the signal?*

RJ—It was the start of a specific chant. Even before the demonstration got there, there were six or seven people in place. And when the demonstrators saw what happened, they said "Yeah!" But I didn't see any of that, because I was inside. We had anticipated the administration was going to say, "You've cut off access to the building." So one of the tasks of those of us inside chaining doors, was to have spray paint and tape, and go down through the tunnels putting up signs saying "This Way Out" all along the route so the administration coudn't say we had made it too difficult for people to exit in case of emergency. The funny part was, I ran into the head of security and a dean coming my way, as I was going the other way, spray painting and putting up signs. They weren't in enough control of the situation to arrest me, which they should have done. So I continued on.

TV—*Did you have plans if it were to run for days or weeks?*

RJ—No. We were deathly afraid the blockade was going to be 25 people, and that people were going to think this was the stupidest thing anybody had ever suggested and it would last, like, three hours. We were thinking we would try to get it to last two days; that would have been a victory. But by the afternoon, it was clear we had something on our hands we had not prepared for. We had done no planning if people decided they were going to stay. But we were a working unit. The first three days were hell, absolute hell. We didn't know what was going on, and the administration kept trying to mess with us. They would send security around, with bullhorns, and they kept harassing us to the point that everybody's nerves were on edge. Nobody slept for the first three days. We were sure they were going to raid us, and carry us out in the middle of the night, when we couldn't get any press. Because during the day, there was a tremendous amount of press, that kept up throughout. But by the end of the third day, we had certain systems in place, and were ready. The problem was that we had split up the steering committee. More than half the committee had gone on a fast, starting the week before, so by the time we did the action, those people were about ready to lie down. They'd been fasting seven days. Only four of us were not fasting, and two of those four were not willing to be arrested, so whenever security came they had to disappear. So by that time everybody that had ever worked anywhere close and come to meetings considered themselves leadership and were willing to take on tasks and responsibilities.

TV—So you had the front steps of Hamilton blockaded though others could come in and out through tunnels. And then what happened?

RJ—We immediately started planning for a large rally. We had posters made up, made contact with some of the unions that brought us everything from blankets to food and gave us money. They also brought the thing that was absolutely most important, and we didn't know it at the time—huge tarpaulins. The first time it rained, we didn't have anything set up, and people just got really soaked. It was disgusting. The unions came in and brought tarps, and we had set up this whole elaborate thing with ropes. People worked really, really hard; it was not a spectator sport. Either they were involved in trying to get their schoolwork done, and still be a part, or they were involved in getting flyers done, cooking food, dealing with the media, with publicity, with maintaining and policing the area. Every night the blankets came out, every morning they had to be put back inside. We swept up and cleaned, and made sure they couldn't throw us out for that. And also because we lived there. By the third or fourth day, there was trash all over the place—cleaning up was one of the details that organized itself every day. The steering committee was always in a position to decide what would and would not happen, but by the time the first week was up, basically the policy was, if you want to do something, find somebody on the steering committee and tell them you're going to do it. And unless they say "Wait, there has to be a decision taken on that," go ahead. But make sure that somebody knows what you're doing. Because we were also very careful about spies, and agents provocateurs and saboteurs, so any time we saw something happening, we wanted to know who initiated it. We had a policy of never going to somebody and saying, "Hey, what are you doing?" We'd go around to the other people on the steering committee and say, "Do you know what's up?"

TV—Were there spies?

RJ—Oh, sure. There were fake reporters, FBI, the administration, New York Police Department.

TV—The event really grew?

RJ—When Jesse Jackson came, we had a crowd of 5,000 people out there. But we also organized four major demonstrations of over 1,000 people—one was on the theme of the Harlem community salutes Columbia for taking a stand against racism, and four or five hundred people from Harlem must have come, and brought banners and food. It was absolutely wonderful. That was one of the things that we wanted to make very, very clear, especially to a lot of the kids who were out there. It's all fine and well and good to demonstrate against South Africa. It's racism, but it's far away, and you don't have to deal with any of the racism that's going on inside your head, your mind, your body. We made a constant and continual effort to make sure that they got an education that they'd never forget. We had speakers come up from the Patrice Lumumba Coalition, from the black community, talking about what it's like to be black in the United States, what the implications of our actions were in a larger context. Teaching, and preaching and educating. There certainly was an element of, "this is a party and I want to be a part of it." But there was also an element of people taking control of their own lives and their own circumstances, and that feels good. "Nobody can tell me what to do except the people I'm doing it with. The university has been messing up, and my educational process has not been the way I wanted it to be and here, I can say something about that." I also have a personal analysis that the level of participation we got from white middle- and upper-class students was a reaction to what was going on across the country, in terms of Reagan, and the control that was being taken away from people's lives. I feel that Reagan really separated the realities of life from people, and separated politics from people. And this was a chance for these people in this situation to get that back somehow.

INTERVIEW

Mark Lurie, Boston University   *December 21, 1986*

After graduating from Boston University, Mark Lurie remained in Boston to help organize region-wide support on college campuses for divestment.

TV—*How do you keep in touch with students active in apartheid work?*

ML—We had this network set up that was medium to strong on about 35 campuses just in New England. We're on a big outreach campaign now, using this new film out of South Africa, called "South Africa Unedited" done by a black-and-white photographic collective called Afrapix during the state of emergency.

TV—*Were connections made with other schools while you were at Boston University?*

ML—Yeah. When BU gave Buthelezi [chief of the South African-desginated Zulu bantustan Gathca Buthelezi] his honorary degree, we did a big rally and got a lot of people from other schools from Boston, and even a couple people from Vermont and New Hampshire. At one earlier BU rally, 14-15 schools just in Boston participated. A year ago, two years ago, well, it was "we'll do our thing on our campus," but now they're really looking outward to other campuses to see what they can learn, and see how they can help, which is kind of exciting.

TV—*How did things start at BU?*

ML—In '82-83 when I got there, there really wasn't anything. I went to a few meetings in my sophomore year, and got really turned off. People didn't know what they were talking about, or where they wanted to go. The following year somebody organized a South Africa Awareness Week. Right after that, it really sparked. People started to get very involved. At the same time, a group formed on campus with some professors, concerned faculty and students, and we met regularly on Tuesdays for two hours, at least, for a whole semester. We put together a rally for student rights, addressing some pretty important issues, looking at the whole university, [BU President John] Silber's role in foreign affairs, the issue of minority involvement, and some professors talked about how BU had failed to give tenure to a lot of professors who have spoken out against the adminstration. It was a pretty big rally. I think the education week sparked everything up.

TV—*Did any coalitions develop?*

ML—Well, the history of the Southern Africa Task Force is that people looked at them, at us, as a bunch of radicals yelling a lot who didn't know what they were talking about, which I think is partly valid. This past year, because a lot of them were suspended, it was a great opportunity for a new group to emerge. A couple of people have been organizing a coalition that includes faculty and unions and headed by some of the black students.

TV—*Was there a black students union at BU?*

ML—Four years ago, they had a very strong union, and Silber or the dean of students decided that, rather than have one big union, they should be divided. In fact, this dean was a black guy, Dean Carter. They decided there should be a minority law students association, a minority liberal arts association, and this and that, obviously in an attempt to weaken the whole thing. And now they're all coming back together again. The Martin Luther King Center is like the union for minority students. The guy in charge just quit his job, reporting that Dean Carter had asked him to spy on the black student union.

TV—*Were there many blacks active in apartheid work at BU?*

ML—I think they weren't involved for the reason that most people at BU weren't involved. They had very little respect for people in the group. They didn't want to work with them. A lot of people in the group were paternalistic. I think that attitude forced a lot of people—both black and white—to not be in the group. Also the group that started up after the rally—before we knew it, it was pretty strong—had no black people involved. And nobody wants to step into a group that's already solid, where some leadership has already emerged. We went to Umoja, the black students union, and to all the minority groups and asked them to be involved, but that's not the way it should be. You shouldn't say, "Here's our group, come and join us." It should all have been done together. Time played a factor in that, and ignorance. We didn't really know what we were doing.

TV—*Some black students say they sometimes resent white students getting so involved in South Africa issues.*

ML—I think that's true, too. I think it's important for people to face that issue. I'm involved because I was born and raised in South Africa, and I saw it and I feel like my voice speaks a little louder than American students because I'm a white South African. For other people, I think it's a lot easier to be involved in South Africa, because you don't have to make personal sacrifices, you don't have to change yourself, your behavior. I think that turned a lot of black students off. Here you are preaching about South Africa, but not bringing it back home to a personal thing, saying how come I still feel uncomfortable sitting next to a black person? Why don't I make eye contact with a black person when I'm walking down the street? It's important for us all to work together, but whites have to change our attitudes on a personal level, as well as preach about non-racism a long way off. I don't think BU people were bringing it back home on the personal level.

TV—*Does the personality of John Silber as president of BU effect political activism there?*

ML—He deals with a fist of steel. Students protest, set up a shantytown, they get arrested, they get kicked out of school. Across the river, students are protesting at Harvard. They block a dinner, do civil disobedience, and nobody gets arrested. Silber's tactics are much more extreme, and he scares the shit out of people. And those who are on the fringe about whether or not to get involved, even those who have been involved, are definitely affected by an attitude that they don't feel that they can change anything.

TV—*Did you change your views about tactics, maybe look at lower profile work, like education?*

ML—Actually it went the other way. We figured the way to get at Silber and BU was through bad press. Apparently, they have the largest p.r. staff in the school's history, and they're constantly pushing his name out, trying to get good press for the school, and that was a way we thought they were vulnerable. We feel like we've done an incredible number of things on campus educationally, yet people are still resigned that they're not going to be able to change anything. And yet, every day they have to read in the paper, something like "Students who protest are ignorant." He lashes out at people, and people don't want to deal with that. And that's what he wants, he wants you to go through there and not make any waves. And one way to do that is to scare people. That's why they photograph you.

TV—*You once said there were about 50 committed people. How does that compare with a few years ago?*

ML—Oh, much more. Even up till six months ago, if you had 10, 12 committed people, it was a lot. I think the numbers are increasing. People are polarizing. One side is moving towards the complacent, the defeatist attitude, and one side is saying we really have to deal with this, to try and resolve some of the problems. But I think there's hope for a much bigger movement, especially with the black students being involved now. Somebody at the rally said that we have the best political organizer, and that's Silber. He just does things that are so outrageous and we react to it. And that's partly true.

INTERVIEW

Josh Nessen, ACOA   *May 2, 1987*

Josh Nessen worked on the preliminary campaigns that led to the first college divestment of holdings in South Africa—in 1977 at Hampshire College in Massachusetts, with a student coalition called Catalyst. He now works with ACOA fulltime on student anti-apartheid and divestment organizing.

TV—*Why was there such a visible explosion of this issue in early 1985?*

JN—First of all, things in South Africa really escalated. By the fall of 1984, there had been several killings, there was a two-day general strike, things were beginning to get going. The other thing was that people were somewhat encouraged by the embassy protests. I think all that educational work over the years built up. People were conscious of a need to break out of a certain bind. There was a meeting that January where people consciously talked about April 4 as a time for direct action tactics. And Columbia played a role, sort of a spark—they were quite conscious that April 4 was a national protest day. They saw it as a key time to do the blockade. And other schools were encouraged to go ahead. At Berkeley, there had been a blockade in the fall of '84.

TV—*Did the press attention to Columbia help much?*

JN—It certainly made people aware and encouraged them. Even without the media, folks knew, through the grapevine, that it was occurring and there was communication within the movement about this. There were a lot of protests. Rutgers students literally came to the blockade and asked how it was done. There was a big event in Washington, April 20. Word went out that April 24 would be another day for protests. There must have been actions on more than a hundred campuses.

TV—*But it was decentralized?*

JN—Decentralized. People knew that April 24 was a day we would try to go to another level. ACOA was in touch with almost all the places and we played a role in communication; we got it announced from the stage on the 20th, during the Washington march. One really key thing was that right before, there was this killing near Sharpeville. It was in the air. Folks sensed that this was the moment—but the organizing had to be in place to take advantage of that moment. If people hadn't been doing divestment work at least for that year, no one would have responded.

TV—*When did shanties appear as an organizing tool?*

JN—At Columbia, they had a "sit-out," not a "sit-in." The idea that you would have something that was more open to people, that wasn't just barricading a building, may have been the origin of the open-air shanties. Cornell was probably the first place to really set up a shantytown in the spring of '85; they set up something like a community, where they would organize. People would move into the building they had set up and people kept being arrested. It was seen as a community. Students put these structures up and moved them to the administration building. The administration tried to bulldoze it a couple of times, and finally succeeded over the summer, then tried to enjoin the students from putting them up again. Cornell people put it up again. It wasn't the idea of a shanty then. They had used it as part of their protest. In the fall, University of Vermont students put up a shanty. It was very successful, because it helped turn around the board of trustees to vote for full divestment. Dartmouth followed on the heels of that in November of '85. (Princeton had had sort of a camp-out.) And then of course there was the attack by the right-wing *Dartmouth Review,* which definitely helped publicize the idea of it. Then it just took off. It wasn't chosen. It symbolized the lives and conditions of black South Africans. But it just didn't happen overnight. Now it continues to be something that people do. At Yale their shanty has been up for over a year; at Johns Hopkins, theirs was fire-bombed. It became a key thing. The media helped with Dartmouth, but paid a lot less attention, given the level of activity, in the spring of '86. It merited a lot more.

TV—*Many people think this issue is over.*

JN—A lot of places have divested. And you could say, for them, the divestment struggle is not key. I think it's not over. New centers emerge—University of Texas has been very active, the University of North Carolina, Illinois, Florida. California divested, but students at UC Santa Barbara have focused on goods being sold in the campus store linked to South Africa. People have broadened their approach. This spring, people who were key in the divestment and anti-apartheid struggles have led the struggles on racism, and the response to racist violence. So the movement hasn't lost its energy or power. This spring you didn't have massive shantytown protests. Without press coverage from South Africa, they're not really covering the local situation, though some of the local press is. But you did have a lot of students focusing on Citibank as a target. I think part of the next strategy is to go beyond just campus divestment but continue to focus on the economic ties. The object of divestment was to force the corporations to get out. The object of sanctions is the same thing. It's part of trying to link the student to the community movements. It's an important strategy. Maybe it won't work in every place, because it's hard for students to go off campus, but it's continued.

TV—*How did you first get interested in this subject?*

JN—I think I got interested in response to Soweto, in '76 when the children were shot down and killed for protesting the presence of guards in their schools. I think I had also been concerned with racism in this country, and always saw the connection between racism and the maintenance of capitalism in this country. With South Africa, I initially reacted to the horrors of apartheid. I was also looking at it as a strategic issue. It's a way of making the connections between racism and capitalism, a way of focusing on the structure of the university, run by trustees who are connected to corporations, undemocratic decision-making. It was a very concrete way of making less political students see those connections. If you look at US policy, change in South Africa is going to have a major impact throughout Africa, and have a worldwide impact. If you think of apartheid as modern day Naziism, the epitome of the worst of colonialism, it's a problem we have to confront. The best favor we could do for black South Africans and the world is to have radical change in this country. That really is the central question—how we can link the foreign policy concern in South Africa to change in this country. Sure, we'll help assist those in the revolution in South Africa by limiting investment and intervention down the road, but it has to connect to something more basic here. I've tried to do that to some extent through the American Committee on Africa. The student movement won't change all society—it's no vanguard—but student activity has been the catalyst in raising these issues. You know, US companies were invested in Nazi Germany, and calls for them to pull out continued to go unheard in the 1930s. I remember seeing footage of what was actually happening in South Africa. One could believe it, but to actually see it moves one to action, and to keep that sense of outrage about it.

TV—*Did you look back to the sixties to investigate strategies?*

JN—To some extent. There was a whole focus on South Africa in the sixties, and I looked back and saw the need for organization, but also some of the pitfalls. SDS played a key catalytic role—that's what students can do. I think sometimes people are wary of national organizations, because too much of their energy goes into internal politics. At least I am. I think the history of SDS has been distorted to focus on what happened at the end, the ideological squabbles, and a lot of the positive things are lost. In the anti-apartheid movement, what counts is what happens and what impact that has, not whether it's formalized or called a national student organization. One can achieve, be active, and have an impact on investment and mobilize students by weeks of protest and regional coordination. Now one may say it's very important that there be national strategizing, to sit down and really look at the movement. The form that that would take is a difficult question, particularly in terms of bringing white and black students together in that process. The sixties, everyone was inspired by that. It would be hard to explain the movement in the seventies and eighties without that. The fact that there was that tradition definitely made it easier for students now to begin.

TV—*Is it possible that much of the student energy that had been focused on apartheid will now move to domestic racism, at the expense of apartheid?*

JN—I wouldn't put it "at the expense." In a sense it's a positive development. To the extent that one moves to make positive changes in this society, apartheid can raise issues of consciousness: that's not a problem. The movement has to win its divestment battle, but it has to move to more active solidarity with struggles in southern Africa, and opposing US policies more generally. Where people put energy on domestic racism, a lot of black students are involved. When white students embrace that perspective, it makes it easier for people to work together. I think people will begin looking at US policy in southern Africa on a more long-term basis if they focus on racism. My worry is that the education about US regional policy isn't being done quickly enough. The fact that the US is engaged in military exercises in southern Zaire, refurbishing a base, is the equivalent to what they're doing in Honduras in long-term contingency. Where's the outcry? I doubt very many people know about that. The problem with students and US policy is: How do you connect it to your campus? And that was the strength of the divestment movement. A 500,000 member national youth congress was just formed in South Africa. Talk about student organizing—they managed to meet, 100 delegates, without the state knowing about it. It took something like six years to build this. That's something the US student movement has to be in touch with. Maybe it's not a spectacular protest like taking over your adminstration building, but it's the kind of quiet, patient work that will allow people to respond when things heat up again in southern Africa.

TV—*Are students seeing that promises to divest are being carried out?*

JN—They are at most places. They've won the public victory, but implementation involves moving through the bureaucracy. ACOA is monitoring this—it's one role we can play. It's hard without the students there, keeping the pressure on. Smith College is a place where they're not divesting fully though the media says they're fully divested.

TV—*How do you deal with the comments that this ought to be a black student run movement?*

JN—At almost every conference we have, the subject of what does black student leadership mean has come to the forefront. On a local level, groups have learned that you can't just have an anti-apartheid movement and invite black students in, you have to structure it so that you have a steering group that's at least 50% black. That's sometimes a difficult transition to make. This is definitely a major issue. From '80 onward, it's been there at every conference. For me, it was part of the anti-nuke movement. In '79 at demonstrations at Wall Street, there were bitter fights in the anti-nuke movement to get them to address the issue of racism. There definitely is a grouping of black student leaders. Not all of them are still students. Most of these leaders are not "nationalists," in the strict sense. In these discussions of racism, a dynamic occurs that makes it difficult to discuss the next step: black students at a conference will pick up on some racist remark, and address it, and the white students will get pretty defensive, or in many cases, are afraid to speak. It's clear that when the issue is domestic racism, that's black student led. I think there'll be less and less questioning from white student organizers about that. At the University of Texas, for example, there may be three different groups, and a changing cast of people. To the extent that you get independent student coalitions, it's possible to work some of this out. It's very hard when there's only one coordinating center, and you have to decentralize it.

TV—*How do you personally deal with criticism about being a white person so active in apartheid work?*

JN—I feel secure in terms of my commitment to dealing with racism. In terms of radical transformation in this country, I know and have written stuff at the heart of dealing with a radical move to deal with racism. I also know that in working in solidarity with the struggle in southern Africa, I'm quite aware that in the ANC and SWAPO a non-racial position is becoming more and more to the fore in southern Africa and I take encouragement from that. I don't think of myself as a liberal who feels guilty about being white. I also think you have to have a sense of humor, and a long-term view that, because you're active and visible, you have to expect that sometimes people will criticize you. To me the struggle is to change society, but the real struggle is to organize ourselves. The transformation is the ability of people to work together and deal with criticism and continue. If people can get organized, almost nothing can stop them. I've never thought this isn't worth fighting on for. You just have to realize what's happening in South Africa, or in this country.

The Struggle Continues

When it comes to campus activism connected with divestment, there are dozens of success stories pointing to the skills and commitment of students. But the struggle over apartheid continues, particularly the process of teaching students that the problem is a regional one that has its roots in white colonialism, and that it is part of a continuum of racist oppression that includes racism in our own country.

Continuing work on this issue will involve not only familiar tactics—sit-ins, shanties, education campaigns, pickets—but moving off-campus to corporations still doing business with South Africa. Boycotts, corporate headquarters picketing and other efforts are actions familiar to students, and give newcomers the opportunity to participate publicly in the kind of political activism they expect.

The work is hard and can be tedious, especially when success is sometimes limited and the actual impact of campus organizing on life in South Africa is unknown. Students understandably grow impatient with the goal of divestment, for example, wondering whether or not it is effective and whether or not it draws focus away from domestic racial problems. According to Yale student Michael Barr, however, who had the opportunity to visit South Africa and meet with students there, black South Africans consider divestment to be an important political goal. "They feel it [divestment] is useful, although obviously not going to make the crucial difference in what happens there... They felt that our student struggles had put pressure on their government, and in another sense, had given them a feeling of outside contact and support that they hadn't had previously. In that sense, it gave them strength... It helped them a lot."[13]

On campuses where university administrations or trustees have pledged to divest, students have drafted monitoring schemes to hold their school to its promise. This work requires intense activity and attention: students must be familiar with the specific investments, the exact nature of the school's commitment and the facts regarding the financial transactions of both the school and the companies involved. This painstaking research and calculating falls to the most committed, to those willing to become knowledgable enough to assess whether or not the university is fulfilling its pledge. If students buckle down and carry out this work, they will not only achieve the goal of true divestment, but they may also gain the respect of university officials who will learn that students are capable of follow-through, of long-range campaigns and of continuity from class to class. Most importantly, however, they will have an effect. The message from the students in South Africa should resonate for today's campus activists, "You have to count every victory, no matter how small it is."[14]

CHAPTER FOUR

Central America

On December 2, 1823, President James Monroe sent a message to Congress declaring that the American hemisphere would no longer be the province of European powers. For a century and a half, the Monroe Doctrine served to keep foreign governments from occupying any new territory in Central and South America—all foreign governments except the United States.

The situation may appear to contain some parallels to Vietnam: intervention into the internal political life of a sovereign nation, with anti-communism used as justification; elements of racism in the mindset that suggests the superiority of a white culture's judgment about what is best for a non-white culture; the jungle setting requiring guerrilla warfare tactics; an American populace disinterested in or uniformed about the region's history. In the Vietnam War, only the mounting deaths of American soldiers eventually captured the nation's attention.

Since 1900, the United States has used military forces in Central and South America more than 40 times to influence or alter the government of another country. In one instance, with the support of US Marines, Rafael Trujillo was set up as dictator of the Dominican Republic in 1924, following eight years of US military occupation. Installed to protect corporate sugar interests, Trujillo ruled until he was assassinated in 1962—by which time he controlled more than 70% of the country's economy. Juan Bosch, a liberal democrat, was then elected president and began instituting some progressive reforms when a US-backed coup toppled his government. When constitutionalists attempted to restore Bosch three years later, 23,000 Marines were sent in to insure their defeat.

With a history similar to the Dominican Republic, Nicaragua has been invaded by its northern neighbor 11 times since 1853 and occupied by US troops for at least two decades since 1900.[1] In 1979, US-supported dictator, Anastasio Somoza, was overthrown by a coalition of revolutionary forces called the Sandinista Front for National Liberation (FSLN)—named for the revolutionary hero Augusto Sandino who had been assassinated with the help of US forces four decades earlier.

While the United States, under President Jimmy Carter, did not support the overthrow of Somoza in 1979, it did not actively oppose it. The situation changed with the election of Ronald Reagan. Acting on campaign promises to "roll back Communist advances," the Reagan administration orchestrated a counter-revolutionary ("contra") movement, led by former Somoza National Guardsmen. At the same time, the administration moved to provide military assistance for the government of El Salvador, which supported America's covert efforts in Nicaragua, and faced a popular insurgency of its own. Covert actions by the US government in supporting the contra forces were judged illegal both domestically and on the international level. In Congress, the Iran-Contra hearings during the summer of 1986 indicted the Reagan administration for violating the Boland Amendment, passed by Congress in 1985 to prohibit American funds from being used for contra suppport. And on June 27, 1986, the World Court found the US guilty of violating international law by supporting the contras, ruling that Washington must make reparations. The US did not send an offical to contest the charges, and did not honor or comply with the ruling.[2]

News reports of the death squad killings of thousands of Salvadoran citizens, as well as Dutch journalists, American nuns and Salvadoran clergy, prompted the creation of solidarity organizations to counteract official US policy. The Committe in Solidarity with the People of El Salvador (CISPES), the Nicaragua Network, the Network in Solidarity with the People of Guatemala (NISGUA), and Madre all worked to raise consciousness by conducting information campaigns, raising money and supplies for export, and lobbying Congress to deny funding for the contra forces. CISPES includes campus chapters, and though it addresses all of Central America, its primary focus is El Salvador; similarly NISGUA and the Nicaragua Network concentrate on their respective countries, and also do some brigade work. Madre grew out of links between American and Nicaraguan women, and also does material aid work. Many campuses are also the sites of anti-contra and material aid campaigns sponsored by local non-affiliated, multi-issue student groups such as the Students for Economic Democracy at East Carolina University in Greenville, North Carolina.

An early target was United Nations Ambassador Jeane Kirkpatrick, who strongly supported right-wing dictators friendly to the Reagan administration. In the spring of 1983, when Kirkpatrick visited Berkeley, she was met by 800 protestors who sat in the audience and chanted, "40,000 dead!" when she mentioned El Salvador; she chose to leave the stage before completing her prepared text. Later that semester, University of Minnesota students rigged a lighting bar to drop a Nazi flag next to her podium. When Smith College president Jill Conway was unable to assure Kirkpatrick that her commencement address would proceed without incident, she cancelled her appearance. The niece of one of the four nuns killed in 1980 by government death squads in El Salvador attended Smith, and helped lead the protests there.

Students joined in prominent actions in 1984: a march in New Orleans on TACA Airlines (accused of flying deported Salvadoran refugees out of the United States), and a Washington, DC protest which blocked entrances to the Jacob Javits Federal Building, and displayed a huge subpoena charging Ronald Reagan and members of his administration with crimes against the people of El Salvador, Nicaragua and Grenada. Protestors, many of them students, dogged the President as he campaigned with shouts of "No Draft, No War...US Out of El Salvador." Revelations that the US had mined Nicaraguan harbors fueled the opposition.

The Pledge of Resistance campaign attracted thousands of students. This project asks people to sign a pledge affirming their commitment to engage in non-violent civil disobedience if the US invades Central America. Students have also played a role in the National Referendum to End the War in Central America, which distributes ballots asking people to vote for an end to support of the contras.

Throughout 1985, attention shifted more to Nicaragua, as US support for the contras, christened by Reagan "Freedom Fighters," received wider publicity. At commencement exercises, members of Ann Arbor's Latin America Solidarity Committee carried large signs which spelled out "Embargo South Africa, Not Nicaragua." Campus reaction increased with revelations tying covert actions to official US government policies, with such targets as CIA recruiters, speakers who support US policies, and members of Congress who have voted for contra funding. Students who occupied Munson Hall on the campus of the University of Massachusetts at Amherst in the fall of 1986 were protesting that school's continued permission for the CIA to recruit on campus. Their trial the following March was used as a public platform to reveal CIA complicity in covert war actions in Central America; their subsequent acquittal provided even more momentum for this movement.

Opposing a nearly invisible war requires unconventional tactics: students who were against US intervention in Central America not only fight to end the conflict but also to educate North Americans about the nature of that conflict, and the role of US imperialism.

Because US strategy has been to conduct a "low-intensity" war, employing regional troops rather than US forces, many here are not aware of the level of death and destruction in Central America. As a consequence, opponents of the policy turn to a variety of methods to make clear the extent of the war, and America's complicity in it.

To meet the challenge, students have borrowed, modified or invented dozens of methods to raise money, collect supplies, alert the uninformed and target those who can effect the changes they seek. Because US policy relies on CIA operations, mutual protests with those opposed to the CIA are common; since US policy creates refugees, students find natural allies in the religious community's sanctuary movement. Organizations concentrating on Central America are now coordinating their efforts more often, a product of the growing understanding that what is occuring in Central America is a regional war. Two of the most significant political events of

1987, the "CIA on Trial" Project and the April March on Washington, grew in part out of opposition to intervention in Central America.

While news reports and official government statements may confuse the issues, students find it hard to dismiss firsthand accounts from fellow students who have been there. Some travel alone but most join work groups called brigades, organized by one of the national organizations. Students are part of nearly every brigade and some are comprised exclusively of students. Almost always, students pay their own expenses, and donate their labor. This direct approach allows the individual student to see the crisis in each country, and to form a personal opinion about its causes and consequences. Students also learn the difference between abstract government statements and daily human details, and that many people in the affected countries do not blindly hate or love Americans, or hate or love communists.

There is some similarity with those who travelled to the South in the early 1960s to do voter registration and become involved in the civil rights protests, and who returned to tell their peers about the issues. Mark Rudd, who helped lead the student strike at Columbia in 1968, and now does Central America political organizing in New Mexico, says, "I think there are comparisons. I think there are also comparisons to Vietnam vets, too, in the sense that Vietnam vets became witnesses to American foreign policy, to American imperialism, and those of us who go to Central America are the current witnesses. I think there are definitely comparisons to the Spanish Civil War, in that we are partisans, not merely witnesses. We're partisans going down there to make positive contributions, in the case of construction brigades, harvest brigades, technical assistance, etc., and I think that that's a very strong comparison."[3]

Students also visited the University of El Salvador, which had been physically destroyed and closed for four years in the mid-eighties. On June 28, 1980, a special force of the military, using tanks, helicopters and machine guns, invaded the campus while classes were still in session. The incident, in which 80 students were killed, began a four-year military occupation of the campus while classes functioned in private homes, storefronts and other underground locations. In 1984, after the demolished campus reopened, a delegation of US students, including CISPES representatives, met with students from AGEUS (the General Association of Salvadoran University Students). These students returned to their campuses to help raise money, gather educational supplies, and mount a student-to-student solidarity campaign for the university.[4]

A sophisticated version of a brigade is the Ann Arbor-Managua Initiative for Soil Testing and Development, a group of graduate students and professionals that flew to Nicaragua in January 1987 to begin work on a soil and water testing and research laboratory. Concerts, money from collected bottles and cans, and a bowl-a-thon raised money for their expenses.

Raising money for material aid campaigns attracts students who might not attend a rally, blockade a building or lobby a congressman. At the University of Wisconsin at Madison, the group Medical Aid to Central America has arranged for the shipment of 100 tons of medical supplies to the region. Another student group, Community Action on Latin America (CALA), founded in 1972, collected more than $10,000 during the 1985-86 school year for material aid to El Salvador, Nicaragua and Guatemala. And the concept was stretched beyond the campus when Madison students were instrumental in creating a sister-city relationship between their city and Arcatao, El Salvador, channeling assistance to the residents of that community.

This work has helped forge connections between activist women. Carolyn Helmke, a Madison student, explains, "I see it happening in a lot of Central American groups, where the women start saying we're going to start organizing separately. We're in solidarity with the women of that country, and we're going to start talking about what's happening with them, because we're sick of it just being the guerrillas and warfare. We're going to talk about the women's issues. It's a real serious issue."[5]

Helmke herself is involved with Movement for Emancipation of Women in Chile (MEMCHA). "It's the united women's support group in Chile. There's a Chilean solidarity group here that's done a lot of work to educate people about what's going on in Chile—show films, have speakers—and send material aid. This group was formed because in Chile the women's movement is really strong and really exciting, and they felt a women's group could work to get people here excited about that. The women are running the movement there."[6]

In El Salvador in 1977, women who had witnessed the death and disappearance of children, husbands, parents and friends joined to create the Committee of Mothers and Relatives of Political Prisoners, Disappeared and Assassinated in El Salvador, known as CoMadres. On US campuses, support groups raise money for their efforts, and do educational work to explain the political situation in El Salvador. These kinds of activities take place all across the country.

- At Cornell College in Iowa, after a study group determined that one basic approach to making a difference in Central America would be to raise money for a material aid campaign, students held a Run for Nicaragua, which raised money for medical supplies.

- At the University of New Mexico at Albuquerque, medical and nursing students helped organize the New Mexico Committee for Health Rights in Central America, and joined with the Campus Committee for Human Rights in Latin America and a Faculty Committee for Human Rights in Latin America in conducting educational and fund-raising projects.

- The New England Central America Network links information and fund-raising among dozens of colleges throughout the northeast.

- The Humanitarian Assistance Project for Independent Agricultural Development in Nicaragua at the Ann Arbor campus of the University of Michigan sends material aid such as farm machinery parts, fertilizer and seeds to Nicaraguan farmers who have been contra targets.

- The National Student Fast for Peace, which involved about a dozen schools in 1986, grew in 1987 to include more than forty, from eighteen states and

Washington, DC and raised more than $40,000 for humanitarian relief in Nicaragua.

But the ability to realize the overriding goal of this movement—to cut off funding for US-backed contras, and to reverse US policy in the region—rests squarely on the movement's ability to pull diverse groups together for coalition work. To exert pressure on the system, coalitions must include the religious community, organized labor, immigrant rights groups, political campaigns and others as well as students. National organizations frequently join with these groups to mount coordinated campaigns. One example is the National Referendum, but individual campus groups often chart their own local course.

In Ann Arbor, students from the Latin America Solidarity Committee at the University of Michigan objected to continued support for the contras by their congressman, Carl Pursell. In the fall of 1985, they began a letter-writing and petition campaign to influence his vote. This was ignored, so the following spring students sat in at Pursell's offices and planted white crosses on the lawn in front of his building, stating that they were not only protesting the representative's votes, but his unwillingness to meet with his constituents. In all, 118 were arrested.

Dean Baker, one of the 118, started working with LASC in April of 1984 when "there were about eight people in the group. But that was when the mining of harbors, a lot was going on, and it looked like we might invade Nicaragua. We felt at the time it was an important issue to work on. It grew incredibly quickly. We did a lot of events in the fall. We had one day when we had speakers all day, videos, workshops, close to 1,000 people attending." They then turned their attention to Pursell, which became "the biggest issue on campus. We had regular meetings of a hundred people, demonstrations of one or two hundred people."[7]

In the spring of 1986, LASC worked with community groups on a ballot initiative opposing Reagan administation policies in Central America and calling for a sister city relationship between Ann Arbor and cities in Central America. When it passed by over 60% "the mayor jumped on. He has been down to our sister city in Nicaragua."[8] Baker, a vetaran of one unsuccessful campaign to unseat and replace Pursell, may again run for Congress.

Pressure to change votes in Congress requires facing the same combination of roadblocks encountered on campuses—educating people, in this case politicians, about the extent of the war, and about their complicity in supporting it.

SCENE

Speaking of Nicaragua

"I had to do it. I had to see for myself."

Kevin Geiger, a sophomore at College of the Atlantic in Bar Harbor, Maine, when he spent two months in Nicaragua, is slumped down in the back row of the Slippery Rock University auditorium, whispering to me about his experience. Up front, two students participating in the 1986 DSA Summer Youth conference lead a discussion. Kevin and I cut out and go for a walk in the Pennsylvania countryside.

"Nicaragua is filled with paradoxes," he says. "Priests hold cabinet posts, the police have poetry workshops and the state security take dance classes. Another shock is that there are so many guns around, and yet I felt safe during my stay. What struck me most was that I was not hated for being a US citizen. In fact, I only heard two nasty remarks during my entire visit."

It's hard for me to imagine this bright-faced, red-haired young man living with people from an entirely different culture, in the middle of a war zone.

"My family lived in Barrio El Calvario, Estelí, which is a mildly poor neighborhood in Nicaraguan terms." He'd gone to Nicaragua expecting crude living conditions, "and I found them. But to my amazement I discovered that I could live comfortably despite the lack of modern conveniences." The family did have electricity which powered their four dangling light bulbs, along with their only appliance, an ancient refrigerator. "I had expected the place to smell, be dirty and uncomfortable. Instead I found things pleasant enough. My house was virtually spotless. The floors were swept and mopped every day. The doorstep was swept off, and even the section of dirt road in front of our house was swept."

Kevin talks of long hot days in the sun picking coffee beans, hauling heavy sacks, the tepid outdoor showers, splinters and thorns that had to be removed from fingers and feet. What he remembers most vividly is his "family." His ready smile and soft-spoken demeanor hide the rage he feels reading news accounts from Nicaragua. He bitterly criticizes not only our goverment's policies that finance the destruction of the country, but the lazy reporting that fails to tell the American people about the culture, the feelings, the conditions and the people he came to know.

He recounts stories of village life, like going fishing with his young "brother" Noel and a friend, who use Soviet-made assault rifles instead of fishing poles. Noel is an Olympic marksman, and shoots fish from a nearby river bank. Kevin chuckles as he recalls two boyish young men, one with a loaded gun over his shoulder, playing in the water, splashing each other. "This didn't fit my preconceived notions of what mustachioed soldiers did." We wander the cracked sidewalks of this small Pennsylvania town, back to the dormitory, where Kevin shares stories with me into the night. His memories include the elderly grandmother who handled most of the washing, the mother's daily routine of grinding corn meal, and cooking rice, beans and tortillas on the open fire, and the flow of nieces, cousins, uncles drifting in and out.

The "cheerful endurance" of the Nicaraguan people, he believes, will give him comfort as he hears about new funds approved to support the contras. But he remembers the sadness, the pain of steady losses of family members and friends that mark their lives, and the frustration.

After he returned to the United States, Kevin Geiger spoke out whenever he could about Central America, giving talks at school, telling people that the situation was not what they'd been led to believe. He is eager to give personal testimony. He brought a contingent of his own from Maine to join the students that blocked the entrance to CIA headquarters in April of 1987.

In a letter, Kevin wrote of his last night with his adopted mother in Esteli. "That night, as a last remark, she clarified that the revolution was not yet over and that it might take 100, maybe 200 years to do the job. And I thought to myself that some-one should have told this woman sitting in a shack under a bare light bulb that there were greater powers in the world than dedicated people, and no matter how hard her people worked, their dreams would fail. Maybe someone had told her after all, maybe many, but I knew she hadn't listened; and by the look in her eyes, I knew they were wrong."

INTERVIEW

Doug Calvin, CISPES   *January 25, 1987*

Doug Calvin left the University of Massachusetts two years ago to work full-time against US intervention in Central America, first on New England campuses then as national college coordinator for the Committee in Solidarity with the People of El Salvador (CISPES).

TV—*Can you tell me something about CISPES?*

DC—It was formed in 1980, around the situation in El Salvador, which at that point was a major issue in the news. It started in Washington and LA, and in 1981 it mush-roomed in terms of size and numbers of chapters. It was formed to support the guer-rilla forces in El Salvador, the armed opposition, and we try to communicate what they're saying, to show there's more than one side in El Salvador. We also focus on supporting, probably more so, the mass movement, the unarmed opposition in El Salvador, teachers, students, human rights organizations, committees for political prisoners, broad labor coalitions, organizations such as that. It started with mainly people working with the left, who were involved in what was going on in Central America, who saw this as a developing issue.

TV—*And how did universities fit in?*

DC—Universities have always been a part of CISPES. In '83, there was a part-time student position at CISPES, to start addressing the student sector specifically, and to start seeing what was out there, and ways of building it. There are now at least 200 campus chapters across the country.

TV—*That sounds like a large number. How do you keep up contact?*

DC—It's hard, because there isn't a real systematic way nationally of keeping up with students, but there are pretty regular contacts, with mailings.

TV—*At Boulder, CISPES looked like any other campus organization with an office and student funding. Is that fairly typical?*

DC—Yes. On most campuses it's actually a Central America group that's a member of CISPES rather than a CISPES chapter, though a lot of places do have CISPES chap-ters. They're very much a campus committee and if there are funds available, they're usually funded.

TV—*So it's not a matter of somebody from the Washington office coming in and setting up a chapter.*

DC—That's the most amazing thing about it. It's real grassroots. We don't try to dictate. With CISPES and the national networks, you can say, "This is the priority need in terms of what's going on right now." For example, we really need to support what's going on in El Salvador and stop contra aid, instead of doing a clothing drive for a cooperative in Nicaragua. We can say that and we definitely lobby to get groups to work on those priorities. But we try to work with what the groups are doing.

TV—*What other groups do you work with?*

DC—The top three on Central America are CISPES, the Nicaragua Network and the Network in Solidarity with the People of Guatemala. CISPES is by far the largest and most consolidated. The other two until real recently wanted to be in touch with committees out there, but didn't see themselves primarily as grassroots organizations, more as coordinating bodies. NISGUA is very small, and they're actually adopting a lot of CISPES programs. Nicaragua Network is pretty broad and just starting to think in terms of consolidating. Their regional coordinators are representatives from large Nicaragua committees.

TV—*Do students tend to make generalizations about this subject?*

DC—That definitely happens. The big problem right now is how people focus only on contra aid. It's a regional crisis and the US war strategy is regional—they have several points going down, with Honduras, with Guatemala, especially with Nicaragua and El Salvador. Because of the way the media have played it, people focus on contra aid, and even refuse to see El Salvador as an issue. It's amazing, because El Salvador is in an extremely dynamic position; changes are very fast-paced. Where the US can determine when and if they want to go into Nicaragua, or the level of harassment, of brutality they want to put against the Nicaraguan people, the US does not have that advantage in El Salvador where the situation is being determined internally by the armed opposition, by the mass movements, and the government the US is propping up is not nearly as stable and united as it was before. It's hard, because people focus on one country, and leave the others out, and don't look at it as a regional issue. Or they go from project to project and don't look at what the people's needs are right now. In the next couple of years, it'll be a very different movement.

TV—*Besides work brigades, what projects are there?*

DC—For a long time, there's been a campaign to stop the bombing in El Salvador, to publicize the amount of aerial bombardments the Salvadoran government was making against its people. The action was focused on Congress and on education. Also, there were efforts to give material aid to civilian victims of the bombings—medical aid, aid to help rebuild towns or schools or whatever. In areas of popular control, there are the local popular governments (PPLs), that literally have their own self-governing systems, with elections and literacy programs, health programs.

They're operating in 30% of the country, and we have worked to support them. Also, there have been projects of sending paramedics with mobile backpacks. Since the earthquake, there's been a big push to support victims. The government's response after the earthquake was to launch counterinsurgency campaigns to halt aid from going down, and to hold on to international aid. So independent channels got set up real fast and we started sending stuff down. They were refusing entrance, and finally the archbishop of El Salvador and the labor unions just took a couple of planeloads and told the government to stop the shit, this stuff is coming in. You can't hold on to it or we're going to expose what you're doing. Human rights emergencies arise a lot, so responding to them quickly has literally saved lives—sending telegrams, calls down right away. You can use that kind of thing to build your campus committee. In the spring there's the Referendum Campaign, which is basically a ballot initiative. In some places, it will be binding and in others, just for publicity, saying we vote against the war in Central America. This is an education issue, because consistently two-thirds of the public is against what is going on in Central America.

TV—*When students raise money, collect food, clothing and medical supplies, are there channels to get it down there?*

DC—There are a few. There are local initiatives working with the national channels. In all areas of the country, the regional offices for regional coordination for the three networks are completely separate for good reason. The organizations are real different in their approaches and levels of organization. In New England, the three organizations are merged under the New England Central America Network (NECAN) and we are working toward real coordination. It's worked very well. It gives us a little bit of autonomy from the national networks, so we can plan a little more and experiment. In the fall of 1985, I helped open the national campaign for support of the University of El Salvador; the following spring I went all down the East Coast doing a material aid project for the University. Then I really started to see what the needs of local campuses were, in terms of building skills and planning, how to use events to build on each other. Committees just started coming to us—we went from being in touch with 25 or 30 schools to being in touch with 60. During the summer of '86, I decided to make it a whole program. It was largely my initiative, starting with fund-raising, because consistently, student work is not a priority. We've done delegations to El Salvador. Each person was sponsored by a local committee with the intent of doing projects in support of the University when they came back. That's started to happen. We have follow-ups planned to keep up with these people. And that builds a committee, too.

TV—*Are the brigades usually all students, or a mix of people?*

DC—Most always it's a mix that includes at least a sprinkling of students on almost every trip. Increasingly, there are exclusively student brigades and delegations.

TV—*Are there conditions besides paying your own costs?*

DC—That depends. On a Nicaragua Network construction brigade they might have specific needs for people with carpentry experience, or masonry experience, and then just general people who are willing to work their tails off. Or cotton brigades—and even then the 11-year-old Nicaraguan will pick twice as much as you do.

TV—*Is there a general length of time?*

DC—Usually two weeks to a month; it depends on the project. One brigade that went down to build a school was there for two months. Cotton brigades or coffee brigades are usually two to four weeks.

TV—*For instance, a coffee brigade—what's the cost to a student?*

DC—Usually around $1,000. It actually might be a little higher. Delegations to El Salvador are usually around $1,000, and some of that goes to the organizations that are meeting with us.

TV—*Has the federal government made it harder for these brigades to operate?*

DC—In Nicaragua, it is getting harder. In late '83, they were harassing a lot of activists who were coming back from Nicaragua, mainly new people they thought could be swayed by that. There's threats of a travel ban on North Americans. El Salvador has tightened up a lot, because US delegations are playing an important role in the day-to-day situation there. They're requiring visas: if you belong to the Catholic Church in San Francisco, it may be difficult; if you have a police record of civil disobedience, it may be difficult. There's also a broad campaign against CISPES, with full page ads.

TV—*Is there a precedent for the brigades?*

DC—Not in Central America, no. The level of US intervention is just tremendous, over a billion dollars this year. In El Salvador, the heaviest bombing ever seen in this hemisphere is going on. In Nicaragua, the US is openly trying to overthrow their revolution. We have a big advantage over the Vietnamese solidarity efforts in the sixties, in that the cultures are close to ours, the countries are pretty close. There's a lot of their cultural influence in our culture already, and the proximity is a big advantage. And the amount of information that's out about Central America and even the amount of media is putting us way ahead of the early solidarity efforts in Vietnam.

TV—*Do students who travel to Central America influence others when they return to campuses?*

DC—I think the growth of activism on campuses is a real sign of that. As more people go down, they have something to plug into when they come back. On a lot of campuses they have groups. We're trying to coordinate that a little bit, and start the process before they go down, with thoughts of coming back and building the organizational basis so there's more of a guarantee that that kind of activism builds, and builds in a productive way. It's real impressive, but real diverse. Large numbers of people have been down.

TV—*Are there coalitions in connection with Central America?*

DC—Usually there are, on the local level. For the April 25 March, we got on the delegation, helped sponsor it. From peace centers and organizations to black student unions, graduate student governments, women's studies organzations, there's a lot of cross-participation, at least on the endorsement level.

TV—*Is there a connection between CISPES and the sanctuary people on campuses?*

DC—The sanctuary movement is not particularly strong on campuses. A few campuses, including Boulder, started sanctuary programs, but it's been mainly religious. Housing people involves a different kind of support than students are capable of.

TV—*What is the place of college students in the national Central America organizations?*

DC—It's taken us a long time to get them to deal with it on a semi-important level. Eventually in terms of national stuff we will create a very accountable but semi-autonomous network to deal with student work. At this point the national organizations have other priorities. But students are starting to say we need to connect more. Students can play a crucial role in solidarity work.

TV—*Will students have to form their own organizations?*

DC—Not necessarily organizations, but networks to address student organizing needs specifically, and to make sure that we all stay connected. In one way, the greatest thing we can do is stop the war, but in the meantime, people are getting killed. Solidarity and anti-intervention are equally important.

TV—*And CISPES is supporting your efforts.*

DC—It's significant that CISPES is building a student program. There are people who feel it's a real struggle to get a thousand people out, to get a protest going on a campus, but we've done it. These new people coming in will say, we've done that. Now we're working from a higher base level.

INTERVIEW

Joy Barrett, University of Colorado   *December 18, 1986*

Joy Barrett is 32 ("I'm probably the oldest person you've talked to here") who balances her work, her studies at the University of Colorado at Boulder, organizing for the campus CISPES chapter, and selling Nicaraguan coffee to raise money for material aid campaigns. She has been to Nicaragua four times.

TV—*How have you worked with churches?*

JB—We work well with a number of churches in town who are always willing to lend us their halls for fund-raising events, concerts, dances.

TV—*Is there a sanctuary movement here?*

JB—Yes! In fact, the campus was declared a sanctuary. I think it was the student government. And as it ended up it was this building, the student union, because the student government runs part of it.

TV—*What general changes have you seen recently?*

JB—In the past, it was harder to recruit people to do mailings or package medical supplies to be hand-carried to Nicaragua, than it was to get people to do some kind of street theater, and I guess that is changing. A lot of people found it gratifying to launch this campaign against CIA recruitment, and the level of militancy is greater than in the past. People seem satisfied with that, and also quite gratified. We mean business when we talk about holding people responsible for the crimes that they commit. We're not just going to step over some stupid line, and then go home at the end of the day and have a beer. I'm pleased.

TV—*Tell me more about the activities of CISPES.*

JB—It's the most active organization on campus. It has the largest membership, it's the best organized, it's the most on fire. We put together a lot of excellent proposals and get funding for these things; we bring films, speakers; we have festivals. We have our material aid campaigns, getting medicines to Nicaragua. And there's support from other groups, coalition work, and an understood political support by a handful of other groups on campus.

TV—*Can you think of an example?*

JB—Student government was voting on whether or not to have check-off funds for student organizations—it was an under-the-table attempt to de-fund a campus gay rights organization. So CISPES people showed up, and everybody put on pink triangles, and some of us spoke, and we basically represented the majority of the audience in this discussion. As a result, there is across-the-board funding for student organizations, which means the continued existence of the gay rights organization and other organizations which are equally unpopular with the right-wing fat cats in student government. We've also made contributions to things like Take Back the Night. And people from other organizations will come and make signs, they'll walk with us in our marches, they take part in the planning of demonstrations, and show up.

TV—*You've been with CISPES here since it started?*

JB—At the beginning of CISPES a lot of us were the same age, more or less, Vietnam-era people with advanced degrees. What's exciting for me to see now is these young whippersnappers, 21 years old, coming in and out of the office. And they're students. Most of us at the beginning were non-students with advanced degrees, working in the community. And all of a sudden there's an incredible group of competent young people, and it's real exciting to see. We have people who have rapidly become very sophisticated politically.

TV—*How is the average student introduced to these subjects?*

JB—For years we've had biweekly educational meetings. We like to show a film every other week—make some flyers, pass them out, put notices in the paper and in the dorms, and get people to come and see a film about a Central American country. And we always make pitches for the various campaigns that CISPES has going on, such as selling Nicaraguan coffee, working on the various material aid projects, a weekly radio show. After we show a movie, we'll have a general rap session, a question and answer period, sometimes with somebody who has particular expertise on what the movie pertained to. A lot of people sign up and get involved that way. They'll get involved in very different levels. The struggle is so huge, people are suffering so much, and dying.

INTERVIEW

Bill Cruices, San Francisco CISPES   *February 28, 1987*

In 1984 after graduating from the University of West Virginia at Morgantown, Bill Cruices moved to San Francisco to work with CISPES where he is subregional coordinator specializing in student work.

TV—*What are you working on now?*

BC—Right now there's the national referendum to end the war in Central America, which has as its sponsors many religious organizations, including Unitarians and lots of Catholic groupings, and DSA. It raises four demands: end aid to the contras, stop aiding the repressive governments of El Salvador, Guatemala and Honduras, promote peaceful solutions within Central America and end the use of the National Guard in Central America. The idea is to get people to vote out on the street, in front of supermarkets, on campuses, etc. The national goal is 500,000 ballots, and the idea is to pressure Congress and the administration. That combined with the spring mobilization for peace, jobs and justice in San Francisco are the two main areas of CISPES programs.

TV—*What about long range plans?*

BC—Long range, we'll probably do more of the same. We tend to focus on educating the community about the war in Central America, about US policy in Central America, to get them activated to do certain things, whether it's write Congress, or join an emergency response network, and send a telegram in response to a human rights violation in El Salvador, or do various actions like the spring mobilization. We do some spur-of-the-moment actions: when the Salvadoran army launched a terror campaign against the civilian population we did a number of civil disobedience non-violent actions at the Salvadoran consulate. The range of tactics depends on what's going on.

TV—*Different students have different views on tactics. What do you think?*

BC—Some think more militant tactics are effective, basically to raise the level of student support. For others, it means just doing non-violent civil disobedience. Others prefer very long-term educational base-building work. I generally think that we're going to end the war in Central America through the longer range approach. It's going to take activation. Poll after poll, Gallup, *New York Times, LA Times,* 70% say no, I don't support the war in Central America, and CISPES's focus is to activate that 70%, to get them to do something. They certainly need more education: in the very same poll, people don't know who the Sandinistas are and who the contras are, but they feel in their bones that something's going wrong in Central America. The goal of CISPES is to end intervention in Central America. The goal of many people on the Berkeley campus is to have a radicalized student movement that can present a challenge on a whole number of different issues, and many think that confronting the administration or the police more directly is going to radicalize students. I think that it may radicalize a few, but it will also turn away a number of students who aren't necessarily into getting their heads beat.

TV—*Who do you work with at Berkeley?*

BC—There's not a CISPES chapter. SAICA [Students Against Intervention in Central America] has done some of the CISPES program, and I work with them a little bit. They've done some work with the University of El Salvador—when the president of the student association there was picked up by the police. Pedro Noguera and some other people from Berkeley went down to San Salvador to try to get him out of jail, and they were successful. SAICA has also used some of our educational materials on US policy. At this point, they would not be considered a CISPES affiliate. We're not unfriendly, but a lot of them have a different approach. They tend to go from action to action, because for a lot of them their goal is to build a student movement: if they stopped US intervention, in the meantime, that's fine, but that's not their objective.

TV—*Do you think CISPES will be on campuses for a while?*

BC—Whether it's CISPES or something else, the movement to stop the war in Central America is going to be an issue for as long as the war continues. The morality is so skewed.

TV—*Do you make connections between policies in Central America, and domestic racism, and the economy?*

BC—You do it to the extent that you need to do it. The objective of CISPES is to end intervention in Central America, not to reshape American society. It's very helpful to bring in how the money being spent on torture in Central America could be better spent here in the United States. There have been times when linking with apartheid has been very important. In most of our literature, we point up what the money spent on war in Central America could be used for, including student loans.

TV—*Is it a problem that there are several different groups all working on Central America issues?*

BC—You work together on those projects where you have common ground. I think it would be foolish to try to have one organization in the United States working on

Central America. It just wouldn't work. There's different sectors of society that like doing their own work, like the religious community and the labor movement. Generally, we like to work with groups that are focused on Central America. We don't work actively with groups that are focused more on anti-militarism in general, and various other issues, and we encourage Central America groups to form alliances with them.

Solid Foundation and a Strong Movement

Just as this is a complicated issue to explain, so too will it be a complicated issue to resolve. Even the definition of a resolution changes from group to group, student to student.

For those who focus only on the military aspect, the cessation of a shooting war would mean an end to the problem. Others look for an end to all covert intervention into other nations' governmental operations; still others seek to correct the economic imbalance between this country and others.

In many ways, work on Central America is largely reactive: US government actions determine where the spotlight shines, and what organizers can use to mobilize students. Certainly, the introduction of US troops would radically alter the situation, and almost no one believes that campuses would remain quiet during such a deployment. Short of that, the amount of involvement often depends on what the press reports, and how well organizers can bring the message to campus with the help of the growing numbers of students who have personally visited the region. While that process is slower, the impact of these witnesses is dramatic and lasting. Any government efforts to prevent other students from visiting Central America would itself be a rallying point for future demonstrations. And Central American issues, so closely linked to the role of the CIA, benefit from campus actions against that agency. But beyond CIA access to campus facilities, the university is rarely the target in Central America work.

Another, related issue that might bring a student response is break-ins at the homes and offices of people active in Central American organizing and sanctuary work. The Center for Constitutional Rights has documented more than 60 such incidents between the spring of 1984 and the spring of 1987, all involving the theft of information, slides, mailing lists, computer access codes, files, work plans and other materials used in political organizing, refugee assistance or other solidarity or support work, while valuables are left untouched.[9]

This movement has been built on a solid foundation. Students linked to a broad community of church, labor, humanitarian and other groups are determined to stay with this issue. The network of national groups with local chapters, as well as autonomous campus groups, further insures a long presence.

Finally, this movement allows students to become involved in a variety of ways, reflecting their degree of commitment, the amount of time they have, and their interpretation of the causes and solutions of the problem. By creating this array of options, organizers have strengthened the likelihood that Central America and all of the issues connected to it will remain a significant part of campus activism for the foreseeable future.

Berkeley, '87: A Day in the Life

Lunchtime at Sproul Plaza. Berkeley is synonymous with student political activism. And its central plaza bustles with activity—not only on special days, but every day, including the mid-March day I arrived.

Part of the nine-campus University of California system, the college spreads over 200 acres, nestled between San Francisco Bay and the beautiful, undeveloped Berkeley hills. The architecture reflects the region's Spanish heritage. Although one of the country's oldest educational institutions (founded in 1868), it's been at the forefront of self-expression and student activism since the thirties. Of its 20,000 plus students, only 7% join sororities or fraternities.

Down the hill on Shattuck Square, *Daily Californian* editor Howard Levine has decided to support the opposition to the English-only movement: tomorrow's *Daily Cal* banner will be printed in Spanish. In the Berkeley Bookstore, an inquiring student is told the store does not carry IBM products, enforcing a ban to protest the corporation's ties to South Africa. At Cody's Cafe, Todd Gitlin meets a friend for lunch to discuss political activism.

And at Sproul Plaza, a noontime crowd of about 100 has elected to stay and listen to an anti-racist, black unity demonstration, in full swing as I stroll back up Telegraph toward the campus. Sproul Plaza, scene of the Free Speech Movement, the surrounded police car, hoardes of chanting students, countless speeches and rallies, television crews and national news photographers and, recently, divestment demonstrations, is alive again. One speaker exhorts, "Do you know your history?" Another promises, "The only one you can depend on is you." Almost every day, some political or student group stages a rally, a speech, something. From the foun-

57

tain and out past the gate, tables line the walkway, with leaflets and literature from dozens of organizations. Down the steps and around the corner, in Lower Sproul Plaza, a band called Mrs. Green entertains another 100 or so, as the surrounding terrace lunchers block out the music and the speeches to talk with friends. A strolling woman dressed all in black velvet blows bubbles to no one in particular. Off to one side the inevitable hacky sack circle carries on, oblivious to everything. Lunch at Sproul Plaza.

The second floor of Eshleman Building faces Lower Sproul Plaza, and the windows of the Associated Students Union look out onto it. Its president, Steve Ganz, remembers that the biggest protests when he was a freshman were about student fees. "In the sixties, because the cost of coming here was so little, people had more time to put into protests and movements. Now because the cost is so much, most of those people have to spend their time working, rather than do progessive movements. They've been indoctrinated to be passive and business-oriented. But people change. Once they get here, they change. When my roomate first came here, he was very conservative. Now there's a total change."

Chris Cabaldan, vice-president for external affairs, joins us. I ask him what it is about Berkeley that compels people to find some political movement to connect with. "That's its reputation. A lot of people come here for that reason. So when you ask them to participate, it's not something strange or odd, it's something that people do in Berkeley." Chris related that "when I first came here, there was nothing happening," except the same students particiapting in fairly routine demonstrating. "As the South Africa thing started to pick up, and the anniversary of the Free Speech Movement, more people started to get involved. I wouldn't have guessed when I first came here that anything would ever happen."

Steve walks me over to the steps of Dwinelle Hall, where 45 students are learning about the growing ethnic studies issue. Teach-ins are still a popular form of education on political topics—informal, often brief, they fill in answers, pull in participants. My friend David Modersbach, a Berkeley freshman, sits cross-legged on the outer edge of the group, listening to the presentation. After a questions period, David hurries off to class.

David hears about my day while we have dinner upstairs at Café Bottega. He confirms that the campus is alive with activity every day. Caught up in learning what's going on, what's possible, excited that activism seems to be an escalating phenomenon on campus, David says, "There is always something going on, that's what's so cool about this place." Walking back to the car, and discussing the best route for us to take tomorrow when we drive to Davis, we pass not one, but five different students stapling and taping notices to the kiosks in the Plaza. David points them out: "See what I mean?"

CHAPTER FIVE

THE CIA

American college students first opposed the presence of CIA recruiters on their campuses in 1966. The agency, and most of the students, were 19 years old.

Founded in September of 1947 under the National Security Act, the Central Intelligence Agency was the post-World War II response to critics who felt intelligence and security information should be coordinated. The compromise which was forged placed the CIA within a kind of intelligence community, within which the Defense Intelligence Agency (DIA), the Federal Bureau of Investigation (FBI), the National Security Agency (NSA), the intelligence branch of the Atomic Energy Commission (AEC), the State Department's intelligence-gathering apparatus, and separate intelligence units within the Army, Navy and Air Force operated in separate but sometimes overlapping jurisdiction.

Possibly the first serious anti-CIA protest took place in February 1966, when students at Grinnell College in Iowa picketed the visit by a recruiter to their campus. One student's sign proclaimed: "Where there is an invisible government, there is no democracy."[1] Since that time, people from all segments of society have come to think of the CIA as an invisible government, keeping its activities secret from the American people, and from elected officials in Congress and even in the White House.

Throughout the late 1960s, the CIA's involvement in clandestine operations in support of the Vietnam War drew protests. The agency's attempts to recruit on campus, implying complicity on the part of the university, drew the most reaction. Since the agency relied on people with advanced degrees, anti-recruiting campaigns seemed a suitable tactic. When *Ramparts* Magazine in April 1966 revealed that

Michigan State University provided support and cover for the CIA in South Vietnam from 1955 to 1959 in connection with a program to train police and public officials, the college community took a closer look at the relationship between the agency and the university. Within a month, Stanford University students staged a protest against their school's participation in classified research, an action that foreshadowed a rising movement.

The following February, students learned that the CIA was not only on campus, it was in their own student governments. *Ramparts* broke the story that the CIA had been secretly funding, and secretly influencing, the National Student Association (NSA), an organization founded in 1948 to represent elected student governments. The agency had used the NSA to recruit students and promote Cold War policies on campuses. (Two future leaders of SDS were unwitting associates of NSA: Tom Hayden was hired to write a policy paper on the civil rights movement which NSA never printed, and Paul Potter served as an NSA vice-president.) The NSA connection was part of an overall design by the CIA which also funneled money to labor unions and media organizations to win favor for US foreign policies. Reacting to the news, SDS spread the word and urged the barring of recruiters on campuses. President Lyndon Johnson issued an executive order prohibiting the use of agency funding for student organizations, labor unions or media outlets.

Throughout the anti-war era, the CIA remained a prime target. Actions erupted at Harvard, Williams, Wisconsin, Brown, Vassar, Penn, Georgetown, Syracuse, Rochester, Utah, Notre Dame and dozens of other schools. Protesters also targeted recruiters for Dow Chemical, which manufactured the napalm used in Vietnam.

The CIA's complicity in southeast Asia was compounded in the mid-1970s by its deep involvement in Watergate. CIA operatives broke into the offices of Daniel Ellsberg's psychiatrist, in an attempt to find ways of pressuring Ellsberg to end his outspoken opposition to the war. A series of articles in the *New York Times* in 1974 revealed that the agency had conducted extensive domestic spying operations, in violation of its charter, from the late 1960s on, maintaining surveillance on as many as 10,000 Americans.

And the landmark 1976 study on the agency, by the Senate Select Committee on Intelligence chaired by Senator Frank Church, pointed out that, despite an executive order forbidding it, the CIA had continued to maintain connections with universities and professors, many of whom were unaware their research was government-backed.

Under Presidents Gerald Ford and Jimmy Carter, the executive branch attempted to rein in the agency's jurisdiction and operations. But under Ronald Reagan, the agency moved back into fullscale covert operations, a complex web further revealed during the joint House-Senate hearings into support for the Nicaraguan contras, partially funded by illegal arms sales to Iran.

Since 1984, students have educated themselves about American intervention in foreign governments, largely through the CIA, and learned about the routine process of keeping secret, or misinforming the public, about these operations. They find that sign at that first protest in 1966 still relevant: "Where there is an invisible government, there is no democracy."

While anti-apartheid protests filled the headlines during the spring of 1985, students were also organizing against the CIA. Revelations of the agency's involvement in the mining of Nicaraguan harbors, and the discovery of a secret assassination manual prepared for contra use by the CIA, fueled these protests. The most active opposition generally came from student groups familiar with its role in Central America, though some were aware of other current involvements, such as in southern Africa. In some cases, the agency's policy of discrimination against gay men and lesbians drew backing for protests from campus gay organizations and their supporters.

At Tufts University in Massachusetts on October 3, 1984, 19 students formed a human chain to block a CIA recruiter from conducting a session on their campus. Their statement proclaimed, "The justification for our action requires that we understand that the CIA is engaged in illegal activities and Tufts University lends this organization institutional support and legitimacy by allowing it to recruit on this campus." Three weeks later, the CIA was at least temporarily banned from the campus. No disciplinary charges were filed against the students.[2]

Later that semester, students at Brown introduced a tactic which found widespread use at other schools. Interrupting a "career information session" led by two CIA recruiters, the students staged a citizens' arrest, citing the violation of domestic and international laws when the agency mined the harbors of another country. In the following weeks, 200 students engaged in a candlelight vigil for CIA victims; 56 were reprimanded by the university council on student affairs, and were sentenced to probation. The campus exploded in controversy over whether the students had violated free speech rights. Students insisted that the CIA was not engaging in free speech, but rather in soliciting. At a public hearing, former CIA agent John Stockwell testified: "If we'd had a hearing like this when I was a senior at the University of Texas, I would not have signed on the dotted line."[3]

In the midwest, a major action at the University of Wisconsin capped five months of petition drives, rallies and other events. On April 10, the Progressive Student Network (PSN) on campus executed a militant "mace in the face" anti-CIA demonstration. About 350 people assembled to block the visiting CIA recruiter including about 100 students who blocked the main hallway at the building where interviews were scheduled. A confrontation with the police erupted.[4]

After a rally at the University of Colorado at Boulder, students issued a proclamation accusing the CIA of assassination, rape, torture and attempts to overthrow the government of Nicaragua. Students then met with the local district attorney and demanded that he indict the CIA recruiters for aiding and abetting the execution of war crimes, saying they would perform citizens' arrests if he refused. After blocking the recruitment effort, 478 students were arrested.

The 1986-87 year saw a new round of protests. The fall of 1986, stoked by revelations in the Iran-Contra Affair, witnessed an explosion of protest at Boulder: anticipating student action, university police erected a cyclone fence around the building where recruitment was to take place. But students in larger numbers than expected were forced into a confrontation with police, resulting in the demolition of the fence, and physical assaults. Arrests, confrontations and a full-scale demonstration involving hundreds of students brought national coverage, and new inspiration to other campuses. Around the country, students staged sit-ins, protest rallies, educational campaigns, petition drives—the full list of political activities—to show they would not be silent about the CIA.

In November, 11 students at the University of Massachusetts at Amherst were arrested for occupying a building in a protest against the CIA. About a week later, 14 others were arrested in the takeover of a building involving more than 100 students. For the first time in 17 years, state police and attack dogs were called onto campus; as they loaded the arrested into police buses, others were arrested for blocking the buses. Because those arrested included veteran political activist Abbie Hoffman and former first daughter Amy Carter, these events generated media attention. The "CIA On Trial" project, as it came to be known, brought together student defendants from half a dozen colleges, media celebrities, the well-known defense attorney Leonard Weinglass, and an array of expert witnesses the following spring. The trial did more to offer concrete direction and inspiration to students opposed to the activities of the CIA than any other single event and offered an excellent opportunity for certain messages to circulate through the country. The eventual acquittal only sweetened the deal.

The following month, students in sizeable numbers journeyed to Washington, DC, to lend their bodies and their voices to the March for Peace and Justice in Central America and South Africa on April 25. Two days later, students comprised a healthy number of those arrested at the gates of CIA headquarters in Langley, Virginia, the first such demonstration ever attempted. These events provided important shared experiences; college students were there not as an adventure, but because they had learned about the CIA's activities and wanted, publicly, to show their objections.

SCENE

Grounding the CIA

In the San Francisco Bay Area, people plant white wooden crosses in their front lawns. Spanish names are written on the crosses, the names of people killed during the fighting in Central America. And along with signs, banners and placards, people carry their wooden Solidarity crosses when they go to demonstrate against the CIA.

The target for this event is Southern Air Transport (SAT), a small private airline which has been implicated in the secret CIA airlifts of weapons and supplies to contra forces fighting in Central America. Southern Air Transport has facilities at the Oakland Airport. The Eugene Hasenfus plane, shot down over Nicaragua while on a mission, was one of the SAT fleet.

Pulled together by an ad hoc group of individuals and organizations called the Contragate Action Committee, the event's publicity flyers list eleven endorsers of the Saturday demonstration, and an additional 23 endorsers of the committee. Three of the organizations, Students Against Intervention in Central America, the

Women's Liberation Front and Get the Pentagon Off Campus, are Berkeley college student groups.

For more than a week, area campuses, bus stops, phone booths and bulletin boards have been sporting brown flyers announcing the upcoming demonstration. The headline: SHUT DOWN THE C.I.A. AIRLINE!

The text promises "This is our first demonstration; we will be back."

As local television crews hustle to set up equipment, more than 200 protestors of all ages assemble in a side parking lot at the airport, located adjacent to the SAT building. About a quarter of them are students. Speakers use the back of a flatbed truck to explain the morning's proposed program. Not a major action, the event's objective is to get some press coverage, make some connections between SAT, the CIA and the war in Central America, and wrap it up before anyone gets arrested.

As more participants trickle in, speakers tell the crowd that SAT is also known for running arms to South Africa-backed UNITA guerrillas in Angola, along with its gun-running and drug-smuggling on behalf of the contras. Once the crowd stabilizes, the march kicks off. The chant begins at the front of the march, and seeps back through the line: "CIA...SAT...Shut 'Em Down!...Throw 'Em Out!"

In an orderly, almost upbeat manner, the crowd follows leaders, walking two abreast, heading for the gate near SAT's locked building. Students there for their first-ever demonstration are excited, enjoying the feeling of making a public stand, and making it with other members of the community. The crowd circles the area for a few minutes, then redirects itself to the main terminal building. After a few loops around the traffic island ("Don't block traffic," admonishes one of the organizers as marchers walk in front of commercial airline passengers. "These people are not who we're here to protest."), they congregate on the traffic island for another round of speeches. Pamphlets with background on CIA involvement filter through the crowd. Across the street, a guerrilla theatre group scurries back and forth, announcing "Ollie North to the Courtesy Telephone! Ollie North to the Courtesy Telephone!"

INTERVIEW

Kevin Harris, University of Colorado   *December 18, 1986*

Kevin Harris helps coordinate the ongoing anti-CIA campaign at the University of Colorado, Boulder. He is one of the organizers of the campus CISPES chapter, sits on an important student government committee, and has attended a United States Student Association (USSA)-sponsored training session called Grassroots Organizing Workshop (GROW).

TV—*What happened during those anti-CIA protests in the autumn of 1986?*

KH—I was one of the founders of Community In Action, the anti-CIA group on campus. This was right after the Psychological Warfare Manual had come out. I wanted to focus on them and not on the university or the police. We made that really clear. We expected only about 15 people would attempt a citizens arrest on the CIA recruiters as they came on campus and we ended up having 478 people try over three days. It is a very orderly means of protest, but it serves a certain purpose in terms of getting people to take what's for them a radical step of getting arrested, and getting them to think about the issues. Everyone on campus knew what was going on in the CIA. And to that extent we were very successful. The next year, we focused a little more on the administration, and tried to force the university into dealing with the issue because they hadn't, really, at all. The protest was a little more escalated, a little more disorderly than the year before—220 were arrested in one day. This past spring CIA recruiters decided not to come back. We definitely think it was a successful protest. When we came back in the fall, people were very frustrated. They didn't want unlimited protest, they wanted something that was organized differently. A lot of the anarchists were involved, and wanted it organized less centrally. One of my key issues was to bring the university into the whole business. So we focused on the university a lot. The kind of thinking that went into this year's planning was the result of some of the training I've had with USSA's GROW. Looking for who's your target. It's the most common question people don't think to ask: who's got the power to give them what they want? They usually just pick a real popular figure or a really non-popular figure on campus, like an administrator, and target them, not asking whether or not those people have the power to give them what they want. In that respect, my organizing changed dramatically since the training. It was revolutionary. Before the training, I didn't analyze the power relations. I didn't know exactly who could give me what I wanted. I didn't know how to analyze those things. We did really successful things before, but I would have designed the campaign a little differently.

TV—*How do people react to the idea that they're going to have to do longer, more intense kind of activity?*

KH—Initially negatively, unless they've gone through a training. Then they realize you're not going to get what you want in a month. You know, we've been working on the CIA for ten years. That's something that we teach in the trainings, that victories are not going to come in a month or two, and that one of the problems in student organizing is that there's a change in leadership every year, which makes it real difficult to keep one campaign going continuously.

TV—*Do students look back and build on what was accomplished last year, or do they want to start all over every September?*

KH—A lot depends on who gets into power in student government. If the other party gets into power, forget it. They'll set up all new issues. I'm on the student organizations committee which allocates money to student groups. The people in power, the three students elected to head the student government, make executive appointments to that committee. I was appointed. There's much difference in who gets funded if there's a progressive person in there, or a person from the College Republicans. Also, we go to Student Council a lot of times for funding for special events, and if the other side is in, we're up shit's creek. So it does influence us and we do work on that in the elections.

TV—*Don't some groups have other sources of money?*

KH—Yeah. In fact three years ago the regents cut off mandatory funding for student groups, because they didn't like COPIRG [Colorado Public Interest Research Group] and turned it into a voluntary check-off, which totally killed a lot of student groups. CISPES, for instance, is the largest group on campus and is the most active and we're always doing fundraising.

TV—*Several people on campus have said that CISPES' anti-CIA work is the best organized here. How do you think people make a judgement like that?*

KH—Visibility, for one. We're really active. We have something going on every other week, big activities three or four times a year: film festivals, speakers. We're always out there organizing an event, organizing demonstrations, organizing CIA things. We just have a reputation of, if we want to get something done, we do it.

Targeting A Large Movement

Any organizer trying to generate opposition to the CIA begins with the strong advantage that there are several different reasons to oppose the agency's actions, its policies and even its existence. The spectrum of opposition includes all types of students from a variety of political backgrounds. It ranges from those who believe the United States has a legitimate need for foreign intelligence information, but maintain that the CIA is unscrupulous and should be reformed, to those who believe that interfering in the internal affairs of other countries is reprehensible and counter to democratic principles, and so should be abolished, to those who believe the CIA discriminates against gay men and lesbians by denying them equal employment opportunity, and so should reform its hiring practices. All three groups have serious positions consistent with the other political work that they do, but they are not formed into any sort of coalition, and the closest they come to working together is mutual support when the CIA is included.

Because students opposed to intervention in Central America are able to point to the CIA's complicity with ease, it is the organizations agitating against the US role in Central America that provide the strongest locus for anti-CIA expression. Thus, CIA recruiters on campus provide students with an easy, ready-made local target. Successfully keeping them off campus, however, only "moves" the problem elsewhere; the agency and its role in foreign policy have in no way been altered. And unlike the anti-apartheid activists who have turned their attention to corporations when divestment is won on campus, those students opposed to the CIA have a far more difficult task relocating their focus.

Still, the agency will continue to seek new staff people from the best and brightest of the universities and this will continue to provide activists with a focal point for their organizing and educating activities. Even with the improbability of a "local" victory such as a university regulation expressly prohibiting CIA recruitment on campus, anti-CIA sentiment is higher than it has been on campuses at any time since the early seventies, and will likely remain that way. The appearance of many free-standing autonomous "CIA Off Campus" groups and the variety of constituencies they represent are testimony to the popularity and importance of this issue. As an issue, CIA recruitment provides one of the easiest and most convenient political rallying points.

The "CIA on Trial" Project

In a media trial, the verdict of the public counts far more than the verdict of the jury. And the "CIA on Trial" trial had all the elements, and then some, to attract public attention.

The core of the event was very serious—opposition to CIA intervention in Central America. Seeking to prevent the CIA from recruiting at the University of Massachusetts at Amherst, students took over a building and obstructed a police bus loaded with arrested protestors. They had tried for more than a year to get their administration to ban the recruiters, with no satisfaction.

But the particulars—the legal questions, the cast of characters—greatly enhanced the attention the proceedings received. Lead attorney Leonard I. Weinglass had previously defended the Chicago Eight, Angela Davis, Jane Fonda and the principals in the *Pentagon Papers* Case. Witnesses would include former CIA agents, *Covert Action Information Bulletin's* editor, a former leader of the contra forces in Nicaragua, the author of the *Pentagon Papers*, and a former US Attorney General. The defendants included students from four different universities, a non-student, anti-war activist who symbolized the sixties, and the daughter of a former US president. I tell my research assistant Miles Pomper, if you saw it in a movie, you'd dismiss it as too unbelievable. Miles observes that, unlike divestment, the anti-CIA movement can only pressure the government to change itself. The need to create political pressure through a strong public impression is greater here than with other issues.

Even the setting befitted an event from popular fiction. Northampton's Hampshire County courthouse, built 101 years earlier on the site of the area's first meetinghouse, circa 1650, nestles peacefully in its small New England town. The three-story granite structure, topped by a gold horse weathervane, guarded by a centuries-old maple, and ringed by black wrought-iron fence, seems to symbolize "justice."

On the second floor of the courthouse, as press and friends settle into long wooden benches, the judge sits down, turns on his globe-bulbed lamp, and continues the jury selection process into its fifth day until both sides agree on the two men and four women, ages 34 to 77, who will sit in the jury box.

Thanking the jury for its patience, attorney Weinglass states that the events of that day are not under contention, only whether they were committed, as the law states, "With no legitimate purpose, and without right," as the prosecution contends. "Was this lawlessness, or an act to stop the lawlessness? Their protest was confined precisely to where the CIA intruded themselves into their lives."

Weinglass and his colleagues put forth a "necessity defense," that it is admissible to commit a crime to prevent the occurrence of a greater evil: you might trespass onto your neighbor's lawn to put out a fire in his house. Use of such a defense is rare, but was used successfully in 1984 by 44 people who occupied New Hampshire Senator Robert Stafford's office to persuade him to change his contra aid vote. Judges determine whether or not to allow its use in a particular case.

Defendant Jennifer Johnston tells the jury, "who we are and why we're doing what we're doing," that the students felt the school was violating its own rule mandating that users of campus facilities "must be law-abiding." Faculty and administration committees had previously advised the board of trustees that the CIA be banned from campus, but no decision was made.

The judge permits a necessity defense, an important step. Slowly, deliberately, background and perspective are established. Witness Ralph McGehee, a CIA officer from 1952 to 1977, recounts how secret CIA operations in Indonesia, Iran and Guatemala, encompassing economic, political, psychological and paramilitary warfare, resulted in the overthrow of governments and the deaths of millions. He also indicates that campus recruitment is vital to the CIA, its most valuable source of new agents. Francis Boyle, University of Illinois law professor and international law scholar, affirms that the United States is bound by the Geneva Convention, the Nuremberg laws and the World Court, all of which have apparently been violated by CIA covert actions. Witness Edgar Chamorro, former contra leader recruited by the CIA, relates how contras disrupt civilian life in Nicaragua by planting land mines to cripple and maim citizens, to strain the hospital system and add financial obligations to the government, and by assassinating judges and security officers. Witness Howard Zinn, author and Boston University political science professor, walks the jury through a history of US social movements, from the Fugitive Slave Act to the lunch counter sit-ins, noting how these actions prompted changes in American society and law. Witness Daniel Ellsberg, former State Department consultant who released the *Pentagon Papers* to the Congress and the press to fuel opposition to the Vietnam War, paints a picture of decision-making in the inner circles of government, where Congress is lied to, and the question "Is this legal?" is never asked. "There's an uncanny resemblance," Ellsberg adds, his voice nearly shaking with emotion, "between decisions made in 1965 [Vietnam], and now [Nicaragua]. The planning process is almost identical." And defendant Nick Komar, a UMass student who has travelled to Central America, testifies that "the CIA represents actions that don't respect the values I was brought up with."

Abbie Hoffman testifies, light-heartedly: "At 50, I'm the oldest of the student demonstrators." Amy Carter tells the jury in a soft voice, "I would have done the same thing even if the general public would not find out about it. I think when a person sacrifices to stop a greater evil, it adds to the cycles of change."

Throughout the nine-day proceedings, a crush of press nearly suffocates the media stars Abbie and Amy, the former first daughter receiving the lion's share of the attention. During short recesses she sneaks up to a third floor landing for a quick, private cigarette. During one of these breaks, she confides how much she hates the press singling her out, but hopes the publicity will result in some people, particularly students, hearing about subjects they'd never heard of before.

In his summation, Weinglass buttons his jacket, removes his glasses and tells the jury, "If this case is about nothing else, it is about morality. That's the standard we're talking about."

The jury files out. We wonder how long the deliberations will take. Outside, the tops of a few old buildings and a crisp blue sky are visible through the windows. The press area swells with reporters fighting for seats. Much of the coverage has been superficial: Amy's clothes and Abbie's age, to the annoyance of the principals. A few defendants take up books, such as *Sandino: General of the Free* and *Undercover: 35 Years of CIA Deception.* Amy leans her head back on the rail that separates the defendants from the spectators, and closes her eyes. Roger Morey reminds me of Abbie's benefit performance at the Iron Horse Café; sitting in the balcony we had heard him joke, "I've certainly been involved in a lot of trials in my life—maybe this time I'll get it right."

At 4:25 p.m., Wednesday, April 16, the jury files back in, looking somber. Abbie signals "thumbs down" to Weinglass. Outside it's a windy 66 degrees, inside, about the same. The defendants—Komar, Carter, Morey, Hoffman, Johnston, Lisa Sheehy, Bill Clay, Tom Landry, Joe Rubin, Mark Caldiera, Emily Katz, Jason Pramas, Jay Allain, Rachel Kolman and Debi Cohen—stand quietly. Members of the jury stand. The crowded chamber shivers with stillness. The first "Not Guilty" is announced and deafening, shattering screams, hugging, shreaking, jumping, whooping all transform the room, reversing the solemn formality of the past eight days. Insisting on order, the judge clears the courtroom. Only the press are permitted to remain.

One by one the defendants are pronounced "not guilty." The jury is thanked; formal closing words are entered into the record; court is adjourned. Again, an eruption.

The defendants, decked out in red "CIA On Trial" T-shirts, come out onto the courthouse steps carrying a black, red and blue banner proclaiming "On To Washington," referring to the upcoming April 25 March. Newspaper stories in days to come assess the victory will lead to more student activism and to more use of the necessity defense. Almost unnoticed, at sunset, a grey-shirted security guard walks to the courthouse yard flagpole and lowers the stars and stripes.

Outside the gate, 300 college students cheer the defendants, chanting "The People United Will Never Be Defeated." A few are selling bus tickets to the Washington March. Asked by a reporter how she feels about the press coverage, Amy replies, pointing to the students, "I'm much more glad that they're here than the media."

CHAPTER SIX

War Machine

For the more than four decades following World War II, the United States has adopted the role of policeman, or "peacekeeper," for the planet. And how did we choose to act out that role? By attempting to establish overwhelming military superiority, amassing the largest arms buildup in history. Through the early years of the Cold War, Americans rarely challenged this position, and the advent of the Korean War seemed to legitimize government pronouncements of an unshakeable need for military superiority. The 1950s proceeded with economic growth spurred on by huge military contracts. The Civil Defense Program assured civilians they could survive a nuclear attack if they socked away enough dried beans, drinking water and board games for a two-week stay in the basement. But by the end of that decade, peace groups started to appear specifically aimed at alerting people to the dangers of the nuclear weapons build-up. President Eisenhower's admonition to be mindful of the dangers of the military-industrial complex verified this fear.

The work of organizing against militarism remained with small peace groups, aligned at times with religion-linked organizations like the American Friends Service Committee. It was not until the mushrooming of the Vietnam War that large, popular support for anti-war efforts surfaced. Fear of the draft and eventual assignment to the jungles of Southeast Asia—and the strong potential for returning maimed or dead—led college students to mount vociferous anti-war campaigns with rallies, draft card burnings, assaults on Selective Service offices, and protests against their own universities which assisted in the draft process by providing information to the system.

After the Vietnam War era, attention shifted to nuclear weapons: nuclear freeze or nuclear disarmament initiatives and test ban treaty developments signaled new rounds of organizing. Campuses joined with municipalities in declaring themselves nuclear-free zones banning the presence or transport of nuclear materials.

By the end of the '70s, the country was engrossed in another military build-up, and when President Reagan announced the creation of the Strategic Defense Initiative (SDI), or Star Wars, faculty members in the various science departments on campuses began to respond. Using research showing the project was unworkable, many signed pledges refusing to work on SDI research. This marked the first significant link between students and faculty in this movement.

Today, interest is growing in the anti-military movement, with different groups addressing different facets of the overall topic. Students in this movement tend to favor educational events that can teach others the complex facts and relationships.

Life and death for everyone on the planet—these are the stakes for students protesting any aspect of the war machine. It's a topic almost too big to comprehend, and certainly extremely difficult to assail.

Three levels of response to the war machine permeate this movement: opposition to SDI, opposition to nuclear weapons, and the drive for complete disarmament. The war machine runs on money, information and public support. Students attack it from all these directions: lobbying to alter federal budget priorities, and to a lesser degree, boycotting companies involved in weapons work; targeting the universities as suppliers of information which is vital to the war machine; and organizing past the campus gate to rally support from the general population in the case of anti-militarism.

And outside that gate, dozens of international, national, regional and local organizations study this issue, distribute publications, sponsor forums, produce films, host lectures and write letters to Congresspeople and newspaper editors, in efforts to alter the direction of the arms race. Students either work within these groups, or use their resources on campus.[1]

The organization aimed specifically at the university is UCAM—United Campuses to Prevent Nuclear War. Founded in 1982, UCAM has grown to more than 70 chapters, and ties together the efforts of students, faculty and staff. Its most ambitious activity is an annual Lobby Day, held in the spring, when delegates from across the country visit Capitol Hill and explain to members of Congress why they should support disarmament, end nuclear deployment, or abandon SDI. In 1987, the contingent involved about 450 students from 55 campuses in 26 states.[2]

UCAM's newsletter compiles relevant information for use in local campaigns. For example, the December 1986 edition reported on a survey, by UCAM co-chair Peter Stein, of 663 physical sciences, engineering and mathematician members of the National Academy of Sciences. Of the 71 percent who responded, more than three-fourths believed that the prospects are "poor" or "extremely poor" that SDI can be made "survivable and cost effective at the margin" in the next 25 years; 98% estimated that SDI would not be capable of destroying a sufficient number of Soviet missiles to make it an "effective defense of the US civilian population."[3] Other newsletters offered tactical advice, for example, using radio talk shows to convey the anti-military message.

On their campuses, students usually turn to education as their principal strategy: lectures, including one on SDI at Connecticut College titled "May the Farce Be With You," panel discussions, and seminars at schools like Adirondack Community College and Western Kentucky University. At Yale, Students for Nuclear Disarmament hold an annual high school training program featuring workshops and lectures. The introduction of peace studies programs into college curricula and the hosting of visiting Soviet students are other methods of educating students to the overall disarmament picture.

Students Against Militarism (SAM) at Columbia chooses educational events. Erica Etelson explains: "We're more on the academic side of the movement— speakers, discussions, films. We're not likely to sponsor rallies, because they sometimes turn off a whole group of people. Our main project was, we had four Soviet students visit for about two weeks, from the USSR Student Council. We sponsored a big forum on US-Soviet relations."[4]

At an annual Week of Education, traditionally in November, UCAM members use a packet prepared by the national office which includes organizational tips, a detailed bibliography and resources list, and a list of available speakers. Areas covered include: comprehensive test ban, nuclear non-proliferation, no first use policy, ban on space weapons, preventing accidental nuclear war, nuclear and conventional force cuts, independent initiatives, complete nuclear disarmament, verification, and building a global peace movement.

Because effective campus organizing requires a local target, students will often protest the presence of nuclear weapons research at their school. A petition drive soliciting pledges from university science professors not to work on Star Wars research was worked out in the summer of 1985 between UCAM members at Cornell and others from the physics department of the University of Illinois-Urbana. From there it spread across the country and a year later, a majority of the physicists in the top 26 physics departments, including 16 Nobel Prize winners, had signed, vowing to neither solicit nor accept SDI research money.

At Columbia, students pinpointed scientists affiliated with "Jason," a think tank project aimed at weapons research. Detailed information about Jason comes from Scientists and Engineers for Social and Political Action (SESPA), based in Berkeley. Brian D'Agostino used the SESPA material to help create a disarmament branch within the New York Democratic Socialists of America (DSA) in the spring of 1987.[5] He describes his work in an interview below.

Opposition to draft registration, a descendant of the draft resistance which generated much anti-war activity in the past, continues to find student support. Campus-based groups, often as affiliates of War Resisters League, the Fellowship of Reconciliation or the Central Committee for Conscientious Objectors (CCCO), counsel their peers about the implications of registering and not registering. The CCCO in particular specializes in this—employing a field worker who travels around the country, visiting campuses and training counselors. CCCO also serves as a networking organization for all students interested in draft resistance.

Some groups have linked their anti-militarism to boycotts of companies doing weapons research. For example, one UCAM packet prepared by John Doris details General Electric's history as a major recipient of nuclear weapons contracts. Students can also use information compiled by Nuclear Free America, which publishes a list of the top 50 nuclear weapons contractors.

Campus groups working on war machine issues often align themselves with organizations opposing US intervention in Central America, or with those dealing with economic concerns, making the point that a reduced military budget could free money for other concerns. Some anti-military actions attract students from women's groups, who see a link between militarism and sexism, or from gay\lesbian groups, who protest the discrimination practiced by the military.

Without question, science and engineering majors are the most influential segment of the student population dedicated to anti-military activity as they bring to their opposition a degree of informed opinion that carries more impact than support from the average student.

SCENE

Damaging Research

Jackie Victor "picked the issue of military research on campus as something I wanted to work on, because it's kind of at a pivotal point." She is working in the Michigan Union Building at the University of Michigan, and shows me the photographs of past student assembly presidents along the walls who silently witness their successors' actions. The pictures change in historical sequence from black-and-white to color, from crew cuts to shoulder-length hair and back again, in some way mirroring the history of anti-war sentiments on most college campuses.

Fifteen years ago, this university adopted guidelines which prohibited conducting research "the intent of which was to kill or inflict permanent damage to human life." Now those guidelines are to be reviewed to permit the school to accept Star Wars research money. Jackie explains, "one regent said we need to research if these guidelines are still relevant, the idea that the sixties are done and we dealt pretty well with that stuff, and luckily we got over it, so let's get on with it and build the country and the university."

Nearby, a woman from the community, Toby Hannah, quietly makes her way around the perimeter of several tables, assembling a large mailing. Opposition to Star Wars research on campuses takes this form more often than public demonstration. Students concerned with this issue see their task as reaching specific people, people with influence and votes in key places. She is a volunteer for WAND, the Women's Action for Nuclear Disarmament, which does joint projects involving university and community people.

On this campus, the Latin American Solidarity Committee frequently provides students with opportunities to show their opposition to American foreign policy. But those opposed to military research on campus are dealing with a less dramatic issue, and one that introduces the question of whether individuals should be free to choose the work they seek.

Jackie has engaged the energies of students on campus, as well as members of the community to lobby the regents. "Letters have gone out to Ann Arbor clergy, getting over sixty signatures, saying to the regents you can't do it. I instigated a project contacting every peace group in Michigan we could get ahold of, sending out packets with background information, sample letters to the editor, sample letters to regents, and these clergy letters. What we're saying to these people is that the University of Michigan is more than Ann Arbor, the regents need to know your input, we need some pressure from you."

The activity is low key, contrasting with Jackie's effervescent personality. "We're planning a big vigil the day of the regents meeting. We decided to call it Progress to Less, the idea being that this is a great opportunity to make some changes in a positive direction."

"What I want to do," she confides as she sits back down, "is draw the links between militarism, racism and sexism. I'm seeing more and more people who are saying I'm ready to commit, but I want to do more than just bitch." Then she thanks me, joins the others, and gets to work.

INTERVIEW

Brian D'Agostino, Columbia   *May 8, 1987*

Graduate student Brian D'Agostino of Students Against Militarism (SAM), has spent years trying to educate others about the complicity between the university and the scientific community in arms proliferation. His particular focus is "Jason," an academic\military think tank made up of top US physicists.

TV—*How organized is the Committee on Jason?*

BA—It's actually a small ad hoc group of students and professors, though we have the support of other faculty and alumni and staff. We see this as an issue that involves everyone, since these people are all part of the Columbia community. It's the arms race, close at home.

TV—*Why have you chosen this focus?*

BA—Actually this is part of a much broader analysis of the arms race. We focus on Jason because we're trying to attack the collaboration between the scientific community and the military, as such, and that's a very hierarchical thing. It's pervasive— many individuals are involved with defense money at Columbia. People don't understand that the whole legitimacy of this thing depends on a much smaller group, about 40 or 50 of the country's top physicists, many of them Nobel Prize winners. And they happen to be in this formal organization called Jason, which meets for six or seven weeks every year. Because they are the most prestigious people in the scientific community, we feel this legitimizes the rest of the scientific community to go along.

TV—*Is Jason an acronym?*

BA—No. I'm not sure where the name came from. It began in the sixties, and it really came about with the obsolescence of the first generation of scientists who developed the atomic bomb. The military sought to renew the kind of ongoing collaboration it had with the scientific community under the Manhattan Project, and it recruited the younger generation of physicists, the best minds in the physics community. During the sixties they worked on the automated battlefield, sometimes known as the McNamara Line, a system of anti-personnel weapons used in Vietnam which killed countless civilians. It couldn't discriminate between military, and women and children. Even then Jason was involved with strategic weapons and after the Vietnam War it returned to dealing almost exclusively with them. They proposed a basing system for the MX missile. They proposed the Cruise missile, instead of the B-1 bomber, and we now have both. The reason we focus on this group is that if you want to stop the arms race, we have to stop people from doing the research. There are so many people doing military research, so many weapons think tanks like Riverside Research Institute or Lawrence Livermore Labs. There are weapons production plants all over the place—the top 500 corporations are deeply enmeshed in the funding and development of weapons. The whole society is deeply enmeshed in keeping the arms race going. So the question is, where can you intervene that's going to count? We're at Columbia, and we know the military depends on tapping the very best minds. If we remain silent at Columbia, it makes it possible for this collaboration to go on, with business as usual. We did a teach-in at Columbia recently as part of a Star Wars demonstration. We try to feed this into existing peace networks. We don't see the need for a national organization to stop Jason. What we're trying to do is public education and feeding it into the existing peace infrastructure.

TV—*Has participation increased?*

BA—For a long time, there was just a core group. Then last November a broader group of people kicked in and got a full-page ad in the Columbia Spectator, and that got a lot of people interested. We have this petition going around, with several hundred signatures—about one out of five students that we ask to sign it actually signs it, and it's a pretty strongly worded condemnation of Jason. So maybe 20% of the student body are willing to ask for action against Jason from the faculty. We're going to present the petitions to individual members of the faculty who are sympathetic to what we're trying to do, but have been reluctant to jump in. It's a can of worms for someone on the faculty. They're easily stigmatized as troublemakers. Our strategy is to build sufficient support among the students so that we can get members of the faculty to take a position and know that there's a substantial body of support for some kind of action. And the core group has grown.

INTERVIEW

John Gourlay, Ohio State University   *June 6, 1987*

John Gourlay is an assistant professor of computer and information sciences at Ohio State University in Columbus. He is one of hundreds of scientists who believe that the Strategic Defense Initiative cannot be executed. He agreed to gather signatures from colleagues on a petition opposing the research.

TV—*What happened to the petition?*

JG—It was officially delivered to Reagan and people in the administration in July of '86.

TV—*Have there been any results?*

JG—I don't know if there's been much official reaction to the petition, but there's been studies done on Star Wars. One was commissioned by the government, which I believe said the same thing that the petition did. That doesn't keep them from asking for money.

TV—*Have students been involved?*

JG—Graduate students—there were actually two petitions, one for graduate students and one for faculty. They basically said the same thing, but as a rule students don't go out soliciting research funds, they just work on whatever projects their faculty has money for. So students signed a petition promising they wouldn't work for any grants funded by Star Wars money.

TV—*What's the university administration's role in this?*

JG—They play a passive role. The faculty writes proposals, and if they get funded, the administration's happy.

TV—*Was there much dissension over this issue within the faculty?*

JG—Maybe in other departments, but in the computer science department, the feeling is virtually unanimous that Star Wars is unbuildable. There are some people who, for one reason or another, won't sign anything, but I got, officially, about 60%, and an unoffocial estimate would be about 75% of the faculty signing it. Everyone that I talked to agreed that Star Wars was a crazy thing to be doing. They had other, almost irrelevant reasons for not signing.

TV—*How did you hear about the petition?*

JG—I was teaching a seminar, and one student in it told me he had this petition he wanted to circulate, and would I help him. The graduate students feel, probably justifiably, that it ought to be a faculty member approaching other faculty members. My only concern was whether or not I had the time to do the job right.

TV—*Do you object to the research because it's a waste of time and money?*

JG—Worse. It's a diversion of one sort or another. It's making liars of all of us who are participating in it. We pretend we're working toward this goal, when we really aren't. We all have ulterior motives, including the President—he must have good advice, it has to be at least as good as ours, yet he persists. Gorbachev's advice has got to be as good, and yet he insists on taking it as a realistic threat. It's all a complicated chess game. It's clearly unfeasible. If it were totally innocuous, then nobody would get excited about it. But the physicists and the computer scientists are being put in the position of justifying some political game the President wants to play.

INTERVIEW

Mary Maloney, UCAM   *June 15, 1987*

Mary Maloney is field director of United Campuses to Prevent Nuclear War (UCAM). Working from Washington, DC, she coordinates information and contacts among the organization's 70-plus chapters. We spoke after UCAM's April 1987 annual conference held in Norman, Oklahoma.

TV—*What was the feeling among the delegates in terms of the next year or two?*

MM—Many of them said they'd like to include more direct action, or public events, like demonstrations or rallies. Some feel they'd like to be more creative in the ways they try to reach out to other students. There's also an interest in expanding our work to more global concerns, a definite feeling of wanting to link things to disarmament, rather than merely arms control. We talked about that a good deal.

TV—*What was the composition of the delegates?*

MM—It was about 50-50 men and women, and maybe 1% were students of color. I can't say if that's an accurate representation or not on the campus level, but we want to try to involve more students of color.

TV—*Has UCAM grown in the past year?*

MM—Just in the past eight months, the number of chapters has increased 30%.

TV—*Where does UCAM's funding come from?*

MM—From a variety of sources: from foundations, large donor members, and a constituency that contributes through dues; we also do some fund-raising events.

TV—*Can you describe a creative educational event?*

MM—Students at Cornell, and UCAM students in Arkansas, wanted to dramatize the size of the military budget. So they made a bar graph using large strips of brightly-colored cloth, and laid it out on the ground. Each foot equalled one billion dollars, and it stretched out for 156 feet! In contrast, the energy budget, for instance, was 15 inches, and the arms control budget was under one inch! They really got a great response. It really grabbed people. And they used it to attract people—they distributed about 2,000 leaflets to passers-by who saw it and stopped to look.

TV—*What do you see, as far as students' interest in this subject?*

MM—There's a realization that the Reagan era has been a very tough one for the movement. But it's coming to a close. They realize there's a lot of work to be done, and I see there's a lot of energy and willingness out there to do it.

Education and Information are Key

The enormous size of the target compels students in this movement to develop a degree of respect for information they need. Most activists opposing the war machine have spent serious time educating themselves about military budgets, weapons systems, historical factors, political considerations and technical jargon, all of them ammunition to counter questions about loss of security, trusting the Russians, accidental war or non-military take-overs.

Though the range of beliefs is broad—from a test ban treaty to complete elimination of all military weapons and systems—students are slowly finding common ground. For the foreseeable future, activists will continue to concentrate on education—speakers, forums, introducing related courses into a curriculum, etc. But there's a murmur of interest in joining students committed to other political causes in public events.

One new tactic discussed briefly at the spring '87 UCAM conference takes a lead from the divestment movement: pressuring universities to divest stocks in those companies doing military and nuclear weapons contract work. Many campus groups already distribute lists of the 50 top corporations doing this work, and urge students to boycott their products. Another idea, put forward by retired Notre Dame president Theodore Hesburgh, would call for a Peace Corps counterpart to ROTC programs that would train students in peace and international development.

As the students connected to this movement graduate and enter the society, their education in these issues could translate into a more informed electorate, better able to challenge politicians on matters of military spending and defense allocations. For now, because the activities are rarely confrontational or likely to lead to arrest or expulsion, students can gravitate to this movement with relatively little risk. This also means they stand a better chance than other movements of attracting the mainstream student whose political consciousness is just beginning to be stirred.

"Greeks for Peace"

On Tuesday, March 3, 1987, the *Michigan Daily* at the University of Michigan at Ann Arbor carried three items about "Greeks"—members of fraternities and sororities.

Across the front page, readers discovered that the Ann Arbor City Council had voted to limit group housing, a severe blow to Greeks looking for houses. The sub-head proclaimed: "Sororities to fight decision," reporting that the pan-Hellenic association had registered 200 new voters to oust the offending politicians come election time.

A small classified ad in the "Greek Gab" department announces Alpha Xi Delta's first annual Bare Your Tan Contest. And on the inside back page, an ad for an event. "Everything You Always Wanted To Know About Sex(ism)." Same night as the Bare Your Tan contest. The sponsor? Greeks for Peace.

"We're aware that it's kind of an odd thing," confesses Matthew Greene. Matthew and co-founder Jeanne Besansine, fresh-scrubbed and able to walk undetected into a Benneton ad, stroll with me through the Michagan Union, talking about an idea that sounds like a cross between a Saturday Night Live skit and a Leap of Faith.

They met at a Democratic state convention, were both really concerned about what was going on in the world, and, Jeanne remembers, "How it doesn't seem real consistent to being in the Greek system." Discovering other Greeks working on the same progressive candidate's local campaign, they decided to give it a shot.

What kind of response do they get to the idea that frat boys and sorority sisters could organize in a political manner? "Disbelief. Surprise. Amazement," Matthew ad-

81

mits. "And as soon as they realize we're serious, they're really interested in at least what it is."

They have begun cautiously. First, they supported existing campaigns, such as a test ban demonstration. Next step: an event of their own to bring people in and to address serious issues. They chose sexism.

Matthew explains, "It's a lot more apolitical. It's a social issue. We're Greeks for Peace, and there's subtle violence every day between men and women. A lot of people in the Greek system are apolitical, or they have some whimsical notion about being conservative, but they haven't had experiences to lead them strongly either way."

Jeanne does not discredit Greek charity and philanthropy work, but adds: "We see that as a band-aid and not really effective change." They will help with a teach-in on Central America. It was exposure to a campus demonstration on divestment that led Matthew to ask questions about what was going on. "I saw a protest and realized, there must be something. I thought, there's got to be a reason these people are doing things, and why they're all upset. So I started investigating. If there is something wrong, I can't just not know."

In their view, many Greeks would become politically active if the climate were changed. Matthew has seen that "people are coming out of the closet" in terms of openly expressing interest in political issues, "and hopefully people in every house will start becoming more concerned. There are a few in every house, it looks like, that are already unhappy with the situation."

They've had general support from activists, many of whom had said "good luck with those people—they're unorganizeable." Their mailing list already contains nearly 100 names.

This is as much about stereotypes as it is about activism, they stress. Mention Greeks to progressive students and you hear reactions like "sexist," "racist," "macho," "conservative" or "apathetic." Maybe the terms fit many Greeks, Jeanne and Matthew concede, but they want to change that, and are ready to deal with large doses of indifference and ridicule to make their point.

"We'd like to break down the stereotypes of both the Greek system and the activists," Matthew says with a tone of conviction. "We feel prejudice in each setting."

CHAPTER SEVEN

Racism

The world of black college students and the world of civil rights came together dramatically and historically in April of 1960.

When the police and city officials of Greensboro, South Carolina heard about sit-ins at the lunch counters of downtown Kress stores, they didn't take it seriously, believing the students were outside agitators. Students were protesting segregated conditions throughout the South, which still mandated separate White Only and Colored drinking fountains, public accommodations, restrooms, waiting rooms and other places of service. Blacks could walk around inside a Woolworth's store and spend ten thousand dollars, but they could not sit down at the lunch counter and order a ten cent cup of coffee.

After two weeks of sit-ins at lunch counters, the police moved in and arrested wave after wave of students, a new group taking the place of those taken away each time arrests were made. Although the students remained non-violent, many were brutally beaten by bystanders and offered no protection by the police. Along with the community members involved, the black students, led by Diane Fisk, John Lewis and Angela Butler, were found guilty of trespassing. Within two weeks, lunch counter sit-ins had spread to 69 cities throughout the country.

As civil rights organizations undertook voter registration drives, boycotts of white-owned businesses, marches and church meetings, students stood on the front lines. And when the Southern Christian Leadership Conference, a leading black civil rights organization, sponsored a conference of more than two hundred politically active black students at Shaw University in Raleigh, N.C., April 15-17, 1960, one of the most influential bits of advice came from longtime activist Ella Baker. She coun-

selled the students to avoid affiliation with a national organization, to remain independent. The Student Non-violent Coordiating Committee (SNCC) followed her advice, and went on to play a major role in shaping the political climate for years to
come.

In October of 1960, a lunch counter sit-in led to the arrest and imprisonment
of Dr. Martin Luther King, Jr. Presidential candidate John F. Kennedy called King's
wife Coretta to offer support; his brother Robert called the Georgia judge and successfully demanded Dr. King's release. The Sunday before the election, black ministers throughout the South endorsed JFK, who went on to win by the smallest
popular majority in history. The following spring, the Congress of Racial Equality
pressured the President to end segregated interstate travel, through the Interstate
Commerce Commission, but help was slow in coming. In response, Freedom Rides,
with blacks and whites travelling together on public buses through the South, were
organized, to pressure the government into establishing an ICC ruling on segregated
interstate travel. After a series of bloody encounters in Alabama with members of
the Ku Klux Klan that left some riders with injuries that would cripple them for life,
the Ride was nearly called off. It was the arrival of, and determination of the students from SNCC that jolted the campaign back on track. The rides resumed, and
forced Attorney General Robert Kennedy to intervene, using federal force to guarantee the safety of the riders. After a series of life-threatening confrontations, challenges in court and disregard for the law, the students had helped to catapult the issue
to national attention. By September, the ICC granted the Attorney General's petition
to outlaw segregated interstate travel and accommodations.

In the following years, northern white students travelled to the South, to learn
from the black students who had generated the activities of SNCC. They joined the
cause, helping with voter registration drives and education campaigns. Abbie Hoffman taught in a SNCC Freedom school. Mario Savio, soon to lead Berkeley's Free
Speech Movement, worked for SNCC's Mississippi Freedom Summer of 1964. And
the Port Huron Statement, manifesto of the Students for a Democratic Society (SDS),
was written by Tom Hayden after he spent time working with SNCC members in
McComb, Mississippi.

In the next few years, white students committed to social and political change
flocked to SNCC, many joining its staff. SNCC's philosophy of organizing locally to
make changes nationally found its way into the agenda of SDS, with its Economic
Research and Action Project campaign. The issues targeted for action addressed conditions which had become ingrained into American life—segregation, systematic
denial of voting rights, inferior education, lack of jobs. The advent of the Vietnam
War, with a disproportionate number of non-white young men being killed in the
jungles of Southeast Asia, added one more atrocity to the list. Black and white students shared many of the same concerns, and adopted many of the same tactics.

But the growing domination of SNCC by white students irritated many blacks,
however unintentional the development may have been. Some blacks resented the
fact that it took the death of two white volunteers in the summer of 1961 to grab
the attention of the national press, which had ignored the deaths of many black
youths killed in earlier organizing efforts. SNCC members also saw some resistance

from southern black community members asked to follow the advice of young white college students. And black women in SNCC resented white women occasionally receiving attention from the young black men in the movement. The young white women found themselves in the position of not wanting to resist their advances, for fear of being accused of racism. Black women saw their status change.

Feelings of resentment and repression within the movement grew, and blacks in SNCC, along with many of the younger militants within CORE, began to evolve the doctrine of black power. They viewed it as a redress of the balance of power, as a vehicle for directing their own destinies, and as a means of consolidating their political and cultural identities. SNCC member Stokeley Carmichael founded a group called the Black Panthers in Oakland to intervene on behalf of blacks in community affairs. SNCC evolved a stance internally to exclude whites from positions of authority, and eventually from the organization itself. A mood of militant separatism began to take hold in the civil rights movement. When in 1966 James Meredith, a black University of Mississippi student, chose to walk across the state to demonstrate that a black man could go anywhere he wanted to, he was shot and killed. This event catalyzed blacks, and by the end of the year, SNCC called for the expulsion of all whites from its organization.

Although the Black Panther Party retained contact with whites, most other groups did not. The idea of Black Power called into question all the views of the origins and continuing causes of oppression. James Forman, a prominent SNCC leader, questioned the Black Power focus, when in 1967 he wrote: "Are the problems we face only ones of color? ...What is upper-, lower- and middle-class? Do they exist among blacks? Why is there a black banker in one town and a starving Negro in the same? ...Do the problems of the black welfare mother arise only from her blackness? If not, then what are the other causes?"[1] Serious consideration of these questions was never offered, and within two years SNCC had died.

On campuses, the overall politicization of students led to some gains by blacks, although many of the promises made during the late 1960s and early 1970s were not kept. Informal or unrecognized black student unions became institutionalized and sanctioned on many campuses. Some increases in the enrollment of non-white students, the hiring of non-white faculty and the introduction of black studies programs were charted. But in most instances, the objectives set out at the height of political agitation were not met.

In other communities, low enrollment figures almost guaranteed an absence of real political power although latinos, chicanos, native Americans and Asians, all formulated support groups on their campuses in the late 1960s. It is only within the last few years, as their enrollment has increased, that their political power on campuses has also surfaced, claiming rights, programs and services for their members.

One legacy of the Black Power movement that remains is the determination of all non-white student groups to retain their cultural integrity within the context of university life. They insist, with varying degrees of militancy, that their heritage, and their history, should not be used as trading cards to get better treatment within the academic community, as trade-offs for career training and job placement.

The Challenge

Racism is the single greatest threat to the emergence of a progressive student movement in the United States.

Racism continues to inject itself into nearly every attempt at unifying college students for political change. While the manifestations of racism in the larger society provide ample cause to organize students who want to change those attitudes and behaviors, relations between students of different races pose at least as big a threat. Students of color, seeing their numbers on a downward spiral, close ranks for survival and uncover broken promises made by anxious administrators at a time, some 20 years before, when confrontations and sit-ins forced admissions offices to recruit more broadly. Now, chicanos make up 12% of Colorado's population, but barely 2% of the University's enrollment;[2] at Berkeley, where the administration made a firm commitment to 10% black enrollment 15 years ago, blacks comprise only 5% of the student body.[3]

This enrollment pattern has affected student political organization. Meetings on divestment at Boston University get sidetracked when someone comments that only one of the 20-odd students present is black. When the 15 most active members of Madison's PSN congregate around the corner booth table in the back room of the Black Bear Tavern, there are no black faces, and all the "CIA On Trial" defendants in Massachusetts are white. Increasingly, white and non-white students find themselves distanced, separate, and unpracticed in how to come together. Blacks have grown suspicious of whites in meeting situations, where white students gravitate toward leadership positions. Whites are unfamiliar with and insensitive to the alienation minority students feel. Too frequently, groups are formed along lines of race and ethnicity, leaving students little opportunity to share social and cultural activities.

Today's students have no personal recollection of the battles fought over voting rights and desegregation; Martin Luther King Jr. exists only on film, in politicians' speeches, and as the name of a national holiday that continues to stir controversy.

Raised in segregated environments, students have had little chance to dispel myths about each other. When the Southwest Residential Area at the University of Massachusetts at Amherst erupted on October 27, 1986, the clearly racist attacks were carried out by students acting solely on the basis of skin color: following the final game of the World Series, fans of the defeated Boston Red Sox ("the white team") harassed, and then attacked—with bats and fists—fans of the victorious New York Mets ("the black team"). An investigation revealed that alcohol was only a catalyst spurring deep-seated racial divisions.[4]

As a student at Yale, Matthew Countryman moved from anti-nuclear to divestment organizing. His mixed-race background provided a unique perspective. "I've certainly been in a number of meetings where, because of my light complexion, people will say 'Oh, there are no blacks in the room. What are we going to do?' Which makes me feel very small.

"I was always very clear about being black in public. Friends of mine, people I have forgiven about this, would say, 'How come Matthew insists on calling himself black. He doesn't act black. He doesn't fit my conception of how an upwardly mobile black Yaley is supposed to operate.' Especially with 18- or 19-year-olds, there's this choice: either I become "Black" and become part of the cultural center and be very much a nationalist, or else I become a Yaley and hang out with all these white folks. There's no middle ground. That's the kind of pressure that black students arriving on campus feel. It's even worse for those who have a left vision and some sense of multi-racialism."[5]

Countryman, who went on to work on DSA staff and helped coordinate the student contingent for the April 25, 1987 March on Washington, used divestment organizing to attempt to bring together the racial factions at Yale. During the summer of 1985, he and some other black graduate students and undergraduate white students, "began to work together, to build trust. We faced directly the issue that we needed a multi-racial movement. And it was my role to say that I thought that we had to understand that racism was a structural issue. It was almost a slogan— we needed a structural solution to a structural problem. Not some sort of good will."[6]

They learned from the multi-racial leadership approach of Columbia's steering committee, "but also tried to figure out ways to guard against criticisms of anti-democratic procedures that had developed at Columbia, and were clearly developing. We had a concern of multi-racialism and how to make this a broad movement, owned by all kinds of progressive segments throughout the campus." They forged a plan in which half the steering committee would be third world students, some representing third world organizations, others members of non-ethnic groups, but all representing their constituencies and not just themselves. "It wasn't a perfect structure. But it created a space for black activists to come in and feel like they had a base from which to operate."[7]

Across the country, in the mid-eighties, divestment and anti-apartheid campaigns on campus were often led by white-dominated student groups. Many ignored the existing black students organizations. As campaigns evolved, so did divisions. Misunderstandings, territorialism, differing styles and other pressures often magnified small rifts and mistrust. A climate of racism encouraged by the federal government's discriminatory policies, waning interest on the part of universities in increasing faculty and student minority representation and a growing number of dramatic racist incidents nationally further exacerbated the problems.

At Berkeley, the division emerged early. Pedro Noguera, then serving as student body president, recalls, "The first organized event was organized by the African Students Association. Right after that, a group of white students who attended said they wanted to form an organization and they wanted us to work with them. They wanted to form an organization, and do a protest. I said we wanted to focus on getting black students more involved. The following week, they had a protest, a picket and things kind of developed from there. They started their organization, the Campaign Against Apartheid, and we started our organization, the Divestment Coalition. They were, basically, parallel. Ours was multi-racial, theirs was basically white. They would initiate an action and then it would be up to us to decide whether we would support it or not. At first, we would support the actions, even though we didn't like the fact that they weren't well organized, and they didn't focus too much on drawing in more people, or conveying effectively why they were doing the protest to reporters, or even the administration. The very first civil disobedience action took place at University Hall in December of 1984, where about 30 or so people were arrested for blockading the entrance. I was one of the people who went inside to present the demands to the administration, but the demands were not worked out ahead of time; they were made up at the time. They also locked arms with each other, which led to many people getting hurt because when the police started prying people off, they were pulling them back. And some people who were not citizens got arrested. From that period, we started having intense discussions and debates over tactics and strategies. And they continued for two years."[8] Noguera's philosophy, of building mass support through education and coalition-building, and by finding common ground with other groups, made others target him as too conservative.

Donald Gallegos, at the University of New Mexico at Albuquerque, chose to exercise his growing political consciousness with the school's chapter of MECHA which "was formed out of the student activism of the late sixties and early seventies. It was first started in Santa Barbara in California, and it stands for Movimento Estudianti Chicano de Aztlan, the Chicano Student Movement of Aztlan. The goals and objectives still stand today: getting more chicanos into education, and keeping them there. The enrollment levels have always been low, and the attrition levels have been very high—up to 50% and more in some places. The strategy was to form organizations and do social support, events, historical consciousness. It's still real active today. We like to focus on recruitment. In New Mexico, we have an hispanic population of about 37%. At UNM alone, maybe 20% are hispanic. New Mexico is a real large rural state so we try to appeal to these kids in rural schools, try and get them into college, because a lot of them are not encouraged to seek higher education—there's work to do on the farm or in the community, or they migrate to another state or to an urban area. The high schools encourage these chicanos into working-class fields and away from any type of profession."[9]

The group also addresses Central American issues. "We have sponsored forums and brought speakers on those issues. This is very important to us, because of Central America being a neighbor. Also, most of the military is comprised of hispanics—the national guard is mostly hispanics, and has a record of being the first sent to any type of conflict. So that involves us directly."

MECHA at UNM sometimes combines its efforts with a minority coalition that includes blacks, native Americans and Arab students. They faced some opposition, Donald recalls, "but it's been short-lived. The College Republicans had a 'Feed the Contras' campaign. They made up another committee, Students for a Better, Balanced Education, but a lot of the membership was from the Young Republicans. They were trying to cut student fees, so they wouldn't be allocated to organizations such as MECHA and the Gay and Lesbian Student Union. But we've been able to rally against them, and beat them at the polls. They have the resources; they have the money. It took a lot of manpower and strategy to work against those things."

In addition, "last year MECHA hosted and co-hosted a series of events on nuclear war and SDI. Some professors here were involved in the Manhattan Project at Los Alamos, and are speaking out now against nuclear war, nuclear armaments."

At Boulder Sonia Pena concurs that much of MECHA's attention is directed at recruitment and retention, but "We do a lot of work with CISPES. Whenever we can, we support them. It's the best organized group on campus, and it's got the widest membership. We also do a lot with Arab students, Palestinian students."[10]

Palestinian rights may be the newest issue to hit campuses in the name of fighting racism. Press and government accounts connecting terrorism and Arabs have led to stereotypes, subjecting students of Arab descent to harassment, discrimination and violence. Two principal groups cover Arab issues on campuses, the November 29th Committee for Palestine (N29) and the Association of Arab-American University Graduates (AAUG).

Hilary Shadroui of N29 at the University of Michigan explains, "We've only been active for a year now, and what we have done is to bring speakers about Palestine, Palestinian history, Zionism. We also do literature tables, and letter writing. Mostly, we try to educate people on Palestinian history and on what Zionism does to the Palestinian people, and what Zionism does to American interests. Rallies aren't as effective for us because we don't have as much support as the South Africa or Central America groups."[11]

Support comes not only from Arab students, but from progressive Jewish students and others. Some Arab students avoid open involvement, Shadroui noted: "There is a fear on the part of a lot of Arab students who haven't finished their studies that they will be harassed by the FBI, or that they will get in trouble when they go back home. This is a very real possibility, and it prevents them from getting involved."[12]

One active student who would only use the name "Tarek" pointed out the difference between the two organizations. "N29 specifically aims at addressing the Palestinian question, while the AAUG tries to cover the whole Arab world. Usually though, both groups wind up addressing the Palestinian-Israeli conflict." Tarek, who has been personally attacked and had his car vandalized, says many of his colleagues try to appear non-threatening. "I think that psychologically a lot of people are constantly trying to say, 'I'm no different from you.' They are trying to Anglicize their activities, just to fit in. It's because they feel like they are really pariahs. They are really afraid to stand up to this tremendous abuse that has gone on."[13]

Coalition-building has been difficult. When his organization offered to co-sponsor a tour by members of the African National Congress, the Free South Africa Committee, "wouldn't give us an endorsement. There's a good reason. There are a lot of Zionists in their organization, and they just didn't want to do it." The tour sought to make the links between Israel and South Africa. "It's just shocking to see the major South African organization not endorsing an ANC tour. This was a major goal, to bring these organizations together in a common struggle, to link them and to make people aware that the way the administration is dealing with this conflict is very similar to the way they are dealing with South Africa and Central America."

Hilary believes their work is beginning to show students that the Palestinian people are refugees, displaced against their will, and have no rights in the international community. "What we're trying to do here is educate people, raise their political awareness, and try to build coalitions—really, just to get the Palestinian issue put on the agenda. It's easy to get depressed; it's a hard pull, especially with the level of opposition. But I do think that in the long run, we have a just cause and that if we can organize and get out the word and educate ourselves and others, then we'll have some effect. But it will take a long time. I think we're at where the anti-apartheid movement was twenty years ago, and some people think that is optimistic."

Although not tied together through national student organizations, native American and Asian students have also injected activism into their campuses. For native American students, they have formed campus support groups that address cultural heritage programs, and align themselves with groups such as MECHA in the struggle for ethnic studies, increase of minority enrollment and faculty members.

Asian students in regional networks, the Asian\Pacific Students Union and the East Coast Asian Students Union, confront stereotypes and mobilize to force universities to teach Asian history, the role of Asians in American society and the importance of Asian culture and heritage.

In the west, the coalition of several third world student groups successfully pulled together the embryo of a new national organization in 1987. Called the National Chicano Student Association, it encompassed 300 representatives of chicano, latino and Asian students from California, Washington, New Mexico, Arizona, Texas, Wyoming, and Colorado, along with a few students from Massachusetts, who convened in Boulder in early April. The resulting structure consolidates the efforts of many smaller groups seeking to forge stronger working political relationships.

Race discrimination has affected students of color working in student government. Ceylonese-born Peter Premarajah Granarajah was treasurer of the student body at Shoreline Community College in Seattle. "I had to prove myself, that I could do the job I was elected to do, whereas somebody else—a white American, even if they don't do a job, people don't object. Every time I took on a certain task, I had to prove that I am good at it, to earn a good reputation. In the election, there were two persons running against me, and they were campaigning on the ground that I was a minority and they were white—but nobody paid any attention. In the budget process, it is hard for me to get money for clubs when there are minority students involved, because they think that since I am a minority I want to get all the funding toward minority programs. If I support a minority, it will hurt them more than if I don't support them."[14]

In coalition or independently, students of color continue to press for change. Following the blockade and arrests at Columbia in 1987, according to Winston Willis, who held a leadership position in the Concerned Black Students there, "the university, whether it wants to admit it or not, has acted on some of the key demands. The most obvious, an African-American studies program, has been instituted. Of course, people in the university say this isn't a political move, we were going to do this anyway. At an Afro-American Studies Committee meeting, a week after the incident, the dean of the college, Pollack, said 'it suits my political interests to get this done.' The university had not moved at all to provide space for an intercultural resource center for the four years I've been on the campus. All of a sudden there were offers for space. We asked that there be a forum on racism during orientation and sure enough, they're planning this forum on racism for orientation. One intangible—a lot of black students have become politicized through all this."[15]

After a year of racist upheaval, Winston thinks "the administrators are completely out of touch with their own racism. The analogy has been used more and more among some of us that in a lot of ways they see themselves as benevolent slave-masters. They think they're doing the right thing, they think they know what's best. They don't really realize, they can't step aside and look objectively at what's going on."[16]

SCENE

Arresting Racism

Allan Freedman is furious. He telephones early Sunday morning, fuming at what he heard below his fifth floor dormitory window the previous night. About 2 a.m. on March 22, 1987 a ruckus had erupted nearby and Allan heard someone say to someone else "I'll get you, you fucking nigger."

Within hours, the Columbia campus is electrified with reports of an early-morning racial brawl involving students and security guards. Details are sketchy. Rumors are abundant. That Sunday afternoon, 150 students march through campus and past the fraternity houses where the accused white students live. Monday's Columbia *Spectator* headline blares: "Racial tensions explode following weekend brawl" and Monday evening, more than 500 students crowd into Wollman Auditorium to hear several of the black students emotionally recount the event—and announce they have retained an attorney, because they do not agree with the university's system of disciplinary hearings, and will bring formal charges against the white students.

The next day, the incident itself is challenged and facts disputed, motivations blurred. In the days that follow, white students claim they were set up, provoked by the black who was eventually beaten up; others point out that the two principals had a history of bad relations. Those who use the campus computer bulletin board say the black student used repeated inflammatory rhetoric over the preceding two months.

To make their case that the university is racist, black students cite other examples, pointing particularly to the fraternities where the whites live, and the football team, since some of those involved play for the team. Campaign posters from a recent student government election are held up, as examples of racist sentiments. Students in the audience boo, discounting the examples.

Two days later at a rally called by the black students, about 600 participants turn out to publicly denounce racism, wherever it lives, however it manifests itself. Students crowd in to hear the speakers, who say Columbia's policy of controlling housing throughout the neighborhood, to the detriment of non-university residents

reflects institutionalized racism. Speakers point out the school's failure to create a
Black Studies program, promised during student protests twenty years ago, and the
low percentage of non-white students. There are fewer than ten black tenured faculty members. The crowd is exhorted to march, and streams out onto Upper Broadway, turning left, heading down to fraternity row.

A few blocks and a few chants later ("Hey, Columbia, Have You Heard? This
Is Not Johannesburg!"), the march stops in front of Sigma Chi, where one black student charges that the fraternity is itself racist and should be banned. A few more
charges, and she begins to lose many in the crowd as they sense exaggeration and
blanket condemnation in her remarks. She brings them back with a few more
moderate statements. A first-year student confides, "I believe in what they have to
say, I mean, I'm really against racism of any kind, but I just don't agree with these
tactics."

Speeches ended, the parade returns to campus, past the emergency room of
St. Luke's Hospital where the injured black student was treated the night of the attacks. On the steps of Low Library, the assembly reaffirms its dedication to fighting
racism. Banners and signs of support appear from the Palestinian students group,
the gay and lesbian organization and a local labor union.

Slowly, the student body splinters. It is not, metaphorically, a black and white
issue. And the situation grows hard to handle. At a hastily-called meeting pulled
together by white students unsure of their feelings, people express sentiments like,
"I have no idea what it means to be black in this society, so who am I to judge?"
and "How can you even think that a university like this, which has, what, maybe
six black faculty members, is anything BUT racist?" or "I know the black student
who got beat up, and he's always confronting people. I can't help but wonder that
he kind of provoked it, and it got out of hand."

Doubts. Conflicting feelings. Then several of the black students arrive, and the
dialogue shifts. They want assurances that this meeting will not turn into an organizing session for a new anti-racist group, because they want solidarity behind their
new ad hoc group, Concerned Black Students of Columbia (CBSC). They apologize
for the name, explaining that it was how they signed a letter to the president, and
it got picked up. The politics of supporting someone's cause, even if you disagree
with some of their tactics and demands, gets kicked around. Someone explains that
labor coalitions hold whatever power they do have by sticking together, providing
mutual, unquestioning support when needed. The blacks get an assurance they will
not be publicly undercut.

During the next few weeks, every campus conversation includes opinions
about the issue. Black students refuse to cooperate with the school's investigation,
gaining allies from those who find the closed proceedings arbitrary and controlled,
and opponents from those who believe that the full story should be told. The white
defendants, on the advice of their attorneys, refuse to talk publicly with anyone
about their case. Posters appear with the legend "WANTED: Racists at Large" with
the names of the four accused white students, and photos of two of them. Observers report seeing the posters in Harlem and in other parts of the city, as well as on
campus.

While the administration makes a few measured responses, condemning racism and promising not to tolerate racism in any form, no action is taken against the accused students. Black students and their supporters decide on a strategy of escalation, and turn to a previously proven scenario: blockading Hamilton Hall.

At about 9:30 a.m. Monday morning, April 21, about 20 students pulled together by CBSC attach shiny new chains and locks to the doors of Hamilton Hall. Two hours later, Columbia security guards remove six of the students, two alumni and a faculty member. Within the hour, the congregation enforcing the blockade swells to more than 100, with almost as many spectators. The mood is jumpy, nervous. Some blockading students implore those on the sidelines to "join us or leave. This isn't a zoo." Two large sheets painted with references to the Citadel, Ann Arbor and other sites of racist incidents, hang from the doorways behind the steps. The students' attorneys give them instructions as curious observers hang from windows in near-by halls. Friends carry food and drinks to the protestors. The day is bright, clear, a warm 75 degrees.

Throughout the afternoon, radio, television and newspaper reporters inject themselves, asking about commitment, racism, the sixties. By early evening, the story seems to be defined: blockade, spring, wait for the next move. Reporters leave. A film previously scheduled to be shown that night, "The People United," about police brutality during desegregation campaigns in Boston in the 1970s, is readied for screening on Hamilton steps. Professor Eric Hirsch begins to assemble the movie screen as others position the projector.

Then a wave of disbelief envelopes the blockaders: someone brings word that the police have been massing at the edge of campus. Almost silently, a security guard contingent inside Hamilton closes all windows. Hartley, the building next door, is sealed off. Columbia security personnel move in to clear by-standers. The film is shut down. An official from the university attempts to read the students their rights, but is drowned out by shouts of "Arrest the racists."

Within minutes, about sixty New York City police, the Blue Line, file into Van Am quad at the foot of Hamilton Hall, two abreast, and proceed to confront those not sitting down. Students, faculty, and press are hustled off; many are pushed. When the arrests begin, students shout to onlookers not to leave: "We need witnesses." Many still reflect disbelief that police are intervening, since no police were called during the three-week anti-apartheid blockade. But police are there, cuffing, escorting, and when they resist, dragging away the protestors and loading them into police vans backed up at the outside end of a walkway. Some are silent, some defiant, and some are crying.

On campus, the number of onlookers grows, and they wander through the crowd to learn bits of news. Shortly after 10 p.m., those still on campus march up Amsterdam Avenue to the 26th police precinct and demand the release of the arrested students. Some comment that it is their first foray into neighboring Harlem, and black teen-agers circling the group on bikes also reflect the novel sight of college students crossing north on 125th street.

In the days ahead, editorials would proclaim support for the cause of the black students, condemn the administration for bringing city police onto the campus, and call for a redress of the conditions that led to the sit-in. A faculty committee would express its outrage that a black faculty member, standing near the site, was pulled in and arrested by police. And though criticisms linger about the CBSC's practice of exaggeration and provocation, most students believe the university has exposed an insensitivity to the true and legitimate concerns of the black students by calling in police to what they saw as a peaceful protest.

INTERVIEW

Barbara Ransby, University of Michigan   *March 6, 1987*

Now getting her degree and teaching at the University of Michigan at Ann Arbor, historian Barbara Ransby was chosen to speak for students at the April 25 March on Washington.

TV—*Why do you think this new visible activism about racism has surfaced?*

BR—I think we see dramatic kinds of protests from time to time. That doesn't mean there aren't struggles going on all along—on this campus, on Columbia's campus, at Berkeley, the University of Chicago, campuses where I know people have been doing work, there have been anti-racist petition drives, efforts to influence the administration on a whole number of levels. There's always a core of people who are struggling. The question is, what is it about the times that pull more people into struggling in a political context—because students of color, by virtue of being in an unfriendly environment, have to struggle in a personal way every day. Over the past seven years while the Reagan administration's been in office there's been a mounting anger about the callousness toward poor people and people of color. The administration has taken a certain tone that I think incited a lot of the more violent manifestations of racism as well as attacks on gays and other oppressed minority groups. There has been a mounting anger about these attacks on a local level, and about the tone on the national level, as well as the specific impact of the Reagan policies. Increasingly people are starting to see that a political response is unavoidable. In times when attacks are not as severe, a lot of people can delude themselves and feel, "I can handle this personally," "I'll deal with these few instances of racism," or "I'll work two jobs." But when things become more blatant, more people look to a political response. I want to stress that I see struggle and resistance as an ongoing thing, not the media images of it—it bursts forth one day. And on this campus that's been the case. The media characterized these recent instances of racism as spontaneous outbursts, as if there's no history to all this. And certainly there is.

TV—*You held some hearings here.*

BR—Over the past few months, there was a series of really blatant racial incidents on campus. Klan-type fliers put under doors to a room where some black women were meeting, declaring open hunting season on blacks, and a campus radio statio broadcast of really anti-black programs, which had jokes like, "Why do black people smell?" "So blind people can hate them too." This was a university-funded station, so students mobilized and gradually formed a new coalition and confronted the administration; we had a rally and got the university to close down the radio station. Then state legislator Morris Hood decided to bring to campus his subcommittee on education, which controls the university's budget, to investigate the problem—which is okay, but that's not going to be our salvation. Over the past few months there's been a really serious mobilization of a lot of forces on campus that had previously not been working together. It really makes me quite optimistic. White leftists and black students and all these different groups are starting to talk to each other and come up with a common platform, which is the most threatening thing we can do.

TV—*Does that coalition include people who had worked on divestment?*

BR—Yes. In fact, the initial rally that sparked the recent round of protest was organized by both the Black Students Union and the Free South Africa Coordinating Committee.

TV—*What's the level of non-white students and faculty here?*

BR—About 2% of the tenured faculty is black, 5% of the student population is black, and the minority student population is around 10%. Of 69 department chairs at the university, none are black and none of the assistant department chairs are black. The problem of racism on campus is not just a student problem. The whole hierarchy with elitist white men at the top and black women concentrated at the bottom is typical of most campuses.

TV—*Did the administration ever commit to changing these levels?*

BR—I think 1970 was probably the last really intense struggle, when a Black Action Movement strike shut the university down. It was led by black students, got wide support and confronted the university with a list of twelve demands centered around increased minority enrollment and increased minority faculty. It led to the formation of the Center for Afro-American and African Studies, but many of their demands have not been met, despite the university's promises. In 1970, the university promised 10% black enrollment and now we're at 5%.

TV—*In 1970 there were strong actions here and elsewhere—why didn't that carry forward on a strong level? What will happen now to carry forward in the next couple of years?*

BR—I don't know that this round of victories will be sustained. What I tell myself, as somebody who has been active for a while, is that there's really no resting place. You just get ready for the next round until we reach a point where fundamental social change can happen. I think the moment we relax is the moment we see the erosion of the gains we have made. That was true of the civil rights movement, it's been true of a whole number of progressive struggles. In a lot of ways, there's parallels with the trade union movement, which started out very militant, with a lot of activism, and now has degenerated into something quite different in most places. I don't know that there's any trick to it, anything we can do now that will guarantee the gains will be permanent. But the way we politicize students, the way we prepare them for an ongoing struggle will determine whether the movement is able to keep itself alive and therefore guarantee that the victories are long-lived.

TV—*What methods do you use?*

BR—Teach-ins and discussions are important; the other part is just helping people understand the struggle as it unfolds. Being involved is one of the big lessons, trying to give people a place in the struggle. That's one of the reasons we try to have not just one or two spokespeople. I push sort of a grassroots democracy similar to what SNCC had: that everyone should learn to be a leader, learn to answer questions, to articulate the ideas we're talking about in their own words, to challenge the leadership, and to really become convinced, as opposed to being sort of carried along with the tide.

TV—*Do you have affiliations with other schools?*

BR—Not at this point. Most of us, graduate students, have been active at undergraduate institutions, so we have personal ties at other places, and bring in students from other places to give people a sense of what's happening.

TV—*Do you think an ethnic studies course should be a mandatory requirement?*

BR—The other day, we went to the administration building, delivering 12 demands. That's one of them. Actually, the way we phrased it is a course on bigotry and ethnic diversity. One way racism gets institutionalized is the message students get when they come to college. What do you need to know to be an informed person? You need to know Western Civlilzation, you need to know Columbus discovered people who were already here, you need to have a science requirement, a whole slew of things—that makes you a fuller person. Nothing about the diversity of the world you live in. There are students who just refuse on principle to read a newspaper, they have no sense of what's going on around them from day to day yet they'll graduate from here and be called educated, informed people.

TV—*Is there resistance to instituting this requirement?*

BR—There are people who believe this should be sort of a comfortable, safe, apolitical haven. Which, of course, it isn't. It's political in the sense that it holds the least common denominators. There are people who see such a course as biased, or think it would be inappropriate to make it mandatory—who want it to be like courses in women's history and Afro-American history, a side dish to the main course. But I think we may very well win, just because the administration is pressured now and hasn't done much else.

TV—*I hear discussions about tactics—confrontation as opposed to education, public versus behind the scenes, integration versus separatist. How are these played out here?*

BR—In terms of the private versus public dialogue, there is a consensus among the leadership of this new coalition that the dialogue must be very public. One of the tactical mistakes in the years between the late sixties and the mid-eighties was to rely on university established committees and formalized mechanisms for handling problems which tend to be a diversion. Our position now is that the university had 17 years since the BAM strike, 17 years of negotiations, dialogue, reflection, introspection—to figure out how to handle the problem and they haven't done it. When I was at Columbia, in my last year I made the mistake of getting involved in a committee to discuss divestment. It was probably the largest waste of my time that I can think of. My position is, the dialogue has to be public, and the more you show people what's going back and forth, the more people will get consolidated to a progressive platform and the more pressure the university will feel. Politics is a struggle to pressure certain people to do things that they may never want to do, and you can only do that in the public arena. We try to create public arenas for presenting demands. The administration tries to pick off certain students—"you seem like a reasonable chap, come on over here and let's have coffee, this is what we're doing, we're nice guys"—but we're resisting that. In terms of the separatism versus multiracial, my position is that black and third world leadership is critical for a movement that focuses on anti-racist issues—in the same sense as we couldn't conceive of a women's movement led primarily by men. The people who bear the brunt of the oppression should be the primary people to interpret that oppression and develop strategies. I also think that in a multi-racial society, it's crazy to think that a struggle for fundamental change is going to happen by any one group alone so the challenge has been to win large numbers of white students to accept black and third world leadership, in the form of organizations and coalitions. The bottom line principle is that the largest shared arena will be a multi-racial one. Black students do need to come together and talk about things and reinforce one another's perspective as black people, but ultimately the struggle is to win white students to a militant anti-racist position.

TV—*I have heard black students tell white students that they need time alone first, that they can't deal with white students yet. And white students are left feeling they had nowhere to go to work on racism. Yet there's a view that it's harder to change an existing white organization than it is to start a new one.*

BR—I think that's true. These various dynamics play themselves out, depending on the individuals involved, the history of the organizations, a number of things. There's a problem when an already established, primarily white organization says to black students—join us, join us.The dynamic of racism in our society is one in which black people have been historically disempowered, and one sort of liberal response has been tokenism, trying to make blacks exactly parallel to a white experience instead of understanding fundamental differences—for example, how black working-class students see being arrested versus how upper-middle-class white students might perceive the very same thing. Sometimes white leftists don't understand these have to be dealt with. If a group's structure is already set up, the ground rules are already set up, they are already comfortable and you're newcomers, then you're in the margins, you have to figure out the rules to gain leadership, you are entering into a dialogue that already has a history—a whole number of things that puts minority students coming into an all-white organization at a disadvantage. So new formations are useful. If a new organization is founded on principles of black and third world leadership, if that's one of the ground rules, if it's built into the politics of the organization, then even if you have a large number of white students coming in, part of their politicization and orientation as new activists is to recognize the importance of black and third world leadership. Black caucuses, separate black organizations, are always useful, but the biggest challenge to my mind is to win white allies and potential allies to black and third world leadership. It's easy for a lot of white leftists to not deal with racism and take themselves off the hook by saying "oh yeah, we support black separatism, go over there and do your thing." It absolves them: they don't have to deal with their own racism, and they don't have to give up any power within their own organization. So what might seem like a progressive position, respecting the autonomy of black political organizations, might also be an excuse for not confronting their own racism. A balance needs to be struck: white activists do have to respect the need for autonomous black and third world groups at points in time, but also be willing to respect the leadership when it comes into their own turf.

TV—*Do you think it's because white students have more opportunity in high school to develop leadership skills?*

BR—I don't think it's that black students lack organizational skills at all. White students have gone to privileged schools, are more comfortable articulating their ideas certainly in a white environment, and know the liberal discourses the administrators are going to engage in. It's not that black students can't analyze racism. It's not that black students can't pull together meetings, because in black communities there's always church groups, block clubs and school groups. Their parents, in order to survive, had to link up with other people in all kinds of formations to get things done in their communities. So black students have organizational skills, but they are not as well received in an academic environment as the white students' language and skills, simply because the institution itself is racist. I've been told by administrators, 'We disagree with what you said, but, my, you certainly are articulate, you certainly speak well.' And I always bristle, because all I've done is put the ideas I would express in my parents' neighborhood, which is a black working-class neighborhood in Detroit, into a language which these middle-class whites can deal with. They like that, it's cute, but they don't appreciate it when it's said in a different form by a high school student or a community resident that comes on campus. They want it on their terms, so obviously they're going to be more receptive to white middle-class students as leaders. But it would be wrong to say black students don't have those skills or that political frame. It's a little different. One example is how white leftists on campus see civil disobedience, or getting arrested. When black students are reluctant to engage in these things, some white leftists take a very self-righteous position and say, 'they're bourgeois' or 'they're inexperienced' or 'they're not as militant as we are.' They do not see that if you come from a black working-class neighborhood, it's no big badge of leftist stance to get arrested. You see people going off with the police and not coming back. You know your parents may not have the resources to get you out, or the judge is going to be harder on you than a white student from an Ivy League school. It's a whole different thing from students who have never known anyone to get arrested other than by choice. Black students have seen people get arrested not by choice, just by looking the wrong way in the wrong situation.

TV—*Can you mention any other examples?*

BR—When people talk socialist politics or Marxist politics, and black students aren't receptive, they are immediately deemed procapitalist or backward or something. A lot of people in the black community have a lot of values that are very much in line with socialist values, at least in the ideal, even if they've never read *Das Kapital* or *State and Revolution*. People don't deal with people where they are, don't try to appreciate how people live their lives, and how people place emphasis on collectivity and do more collective things. For example, black students understand they need each other to survive in this context, so they may be more collective in terms of studying than some white students. But they don't express that in very formal academic language. The struggle for a common language is something that has to be done. Now people talk about similar things in different languages, and deem something fundamentally antagonistic when it isn't.

TV—*Is there a danger that, because there is so much work to be done on issues of race and color, black students may feel an obligation to work on them even if they might be interested in other issues, like anti-nuclear issues, the economy?*

BR—Yes, black students are more concerned with racism just because it's not an abstract thing. Of course, there are privileged black students. For a lot of black students who either come from working-class parents or have some connection to people who are still struggling in a fundamental way, resisting racism is something they have to do. When they consider political activity, it's just a natural extension. But a lot of the anti-intervention groups, the Latin American solidarity groups, even the white-led sections of the anti-apartheid movement, have really made a big political mistake in not seeing the ways to link the struggle around domestic racism with these other issues. You know, W. E. B. DuBois once said "the color line is the question of the twentieth century," and I think it's true in a lot of ways. We can see manifestations of racism in US foreign policy, in the justification for domestic policies, in increased militarism, in terms of who's going to be fighting a war and where. If we have that kind of analysis, and we incorporate an anti-racist perspective into an analysis of what's happening in Central America and in South Africa, and in terms of the military build-up here, that becomes a way to link these struggles that is meaningful and real, a way that students who are focusing on domestic racism can deal with and respect. For example, look at the anti-militarist movement. I won't include the anti-nuclear movement because of how a lot of leaders have defined it. I would never be a part of a movement that was just anti-nuke because one argument for combatting the nuclear buildup is that we maintain a conventional force, and that translates into taking a large section of black and hispanic people from this country, sending them to another poor country populated by people of color, fighting a war, and leaving the suburbs intact, whereas nuclear war is all-pervasive. I have some problems with that. But in terms of fighting militarism, increasingly the choice for a lot of black youth is unemployment or the military. An increased percentage of those soldiers are black working-class people who, in a lot of ways, have the least stake in defending this society which has offered them so little. To make that connection, to show how the military machine is exploiting the black community would offer an entry point for black students who already have some commitment to fighting racism. But I don't see that done very often.

TV—*Is there any discussion that black students should show they also have an interest in issues that are not race-related?*

BR—Absent a larger progressive political movement, most people's entry into politics is through the single issue, and most people get attached to it as if it's the only thing, and get protective of it. "This is the most important thing, because it's what I do four nights a week." So if the perception is that black students are single issue because they deal primarily with racism, I don't think that's any more of an indictment of their narrowness than students only involved in Central America.

TV—*The single biggest issue seems to be lack of opportunity for people to work together.*

BR—There are coalition efforts. The idea for this United Coalition Against Racism here is explicitly anti-racist but we are trying to bring in progressive forces. Racism, not only in US policy but also within the left and progressive movements, has been one of the key factors that has divided and held back these movements, a key bone of contention. If that's not at the center of our politics, then many mistakes are going to be made all over again.

TV—*After a student begins to make the connections, what can she or he move to?*

BR—A campus-wide progressive coalition.

TV—*But a coalition is again a group of single-issue organizations.*

BR—The reality is people come to politics through these issues. I don't think we can pretend that reality doesn't exist. We can say let's take these as the channels through which people will come to a more central point of analyzing things in a broader context. And let's set up a platform, a set of unifying principles, a leadership that brings together these various groups, but has a broader platform than all of them. For example, in our coalition here, there are people who have gone through a single-issue thing and have found it inadequate and are just involved in the coalition's committees. And there are people who are still working on one particular front or another. The combination is fine: because you have other people around, you have to start translating your politics into broader terms. But I definitely don't see coalition politics as an answer, and I don't see electoral politics as an alternative either. When more links are made between various organizations and sets of issues, then we get something we can begin to call a movement. Until we have these coalitions form, and gradually grow into a more coherent movement, it's going to be hard to have an explicitly progressive political organization or party that's going to offer an alternative.

TV—*Can you see similarities and differences between now and the early sixties?*

BR—In the early days of SNCC, people were doing sit-ins, looking for strategies, looking for issues: was it going to be integration of lunch counters, or voter registration? There was a lot of energy and a lot of regional connections among different groups of students that had been struggling locally, and all that's happening now. And there was an increased militancy. There were students who, by the mid-sixties had had several years of experience, and were still in school, primarily because they had been involved in political work, and were increasingly developing a sharper, more progressive analysis of the problem, and were willing to engage in more confrontational tactics. People always have meetings, and there's this debate and that debate, and that always gets me excited, because it means that people are not just coming and thinking the answers are simple. It means they're taking them home and grappling with them, and some of the vigor of political debate that existed in the sixties is starting to re-emerge. People are going back and reading things and coming up with an analysis. That's what we've got to do, as opposed to a sort of passive political involvement—you have three candidates, you pick one, you go home, and you're done. Surprisingly, a lot of the issues are similar—the question of racism and war. When you think of the black civil rights struggle and the anti-war movement, these were the galvanizing issues, and unfortunately they're still around.

TV—*And differences?*

BR—We've seen racism take on new forms. And a certain number of people have been incorporated into the system, and that creates a different dynamic. In the Jim Crow South, it really was clear cut: all blacks were excluded at every level. Now you see a few black people, black conservatives, advocating reactionary positions, and claiming that is a black perspective, which confuses some people. They say "you've got this person and this person in power," and don't see racism for what it is, which is the oppression of the majority of black people. That's a different thing to combat. With anti-militarism and anti-interventionism in Central America, one thing that's key is that you don't have American troops engaged actively. It's easier for people to be abstract than feel connected to it. I'm also interested to see how the media's going to handle things. The media is a powerful force in this society and tragically is very easily manipulated by the powers that be. I shouldn't say that— it's not that simple. Many of the people who control the media are in fact part of the powers that be. In the sixties you saw scenes of people in the civil rights movement being attacked by dogs, and that infuriated people and fuelled the movement; I don't think we can minimize that—it did. Similarly seeing the scenes from Vietnam gave people a visual image of what was actually happening. You can't abstract that into meaninglessness. Today I think the media has taken a much softer view of things. The coverage of the anti-apartheid struggle in South Africa was very vivid for a while, but when the blackout happened there didn't seem to be any real resistance on the part of the media, or any creative attempt to continue to keep those images in the forefront. Simultaneously, we saw a decrease in activism on the campuses. And the coverage of Central America has been scandalous—nothing. Journalists are there, but nothing is making its way back.

TV—*How about the role of women?*

BR—I think that's going to be different this go-round. A lot of people in the key movements that exist around the country are women. Despite all of its weaknesses and internal problems and elitism, the women's movement has contributed to that. I think that's an important difference. In SNCC, and even SCLC to a large degree, women played a tremendous role. They were just not touted as the leaders, they were not the people who got the recognition or credit. But they were on the very, very front lines. When I think of SNCC and those voter registration drives, I think of the Mississippi Freedom Democratic Party, which had a large array of women candidates, Fanny Lou Hamer. Women were playing a role then, but I think now they're going to insist a lot more on being visible.

TV—*Do you still see resistance to women taking leadership positions?*

BR—Yeah, I do. We have a long way to go in terms of combatting sexism, in and outside the movement. On the local level, women's leadership has always been accepted a lot more: when you talked about people you could count on, women were always going to emerge as the people who would get things done, who could get other people off their butt. Whatever your philosophical biases were, the reality was that women were relied upon and respected. When you get to national leadership, it was a little bit different. It was summarizing and articulating, and being charismatic, and galvanizing the force of these local struggles. The kind of people the media was most comfortable with and most impressed with were strong male leaders, and consequently a lot of people saw it as more appropriate to put those figures forward. In the black community, too, the role of ministers as key leadership figures was important.

TV—*What about openly gay and lesbian leadership?*

BR—I think that's more problematic. Two spokespersons from the gay and lesbian task force on campus came to the hearing, and there was a mixed reaction. Nobody was hostile, but there were some people who felt, "that's not a minority issue; that's not racism; it's something different, we're not here to deal with that," that kind of sentiment. On the other hand, there are people who see the need to link these various struggles and recognize the same kind of intolerance and bigotry that is manifested in homophobia is also what fuels racist attacks.

TV—*What about homophobia within a group like UCAR?*

BR—The clearest symptom of the problem is probably that there aren't a lot of open gay and lesbian people. That says something. I resist drawing too many parallels, because there are too many critical differences, and we become reductionists if we say there are people experiencing oppression so there are parallels. It's very different. A lot of gay and lesbian people on campus are not out, because of the environment, and they have that choice. Racism is a little different. Dealing with the matter of black and third world leadership in a coalition is not a question of anybody's choice, but the whole issue of gay and lesbian leadership is easier to sweep under the rug, because unless people identify themselves that way, it's not an issue. Also, our group defined itself as focused on racism.

INTERVIEW

Ricardo Velasquez, University of California   *February 27, 1987*

A champion debater in high school, Ricardo Velasquez is now an active MECHA member at Berkeley.

TV—*What's the origin of the campaign to introduce a mandatory ethnic studies course?*

RV—After the civil rights movement and the free speech movement, at Berkeley and San Francisco State, there came the notion of an ethnic studies, third world college that would give ethnic studies and third world scholars, and civil rights scholars, a chance to teach with a good degree of autonomy, without having to fear any repercussions or questions of tenure. They could inspire students, create self-esteem, and also propogate future scholars. In 1969, the UC Berkeley Academic Senate voted 550 to 4 to create an ethnic studies department that would ultimately evolve into a third world college. Now, 18 years later, no hints of that college have materialized. Today, what students are pushing for, on this campus and state-wide, is an ethnic studies requirement. They're saying, "let's be sure that students take at least one course in the area of race relations, so people come out with accurate history and the factors that contribute to today's racial tensions."

TV—*What's the likelihood that this will happen?*

RV—In the minds of the powers that be, probably not terribly likely. The academic senate has a procedural gauntlet that they're using to slow this movement. But we've received very good press and that gives me hope. And we have a lot of history on our side. There's also hope in the fact that the UC-wide academic council has asked every school to develop a written policy on ethnic studies and race relations, because it recognizes the severe need to address those issues system-wide. We can incorporate our needs into that. We ask an undergraduate requirement: a typical student has to take two social science courses and two humanities courses and we ask simply that one of those four courses be in ethnic studies.

TV—*Is MECHA the principle organizer?*

RV—No, it's United People of Color, which is a coalition of the various groups, including the Asian Students Union, MECHA, the African Students Association, and others. We are wary of appearing to limit ourselves to a special interest. We'd like to say this is the work of concerned students, who happen to be members of those other groups.

TV—*What is going on in MECHA?*

RV—For the outside world, it has interests in retention of chicano-latino students. It wants action taken on community levels to help alleviate the poverty and educational deprivation of chicano and latino students. The word "hispanic" in and of itself is an issue. Most politicized latinos and chicanos will squeal and squirm at the word "hispanic," because it means a Spaniard or a lover of Spanish culture, which upholds our European side, saying nothing of our Indian side. It replaces a word that serves the same function and existed long before hispanic did, and that's the word latino, the phrase of choice. The word chicano had a Mexican-American link, and there are chicanos who wish to not make that link, but make a link to consciousness, an affinity to those who agree we're all in this together, so a chicano would be a latino of any descent who is politicized. That is the long-term objective of what chicano will emphasize. For now, chicanos are latinos who are Mexican-American. Hispanic came from the census people, to embrace all people who spoke Spanish, as if they were all the same.

TV—*Students in a variety of organizations often say they find themselves divided along race lines, and discover they have prejudices they didn't know about. What's the situation here?*

RV—In every group, there will be a nationalistic element. For example, with chicanos, there will be many who have a nationalistic bent who will want chicano issues to take precedence over everything else. Among the black groups, the vestiges of pan-africanism will sometimes take hold. With any group, there are a small number interested in extremes.

TV—*Do they sidetrack the flow of any progress that might already be underway?*

RV—In terms of the ethnic studies program, that problem hasn't surfaced. The vestiges of the divestment campaign may have a negative impact. There was a largely white pro-divestment group, called the Campaign Against Apartheid, and they had good intentions, but they didn't realize sometimes what their prejudices were. All of us must have internalized certain aspects of our conditioning to the point that we don't even recognize it. On Sproul Hall steps, where we had a sit-in, the radical, the black groups, the chicanos would caucus over what we should do, and the white group would walk over and say, "no, no, fellows, we're pros, let us handle this. Our parents were participants in the sixties movements. Just listen to us. We're in the know." That wasn't taken too well by the black students who felt they had as much stake in it as anyone else. Some reacted too harshly—perhaps they were overly sensitive; on the other hand, these white youngsters had no business being so presumptuous. When students who were members of the Campaign Against Apartheid approach students from the United People of Color, there will be some conflict: "Are you going to go off on your own thing, not listen to us, because you've read a lot about the movement, and you *know?*" I can see that happening, but I hope we'll be cool enough to avoid it from the start.

TV—*Do you see some potential for organizing done around class?*

RV—Yeah, I think people are becoming aware that's an important principle. If you fail to underscore that, then you get into the rut of having the few upper-class latinos, blacks, native Americans being the ones who make it here—which is not to say they shouldn't make it here. But the whole point of affirmative action wasn't that you would be chosen on the basis of your color. You want to show that it goes to the people who most deserve it. Almost every person of color deserves it, because you'll have teachers who don't want to give you the full measure of your grade, to fully appreciate your potential. Also, you have the problem of white students complaining, "this person was richer than I was—this latino, this black—where do you get off saying that he was more deprived than I was?" You want to avoid those arguments and give it to the people who really do need it the most, the many brilliant youngsters whose academic and social growth gets stunted at the high school level, or before. Many dreamers stop dreaming long before they hit high school.

TV—*Some latino students say their own culture does not pay enough attention to instilling a drive for higher education compared perhaps to Jewish or Asian families.*

RV—I have heard this before. You don't want to dismiss it out-of-hand. You can go down to the ghetto areas of Los Angeles, where I'm from, and you'll see that stark reality. But you're just looking at the after-effects of a long process. What causes it? Is it that they don't care enough, or are things happening that make them not care? That make them incapable of having much faith in the system? In a ghetto area, the American dream falls tragically on its face. If the education offered you is so poor, even if you get straight A's, you will not learn enough to master the SAT's. You choose not to apply to the big schools because you feel, other students are submitting what they did last summer, while I had to work for my mother or my grandfather, and I didn't get any internships and my SAT's aren't particularly good. That's where the work ethic falls on its face. It says Effort Equals Results. And it's just not true in the ghettos.

TV—*But is there a difference? Certainly poor economic conditions exist in Asian ghettos today, and they did for other immigrants several generations ago. Are there elements that continue to associate education with an anglo culture?*

RV—One needs to look at the historical content. When you look at the Irish, the Italians and perhaps the Jewish people, and the German-Americans, they came at certain.times, when the dreg occupations in society were policemen, firefighters, certainly not the dreg positions today. The unskilled labor of today is not the unskilled labor of yesterday. The unskilled labor of yesterday gave these people a greater chance for politicization. You might be a policeman, but a policeman wasn't the worst position to be in. You may have been a steelworker, but that takes on a greater respect than whatever society builds into industry, creates lower and lower jobs for the masses.

TV—*It seems particularly harsh for women.*

RV—Sometimes hispanic women are not encouraged to go to college at all. That can be attributed to the overemphasis on machismo.

TV—*Women and gay students say they have a harder time with prejudices coming from black and hispanic cultures.*

RV—I am probably one of the most feminist-minded males in MECHA, and even I see the shackles of my conditioning. If somebody openly gay were to run for the presidency of MECHA, it would be ridiculously hard.

TV—*Isn't it inconsistent to ask other people to confront their prejudices about color and not to confront your prejudices about sexuality and gender?*

RV—Yeah, it is inconsistent. I don't pretend to defend that.

TV—*How did you decide to spend time on the activities that MECHA is involved with?*

RV—The decision comes down to this. I'm sympathetic with the anti-nuclear movement; I could choose to do that. But because racial and class lines are such that students who are privy to a good education are largely white, if you are one of the few students of color lucky enough to hold your own in academic debate, against the best of anyone, then you do need to be here fighting it out for color issues or race issues, because someone can fill your place on the nuclear platform, but cannot fill your place on this issue. You go where you're most needed. I am most needed here.

INTERVIEW

John Adamson, University of Wisconsin   *March 9, 1987*

Progressive movements seem to thrive on the campus of the University of Wisconsin at Madison. But John Adamson, a senior pre-law student says students of color feel alienation and discrimination.

JA—In my opinion, Madison is a pretty racist, pretty segregated place given the fact that it's supposed to be so liberal in nature, so progressive, forward thinking. On the campus, there's probably not a lot of overt racism, in terms of racial slurs, epithets, attacks on students. It's more covert in nature. There's not a lot of interaction.

TV—*How does it show up?*

JA—In a variety of ways. For example, you probably wouldn't see too much racial interaction at the union, even among blacks and hispanic students. Coming from Chicago, I'm used to a little more interaction.

TV—*Doesn't Madison attract progressive students who are willing to deal with their own, perhaps unconscious, racism?*

JA—When you talk about liberal and progressive, I think you have to look at what that really means. Does that include attention to racial issues, or just concern with Central America or South Africa or a nuclear freeze or disarmament? Someone with a progressive tag can just jump on a bandwagon on any issue, and exclude other aspects of society that are just as important, like racism on campus or racism across the country. It's a lot easier to attack something that's distant, that's foreign, than something that you might actually contribute to. I know a lot of supposed liberals, who really don't consider racism a problem because they're not affected by it, or at least they don't see how they're affected by it. Consequently, they ignore it. I'm not making a sweeping indictment of everybody on campus by any means. There are people who are honestly concerned with racism and race relations, and also a myriad of other issues.

TV—*Have you seen attempts by either black or white students to get together, socially?*

JA—Not on any large scale. Within any community there are whites and blacks who get together and have good relations. Not to make a patronizing statement, but I have quite a few friends who happen to be white. I have no problem with the white race—it's people who are racist that I can't get along with. Racism doesn't always connote hatred. I don't think blacks, as a whole on campus, know whites. It's like this in America, white America, and certainly the student body here is a microcosm of some of the attitudes that exist. The only way you can really get along with a lot of the cats who are frat boys or sorority girls, or the other students who grew up in very narrow, sterile environments, is to portray some image that's very Euroamerican. You have to want to assimilate, basically, to fit in. And a lot of black students here don't want to give up what they feel is their culture, their self, their identity. Assimilation is not really accepting the other person's qualities and traits. It's "Look, if you want to deal with me, assimilate." The reasons why are very deep in our society. A black student who has a bad encounter with a narrow-minded person who happens to be white during their first year, will build up a defense, where they wrongfully stereotype all whites. There's a propensity to run into both types of minds here. More often, you'll run into liberal, open minds—most of the whites I get along with are from other cities. Eighty percent of the students are from Wisconsin, and a lot of them haven't been out of Fon-du-Lac or Eau Claire; the only exposure they've had to blacks have been media projections. If they are friendly and attempt to bridge that gap, it seems like it'll be in a patronizing way, a sort of very plastic, phony, artifical way. They'll say things like "I like the Cosby Show, that's my favorite show," or "I have Michael Jackson and Prince albums, just the biggest collection." Things like that, sometimes out of context of the situation or conversation. Most black students are not stupid. They detect something's wrong. It's phony, and they don't want to deal with it. Quite a lot of black students come here with preconceptions about white students, and they don't want to deal with these hicks, or else they'll say, "I just came here to get a good education."

TV—*It sounds hard to turn the intentions into behavior. I hear young white students wanting to address their newly-discovered racism, and doing it clumsily, while black students don't know how or aren't willing to take the first step.*

JA—I agree. It's been a part of America that's been a problem.

TV—*At black student union meetings, do you discuss how to achieve a more multi-racial environment?*

JA—As a whole, no. Most of our meetings are concerned with making the environment more hospitable to the black students. We don't expect any white students to be concerned enough about multi-racial activities or about a non-ethnocentric environment to take positive steps. There doesn't seem to be that degree of concern on this campus. And even when we try to create some multi-racial constituency, quite often there seems to be a condescending attitude. "We know what's best. Why don't you just listen to us. We're the educated Marxists, and we'll teach you how to escape your oppression." It's a given that everybody here is racist, and the small number who aren't racist aren't really concerned about creating active widespread multi-racial constituencies. I'm sure they have their share of minority, black friends but in terms of actually getting involved in something…We don't discuss it as a whole, because it's a given to us.

TV—*So that assumption is passed along to new black students?*

JA—I don't think so. I think most first-year students develop that assumption themselves. In reality, they're exposed to a disproportionate amount of negativism and racism. Even if they run into the counter situation, it's not enough to offset those negative images. Quite a few blacks have left this school, and no one had to coax them into believing this.

TV—*What are some examples?*

JA—Most first year students are required to live in dormitories. My experiences at Boston University, and what I've heard here are fairly consistent. Black students at predominantly white universities face a patronizing attitude quite often, racial jokes. Questions like, "how do you comb your hair?" or "how do you wash your hair?"

TV—*White students are bewildered when their questions are taken as an affront, instead of a genuine, sincere attempt to get to know someone.*

JA—I can understand that. I realize these questions come from a genuine curiosity. But the way in which they're brought up can also appear very callous. It's akin to speaking about a very delicate issue, like asking someone their salary. It's an accepted part of our society that that's a personal, private thing; if you want to determine it, you don't come out and ask, "What do you make?"

TV—*But a person may grow up in an entirely Christian environment, and meet someone who is Jewish, or Muslim, or Buddhist, and ask questions about something that person thinks of as sacred or unspoken. So one might say, "If I'm accused of being insensitive, how am I going to get any better if I don't ask?"*

JA—It's the manner in which the questions are asked. Try to put yourself in their shoes. Here is someone who is a member of a minority. We can assume they have some knowledge about the history of their race in America. More often than not, it came from their parents. You're an enigma with a stigma. You have to constantly be under scrutiny, like you're some type of microbe. If you want to get to know someone, get to know them first. You don't go up to some white person on the street, if you're white, and ask, "How do you comb your hair?" What you do is, get to know them as a person first, not as some type of case. Don't ask them all types of questions about personal grooming and do you tan? Ask what type of books do you read, do you play sports. I'm not saying lie about your curiosity, or try to cover it up. Later, observe them combing their hair and say, "That's how they do it." I'm saying I treat anyone—any race, religion—with a certain degree of respect. Because of my experiences in life, I put myself in their shoes. And if I have that much curiosity, I'll go read, I'll go pick up a book before I'll ask.

TV—*Whose responsibility is it to show white students just how insensitive they appear?*

JA—On the collegiate level, in reality, the burden may be on the black student body. However, the burden also lies on the school, to some degree, because the school is the mechanism of socialization, endowed with the power to educate, and that also means to socialize. I believe that if students are required to learn about American history, Euroamerican history, perhaps precolonial history, they should also be required to learn about modern day American history, about problems that are relevant today. And I would consider racism one of the preeminent problems. I think that should be a required course. Before I leave this campus, I want to try and facilitate some form of communication between the black students on campus, the black and other minority students, and the black and white students on campus. Raising consciousness first means developing channels of communication.

TV—*How is the problem of retention addressed here?*

JA—On this campus there's a downward spiral. People think it's because they come from inferior high schools, inferior backgrounds. I don't think that's true, because I've known quite a few people who leave for other comparable, competitive and demanding universities, and performed well because they've gotten out of this environment.

TV—*To those who don't experience it, that is very intangible—what makes it more difficult for a black student?*

JA—Separating performance from social interaction and extracurricular activities is impossible. A person's academic performance hinges (at least mine does) a great deal on my satisfaction with the situation I'm in—socially, spiritually, and everything else. When I came here, I had experienced the same thing at Boston University that a lot of black students experience here. That's why I transferred. First I contemplated going to an all-black university, because I was sick of the racism I encountered. Then I spoke to a friend who told me I'd run into a lot of elitism at an all-black institution. So I decided I'm just going to go through school, do well, whether it's predominantly black or white. But when I came here, I encountered a lot of the same crap that other black students go through. And I realized that this place was even more oppressive than Boston University.

TV—*Specifically?*

JA—Okay. If you're the only black student in a classroom, they may talk about an issue that everyone in the room perceives is more relevant to you because you're black, like slavery. No one I know today has ever been a slave. They're exposed to racism, so they might understand some of the tragedies slaves had to endure, but they'll never really understand because they weren't actually exposed to it. Regardless, when an issue like that comes up in class, an excessive number of students will look to them, the professor might even solicit their opinion. Nothing's wrong with that. But no one wants to stand out. Well, some people relish it, but most don't want to feel different, to be "salient." Wisconsin obviously has a strong German influence. At the union, the Rathskeller, the whole environment can be intimidating to a student who's never been exposed to that type of strong Euroamerican ethnocentrism. If you go there and no one talks to you, it affects you. When you go to the library later to study, this sticks in your head. You can't just sit in a booth, study, go home, study some more, and go to sleep, and get up the next day. All this depression leads to ineptitude in academics, a lack of motivation. People come to college with more than an idea of just going to class, going to the library, coming home, washing the dishes and going to bed. They think they'll want to go to the basketball games or football games, and have school spirit. I've spoken to a number of people who regret the fact that they can't honestly say they're proud and happy to have graduated from this school.

TV—*What would you advocate to make things better?*

JA—If I could be omnipotent...

TV—*I just made you omnipotent.*

JA—First, I'd have to clean out a lot of the administration hierarchy. I'd put in people who are concerned and sensitive and educated on the issues, motivated to make some change. I'd initiate a number of programs, some of which would center around increased retention and recruitment campaigns, emphasizing the fact that this university has a preeminent goal of creating a culturally diverse and stimulating atmosphere. I wouldn't hide that from the white students. The literature or brochures would say, this university is striving for a truly multi-racial atmosphere. I would do the same thing with black and other minority students. If necessary, I would recruit from out-of-state, to increase the number of incoming minority students, but I don't think that's necessary. There are quite a few high schools in Milwaukee that are never recruited by the university. I'd have a program for incoming freshmen, to be completed by the end of their sophomore year, some type of cultural awareness program, perhaps one course or two, that would give some necessary background on race relations in America, from its inception to the present. And then, what should be done, what are the consequences, for them and their family and their lives? To give them some awareness, some consciousness, since they haven't been exposed to that. This is the time where you're supposed to expand your horizons. That doesn't just mean picking up vocational skills, or learning how to be an electrician or a biochemist. It means developing critical thinking skills. It means being receptive to different ideas, being open to possibilities that one has never conceived of before.

TV—*But, in the short run, you think opening up lines of communication is a first priority?*

JA—Definitely. That's what I hope to do with this newspaper. I also believe that the major problem would be sensitizing these constituencies to the need to address problems in America and on this campus that are relevant to black students also. Which is race relations or minority retention. Should we just focus on the Star Wars program? On Central America? Or can it embody all of these? Can we also encompass the labor movement, and what happens in Poland and in South Africa? I'm not trying to be a knee-jerk liberal, and when something happens, just jump on the bandwagon. But these are all relevant, intertwined; they all have to do with some degree of class conflict, some degree of exploitation of someone else by someone who has power. People have to see the relationships. If they want to avoid that, in terms of race relations and racism on this campus, then I don't want to have anything to do with them, because they're wearing blinders. And they're not going to get my support. And they're not going to get the support of the majority of black students.

INTERVIEW

Jacqueline Ross, University of California   *February 26, 1987*

When Jackie Ross of the University of California at Davis was interviewed, she had just been selected to serve as student member of the state Board of Regents.

TV—*As someone with a native American heritage, how do you experience racism?*

JR—We get the feeling of a lot of guilt directed toward us. Not that we are guilty, but a lot of students react to our educational and cultural sharing programs with a lot of guilt. Very much so. I am also a reader for one of the ethnic studies programs so I see students reflecting that in their academic work as well. It affects me when teachers don't regard a native American perspective as valuable or valid. They try to invalidate students a lot. I do a lot of counselling and heard from a student who asked to present a paper in history class about native American perspectives at the time of the pilgrim contact in the United States. She was rejected. And that's not uncommon. In the academic community as well as in the student community, there's also a real lack of awareness as far as nonverbal contact is concerned, a real lack of understanding of extended family.

TV—*What do you mean by that?*

JR—A lot of white students don't understand how two women or two men who haven't grown up together can call each other brother and sister. How you can have a group of twenty or thirty people on campus who regard themselves as family on the basis of cultural ties rather than blood lines. There is a lot of resentment of that;

it's as though these people are some kind of gang. For me it's a real sense of family. Even when we really dislike each other, we recognize that we have a responsibility for each other whether it be helping out with studying or money or housing their family. When someone is graduating and leaving campus, we may not know them, but if we know that they are native American, we have a responsibility to celebrate that for them and send them off in a good way. That may be particular to us. At Davis, the stratification is so absolutely clear. Black students make a point of saying hello to each other when they see each other on campus. Native Americans make a point of doing that, too. I can't speak for the chicano and Asian groups. My sense is that they don't have that same thing, that same connectedness.

TV—*And is there a particular reaction on the part of white students?*

JR—Oh, yeah. "You all hang out together." "We don't feel comfortable approaching you." That kind of thing. Also going into a white group and meeting with white students there's not an immediate acceptance.

TV—*In a mixed group not centered around ethnicity have you ever perceived a reaction to you that's different from others?*

JR—I've never really had a situation where it hasn't become a factor. I try to make it a factor. Women's groups on campus are really excited to get a woman of color in because it makes the movement look more united. Yet they seem reluctant to take the time that is absolutely essential to gain an understanding of those other groups. It's almost as if learning about another culture would pull the movement back—we can't stop now to learn this because we have this movement going. Well, to me that's going to make them fall flat on their faces.

TV—*Do male native American students feel less of a problem with being accepted?*

JR—I don't think so. I've seen my brothers go through a lot of the same things, because, they get caught up in the macho aspect of it all. In a lot of native cultures, there's a real respect for the man who recognizes woman's power. When they go into a white culture with that automatic respect for women, it is really unusual. Respect for the elders, too, is really unusual in white culture.

TV—*What about sexism in your culture?*

JR—For the most part, I don't see any native women accepting or tolerating men that don't recognize our equality. In terms of equality with men, in some ways we have that, in some ways we don't. But for us it's a problem when we come into contact with white women, because it's not easy for us to recognize why other women don't expect that.

INTERVIEW

Peter Kiang, Harvard University   *June 9, 1987*

Peter Kiang, a graduate student at Harvard University, talked about the East Coast Asian Students Union (ECASU).

TV—*How does ECASU relate to other student organizations?*

PK—There's a loose communication with the Asian Pacific Students Union, on the West Coast. Usually there's an ECASU representative at their annual conference, and vice versa. There is no national Asian students organization. ECASU itself is probably the most advanced network of any student organization on the east coast. It has been able to survive since '78. It does annual conferences, meets regularly, and has a real impact on more than 40 campuses in just the Northeast.

TV—*What led to its creation?*

PK—A recognition that there were common issues facing each of the campuses, and to have a way for people from different schools to come together and talk about common problems and strategies.

TV—*What were some of the common problems?*

PK—Whenever the issues of minority students were raised—in admissions, in ethnic studies, or counselling—Asian students' needs were never represented. In the earlier years, that was partly because numbers were much smaller than they are now. But the more important reason, the most important issue that faces Asian students, is the "model minority" stereotype—that Asian students don't have any problems, that they're really not a minority.

TV—*Where did that come from?*

PK—You can pin it down very clearly. The first references to Asians as the model minority come in 1966 and 1967, right after Watts and some of the other riots in black communities, where the national media like *US News and World Report,* the *New York Times Magazine, Time, Newsweek,* juxtaposed images of black urban rebellion with images of the stereotypical quiet, hard-working, obedient Asian minority that pulled itself up by its own bootstraps, doesn't need welfare, doesn't riot in the streets, etc. And at different points since then, that image gets whipped up again. In the '80s it's come up again a lot. Asians have been used as an example, part of the attack on the principle of affirmative action. The argument is that Asians are overrepresented and don't need affirmative action.

TV—*Do Asians need affirmative action?*

PK—Asians are a very diverse group. Large sectors of the Asian population clearly need affirmative action, and should be considered as an oppressed minority—large working-class populations in the cities, in the Chinatowns, and large immigrant populations. A significant portion are suburban professionals, well-educated; in a sense they should not be considered the same way, but they also face a lot of racism and discrimination on the job. It's very complicated, but generally, whenever the "model minority" image is promoted, it's never being used in the interests of Asian people. It's either used to shift attention away from real needs in the Asian community—Asians have made it, they don't have any problems—or it's used to create this really serious division between Asians, and blacks and latinos. It has the biggest impact on the campus. It's a real issue.

TV—*Tell me what you've seen.*

PK—When I was an undergraduate, the sense of third world solidarity was much higher than it is today. When I went back to graduate school, conditions had changed a lot: the whole notion of third world unity, particularly between blacks and Asians, was much more in question. I feel it's still essential to form third world coalitions to take on common problems. The day-to-day work of trying to organize that is difficult, because you really have to take on this model minority image, and cut through it, and show how it's divisive, and where it comes from, and how a lot of its assumptions are inaccurate. That's not easy. It's so widely promoted in the media.

TV—*On many campuses, relatively few Asian students are involved in multi-issue political organizations.*

PK—On a lot of campuses, the involvement of Asian students in South Africa work and Central America work is pretty low. But this past year Asian students have really been on the move in terms of issues like ethnic studies. Not only Asian studies—they make the connections.

TV—*Are they welcomed when the process also involves black and latino students?*

PK—At a lot of the east coast schools, in part because of ECASU, the Asian students have tried to form third world coalitions, and their level of organizing, their organizations have been stronger than the black and the chicano organizations. It hasn't been easy to develop and sustain a local coalition for a variety of reasons. But at least at the schools that I've seen, there's a general weakness in the organizational level of the black and chicano organizations, more at the elite schools than the public schools.

TV—*Why do you think that is?*

PK—For the chicanos, I think because their numbers are really small, and they feel really isolated. Chicano friends tell me it's a struggle just to be able to stay in school. For the black students, it's different because the school administrations have paid a lot more attention to buying them off, and trying to bring them much more into the mainstream of university life, and so the black student leadership at a lot of schools I've been to has been much more reluctant to take up issues in opposition to the administration.

TV—*So it's not easy to pull a coalition together?*

PK—No. Very difficult.

TV—*Do you think a coalition is necessary?*

PK—This past year there was a resurgence of outright racist violence on campuses. At the same time, all the issues that were important in earlier years, like ethnic studies, are still real. When you combine these the need for a third world coalition becomes more important. At Cornell, a very strong third world coalition was formed. It was multi-issue, involved with divestment, with ethnic studies, with support services, and also with community issues. One of the main things it took up was the issue of English Only—the English Only movement was really pushing hard in New York state to get a bill passed and the Cornell group did a lot of really good work, rallies, a lot of education.

TV—*Do Asian students employ strategies that other student groups don't use?*

PK—One additional thing can be using the resources of the community. In areas like Boston or New York, where there are significant Asian communities and progressive Asian organizations, campus organizations are able to draw from their strength and resources.

TV—*What kinds of problems does an Asian first-year student face?*

PK—It depends on their background—for the working-class immigrant or refugee student, it's very alienating. It also depends on the campus—at the private schools it's very hard just to feel like they belong. For the well-educated students, it's more that they want to really fit in to the mainstream of the institution, but because of racism, they don't, so a lot of them go through an identity crisis in their college years, and that usually involves becoming really politicized about their own identity as Asian-Americans, and having to confront the issue of racism head-on. For Asian students, there's a very strong pull to assimilate, to make it. The model minority myth is a big part of that. So when they come up against racism, it throws them into this identity crisis.

TV—*How does some of this prejudice show up?*

PK—It's very common for Asian students to be asked, "Where are you from?" like you are a foreigner. Or, "You speak English very well."

TV—*Many third world students want to hold on to their heritage and their culture.*

PK—That's one of the main issues that Asian students have to confront—how to deal with wanting to be a part of those institutions, but at the same time not wanting to assimilate. That's a real tension, and I think it's because the administration creates a situation where they have to choose one or the other. It's really a drag. One common example is when any easily identifiable minority group sits together in the dining hall, and it's called separatism. It drives third world students crazy to hear that, because it says it's not legitimate for third world students to get together. For every third world student group, there's a feeling that to be among your own people in a very basic way is a good thing, not a bad thing. You should be proud of your heritage and your culture. It's a real strength that you have, not a threat to anybody else. If there was real respect between groups, it wouldn't be an issue.

TV—*There's resentment toward Asian students who do well academically. Is that common, and is that generalization true?*

PK—That's very complicated. On the one hand, the Asian population as a whole is predominantly immigrants, so the sense of language and culture is quite strong, but so is the American dream image, particularly among parents who worked long hours and put a lot of pressure on their kids to study hard because they see education as the key to a better future. Some people say it's cultural, Confucian values, but I think that's nonsense. Education is a big deal for Asian students and a lot of them can't hack the pressure of family expectations, and stereotypes on the part of teachers that we do well in math and science. Tracking goes on, moving Asians into the sciences and away from the humanities and the social sciences. The dynamics are complex. The failure rate is also very high. So support services for Asian students are very important. At MIT there were a couple of suicides.

TV—*How does racism against Asians show up?*

PK—There has been actual violence, at some of the West Coast schools. But there's a lot of racist name-calling, racist graffiti. At Tufts a couple of years ago, there was a frat that had a group of their pledges do calisthenics and shouted anti-Asian slogans in front of this house where a lot of Asian students lived. There's a lot of that that goes on.

TV—*Where do you see the direction for ECASU and APSU?*

PK—For ECASU, I would say the main agenda item is educational rights, and a real commitment to working with the chicano movement, blacks, native Americans and progressive white students groups, building statewide networks that are not just Asians. In the east, I think we're not yet at that stage. For ECASU, it's related to education, ethnic studies and confronting the model minority myth. There's been real significant growth in ECASU in the last two years. The organizational level and the level of consciousness has really developed, and a lot of new Asian student organizations are showing up, and getting involved. It's exciting.

Questions for Multi-racial Organizing

On campus, the long overdue introduction of ethnic studies may be a sign that administrations are paying some attention to race, but merely listing courses and tossing them into the academic mix will not be enough. Students of color realize that adding a few sessions on the history of African, Asian, native American, latino, Middle Eastern or any other peoples will not rectify the imbalance. What they want, and will continue to agitate for, is a reassessment, in all courses and all departments, of the roles of the world's various cultures and heritages. As students urging an ethnic studies requirements at Berkeley point out, California will be majority non-white by 1999. Educating people to be able to deal with, do business with, live next door to, work with and vote for people of other races must begin now.

Increasing the percentage of non-white students on campuses cannot be handled with one sweeping recruitment campaign. Universities need to look at each affected group separately, assess the conditions within each group, and stop lumping all non-white students into a single category, which is offensive and alienating to politically aware students in every category. To find college-prepared blacks, latinos and native Americans, the university establishment must reach down into local school systems, urging them to upgrade elementary and secondary education. College students realize that universities could exert such influence on many levels. In a study conducted by Signithia Fordham of the University of the District of Columbia, and John Ogbu, of the University of California, they reported that academically capable black high school students do poorly because their peers tell them that working hard doesn't pay off, and that achieving academically is "acting white," an outgrowth of having internalized white racism, and because of the reduced expectations for black students by some educators.[18] MECHA's efforts to contact promising latino high school students and encourage them to apply to college is an example that other ethnic student organizations may soon follow.

Racism, like sexism and homophobia, affects the entire society, and like those issues, needs the contributions of strong, articulate leaders. Whites, who may not be accustomed to seeing blacks in those roles, must be taught that, like sexism and homophobia, the movement against racism must be led by those closest to its effects. Male-dominated leadership in the women's movement, or heterosexuals speaking for the gay rights movement would be considered inappropriate, and whites must learn to see the role of blacks in leadership positions in this fight in the same way.

Each of the nationals has at least begun to deal with racism. The USSA offers support to the National Third World Student Coalition, an educational and resource affiliate. DSA produced some position papers on the subject, and the PSN has also supported local anti-racism campaigns. But no amount of national attention will matter if local campus organizing is not equipped to absorb it. It is at the grassroots level that students are provoked to deal with the important political issues of organizing against racism: the question of exclusive black leadership, the importance of minority populations being able to define their own oppression, white racism and\or ignorance of black issues, and the potential for linking political struggles. Multi-issue groups must open up the discussion, talk frankly, be willing to fail—but admit there is much serious work that needs to get done before multi-racial efforts of any kind can proceed with any success.

Whether organizing is oriented toward reforming the institution, educating students, or broadening and redefining the program of study, it is the university community as a whole—the administration, students and faculty—that must take responsibility for racism in all the many different ways it manifests itself in campus life.

Students blockade Hamilton Hall in the spring of 1985 to protest the refusal of Columbia's board of trustees to divest its South African holdings (above). University of Wisconsin students march to the capitol in April 1985 to protest investments in South Africa (below).

Dartmouth students protesting their school's failure to divest South Africa hold-ings construct symbolic shanties on campus in November 1985 (above). Right-wing students who support the school's position tear down the shanties (below).

Students organize a Take
Back the Night March on the
University of Wisconsin campus in the fall of 1987 (above).
Material aid supplies are collected for Central America by
students at the University of
Rhode Island in the spring of
1987 (right).

Students organize the National Chicano Student Association at a conference in Boulder in the winter of 1987.

A campaign to boycott Coors beer in the winter of 1987 results in students getting assistance from a local tavern owner near New York University.

The CIA on Trial Project in the spring of 1987 in Northampton, Massachusetts. Clockwise from upper left: defendant Amy Carter during press conference; defendant Nick Komar testifying; attorney Len Weinglass with the press; defendant Mark Caldiera after the defendants have been acquitted.

Marchers in San Francisco convene from several western states for the April 25, 1987 march.

The April 25 weekend in Washington, DC: Students march to protest CIA involvement in Central America (above); students prepare to block access to the CIA headquarters in Langley, Virginia (right); students are arrested during the civil disobedience action (lower right).

American students join with members of the General Association of Salvadoran University Students during the July 1987 march in El Salvador (left). The March for Gay and Lesbian Rights, held in Washington, DC, in October 1987 includes students from the Columbia Gay and Lesbian Association.

More than 700 students gathered for the first National Student Convention, held February 5-7, 1988 at Rutgers University.

The April 25th Weekend

Big national political marches are devised to exert public pressure and develop private contacts. For the student movement, the April 25 March led to more of the second than the first.

Early in 1987, students heard that a march on Washington in late April was in the works. When a printed call finally appeared, "A Mobilization for Justice and Peace in Central America and Southern Africa," it was signed by 24 prominent labor leaders, and 54 members of the religious community.

The call sent several signals to student activists: issues of concern to them—Central America and Southern Africa, and by easy extension the CIA—would be the focus; concern about racism, women's rights, gay rights or economic inequality, could be inferred by the "Justice and Peace" designation. The coalition of major labor, religious and political groups heralded a relationship that had not existed even during the Vietnam War era. And there was no mention of students.

But students mobilized anyway. The national groups passed the word. Buses, vans, carpools and sleeping accommodations materialized in a flurry of phone calls and meetings. And to carve out their place in this action, a student subcommittee was pulled together, headed by Tom Reiffer and Doug Calvin of CISPES and Matt Countryman of DSA. Their talks with other students created plans for a separate student action Monday morning, April 27, at the CIA headquarters, while the non-students were to lobby Capitol Hill. When students refused to cancel this separate action, Mobilization organizers adopted it as an official event and other activists planned to join in the event.

Friday evening, April 24, the van rolls up to drive me and Peter Anderson to Washington, DC. Peter, a 1986 Middlebury College graduate, spent one spring break in South Africa disguised as a black American student. Mark Caldiera, a CIA on Trial defendant, has made the arrangements, and six others fill the van with anticipation reminiscent of rock concert trips and summer cross-country adventures amidst blankets, mattresses, music, cookies, beer and other paraphernalia—definitely a celebration atmosphere.

Saturday morning at the Ellipse, tables—Asian-Americans Against Imperialism, the Christic Institute, the War Resisters League and 100 others—ring the perimeter. Wide banners tell contingents where to assemble: "Seniors," "Environment," "Gay and Lesbian" or "Disarmament" and many others. People carry white crosses; four shoulder a plain wooden coffin.

And at the center of the milling crowd, college students gather from as far away as Wisconsin, Iowa and Florida. The same celebration feel, the Woodstock feel, colors this public coming together. Some are positively spiffy with ironed collars and creased pants; others look like they walked all night. But everybody looks happy to be there in the chilly drizzle as the lawn starts to muddy up and Peter, Paul and Mary sing out from the far-end stage.

Where the students "belong" is not clear as the march assembles. Labor is first, a statement—that working people support the march—both to the public and to the columnists and Lane Kirkland, who have red-baited the proceedings and warned people to stay away. Church groups follow, and somewhere, back there, students are instructed to group themselves. Their position may be uncertain, but there is no question about their numbers. As the march snakes out of the Ellipse, paraders walk four abreast. But when the students hit the street, they are eight abreast, filling the street from curb to curb. Streaming out of the Ellipse, toting their school banners, they provide an hour's worth of flow to the march.

At the head of the procession, Mobilization staff people in orange shirts set the pace ahead of the first line, the "faces" who make it to the evening news: Dan Ellsberg, Ruth Messinger, Ed Asner, Ben Spock, Jesse Jackson, Ellie Smeal and William Sloane Coffin. At the Capitol, the great lawn starts to fill up, like sand trickling into the bottom of an hourglass. In less than 20 minutes, there is not an empty spot of grass. Speaker after speaker, from CoMadre Maria Theresa Tula and the AFGE's Ken Blaylock, to the Reverend Patricia McClurg of the National Council of Churches and Rep. Walter Fauntroy, tells the people why they're there. Crowd estimates range from 125,000 to half a million. An hour into the speeches, people are still marching past the White House up on Pennsylvania Avenue. As Jackson Browne sings "Lives in the Balance," Natalie Budelis, from New York's WBAI, engineers live satellite radio broadcasts to Pacifica affiliates around the country. While these events are predictable, the responses continue to be vigorous. Ed Asner introduces Holly Near, who captivates the crowd with an anti-homophobia song. A policewoman obligingly snaps a photo for a yound couple standing at the waist-high wall separating marchers from speakers. I grab a chair in the press area and stand on it to view the crowd. It's the cliché come to life—a sea of faces.

Very late in the afternoon, introduced by Ruby Dee, Barbara Ransby from the University of Michigan takes the microphone. A veteran student organizer, her inclusion is a token nod to the students. By that hour, the vast majority of people have drifted off, many to waiting buses chartered only for the day. She is the first speaker to address and thank students.

That night, DSA hosts a reception at a local church where Michael Harrington notes that the coalition of labor, religion and political groups far surpassed anything comparable in the late sixties and seventies. "This is the beginning of the end of the eighties."

At a meeting of student activists Sunday morning, specific goals are not clear. At American University the lobby is filled with students exchanging literature, trading stories, renewing acquaintances and talking about the need for a national convention of student activists. Proceedings kick in about 11:30 a.m., and some 200 students from 38 schools nearly fill the auditorium. Doug Calvin reports the weekend's coordinated student involvement grew out of a combined effort by CISPES, DSA Youth Section, USSA, National Student Action Center, PSN, ACOA, UCAM, Young Socialists and Third World Students Alliance. Matt Countryman ticks off the issues students are working on around the country. Doug gets the biggest round of hoots and applause when he proclaims, "People will not look back on the '80s as a dead decade."

For the next hour, people split up into small caucuses. I keep running into familiar faces—Sibby Burpee from Boulder, Chris Babiarz from Madison, Gus Glazer from Worcester Polytechnic Institute. We reconvene for brief reports and statements of continuing dedication, but, surprisingly, no discussion of a national meeting. People expecting to be arrested the next morning at the CIA must leave for nonviolence training. The session breaks up with people feeling generally upbeat about coming together and generally disappointed that a "next step" has not materialized.

Monday morning the aim is to block CIA workers from entering the agency's suburban Langley, Virginia, headquarters. The unprecedented action is called the "Non-violent Civil Disobedience and Legal Protest at CIA Headquarters."

Barely awake, my friend Peter and I make it to the Martin Luther King Library where buses will pick up demonstrators needing a ride to Langley. It's a quarter to five. Somebody's radio reports FBI Director William Casey, hospitalized the day before he was to testify to the Congressional Iran-Contra Committee, has been moved to intensive care. The contingent starts to build on the sidewalk, toting signs, placards and rolled-up banners. Some wear plastic bags against the threat of rain.

Steel blue interstate coaches and clunky old yellow schoolbuses load up, and bus captains warn, "Use the bathroom on the bus. The CIA is not providing facilities." The ride to Langley is almost restful, like an organized excursion to a mountain resort. The Washington Monument, mirrored in the Potomac, reflects the pink blush of sunrise. Then overhead, a loud, insistent whirring, a motor noise breaks the mood. Helicopters patrol back and forth, charting the caravan's progress.

Suddenly, the scene becomes serious. Fairfax County and Virginia state police, out in force, redirect the buses to a holding area, slowing the flow of protestors into the CIA vicinity. People get impatient, looking out the bus windows as others in the distance walk to the site. After ten minutes of not moving, Peter and I ask the driver to let us out.

It's barely 50 degrees, see-your-breath cool, and decidedly damp. In a stretch of grass next to a parking area the careful planning shows up, as affinity group delegates meet to discuss dealing with the police maneuvers, and how to proceed with the action. We hook up with those heading for the closest of the CIA's three entrance gates.

Protestors traipse across the field and onto a small footpath which parallels the road to the gate. Up ahead, a green, white, red and black banner announces "Vermont Says NO." Someone has set up a mock graveyard on a sloping hillock. We keep moving past a counter-demonstration: 11 angry CIA supporters, and a large American flag, are kept by police well away from the hundreds there for a different mission. The massing hundreds have some success—employees' cars have been prevented from reaching their usual destinations.

From the back of a pick-up truck, organizers remind everyone where to walk, how to group, when to act. At 7:45, as the sun dodges through branches of the tall trees that line the unmarked driveway, the action takes shape; the first wave of blockaders sits down in the road. Rings of police separate them from the gate. Delineations firm up: people expecting to be arrested, in the street; people there to witness or show support, on the grass; between the two, the press. And police, wherever they want to be, trying to separate the other groups.

An older voice, a member of the Lincoln Brigade in the Spanish Civil War, praises the crowd through the makeshift sound system. He tells them they're part of the tradition of people of conscience opposing government policies when they disagree with them.

The message is serious, but a celebratory mood erupts again and again. UMass students break out a collection of cowbells, cookie tins and toy drums to make music. Others with tambourines and bells join in, launching into chants of "USA - CIA - Out of Nicaragua."

Arrests begin. Most comply, permitting cuffs to be put on and walking to the waiting police van. A few resist, or go limp, and are dragged off. A grey-haired woman wearing an embroidered white sweater and carrying a blue purse raises her cuffed hands, and smiles to the cheering crowd. As people are arrested, others take their place. Joe Iosbaker moves in to fill up an empty spot. Dan Ellsberg takes a picture with his pocket camera before he finds a place and sits down. Throughout the morning, people ride waves of nervous agitation, adrenalin spurts, jolts of fierce conviction. In all, 550 are arrested, employees are delayed in getting to work, and demonstrators enter another phase of opposition to the CIA.

By mid-morning, traffic is snarled for miles along the Washington Memorial Parkway. News reporting for the entire weekend has predictably concentrated on the cosmetic: police crowd estimates, familiar faces, the '60s nostalgia references—lazy reporting. Organizers resent the lack of substance in most press accounts, which downplay the issues the march addressed. Monday's action elicits stronger responses from the press, partly because the message is simpler: people who oppose the CIA tried to prevent them from functioning.

For most students, the weekend was a first, a mass expression of their convictions, an opportunity to see their growing numbers. Riding back home, Peter says, "It was inspiring to me to see so many people my age who felt the same way I do about social and political issues—to see that strength."

A few days later, Doug Calvin assesses the weekend. "Students were there, and students were largely unrecognized by the officials. I think between 30 and 60% of the crowd were students. We definitely had a big impact." I ask him who determined the place of the students. He tells me it's "older organizers who have been doing this for a while, but they don't see the students as a sector. It's this attitude—I hate to use Abbie Hoffman's phrase, but people don't trust people UNDER 30, these older people. They're not in touch with the surge in student activism very directly, they don't see the growth, and they're still on the rebound from the right-wing media campaigns of student conservatism. They don't recognize it, and it's a pain in the ass."

CHAPTER EIGHT

The Economy and the General Welfare

More than an abstraction or the topic in an elective course, the state of the economy directly affects the lives of students. The cost of attending college—tuition, fees, books, housing, food, services—represents the single largest investment most people make. Access to loans and grants mirrors economic conditions. The projections on the nation's economic health in years to come affect students' abilities to repay those loans, and often influence decisions on which career to choose. Furthermore, every student will move into the larger society in one way or another. How it operates, what shapes its direction, what governs its health and vitality are questions that will touch every one of them.

A glance back at a couple of moments in our economic history shows students engaged in a variety of political activities having to do with the economy. In the 1930s, with the economy in near collapse, students joined workers marching in the streets for reforms. College students, aware of the problems facing parents, neighbors and friends, and seeing no hope in their future, stood up and made their voices heard. Many moved into positions in newly-founded labor unions, to insure the continuation of economic reform. (Today, students involved in labor issues usually offer support to workers, though sometimes the disagreement involves the union itself.)

In the 1950s the government created the National Defense Education Act, a program of federal loans to college students. When the baby boom generation left high school, the flood of applicants overwhelmed many university loan programs, and the government responded with a host of potential sources. But with the Reagan deficits, student funds have been targeted as one place to reduce federal spending. The response, particularly from members of the USSA, has led to education and lobbying efforts.

When the environmental movement burst into public view on Earth Day 1970, with outdoor festivals, events and rallies across the country, students began to draw connections between environmental problems and the needs of the economy. Campus activists turned to such tactics as boycotts and consumer education in an attempt to influence corporate decisions about waste disposal and abuse of natural resources. As the seventies wore on, through gasoline shortages, water shortages, Love Canal and other events, patience wore thin with promises and studies. Now, even more radical college groups confront the issues head-on, spurred by what they see is a lack of understanding about the seriousness of the problem and a lack of commitment to make the needed changes.

One beneficiary of the environmental movement has been the Public Interest Research Group (PIRG) concept, independent state-based organizations using fees from students to fund environmental and consumer activism, founded in 1971. Often attracting concerned but not politically active students, they have grown into effective, multi-issue groups involving many topics related to environmental and consumer problems, and some that are not.

As the rich get richer and the poor get poorer, as the environment continues to deteriorate because ecologically sound policies are not "cost-effective," as problems of homelessness and hungry grow, students in the 1980s have found various ways to engage in and organize around economic issues. While campus-based religious groups have a long history of providing aid to the needy, the explosion of volunteer activism has helped students forge their own organizations for fighting the effects of poverty. Furthermore, *all* groups on campus are beginning to recognize the economic component of any political struggle and see it as a necessary part of their efforts to bring about change.

A Critical Component of Organizing

It affects all of us, but in radically different ways. In a sense, the US economic system, its care and maintenance, can be seen behind any of the issues addressed in this book, whether it's the perpetuation of an economic underclass which weighs most heavily on women, people of color, or anyone who varies from white, heterosexual, middle-class and male, or the drive to feed a growth-based economy with weapons and arms production, or the fear of losing dominance in the world which rationalizes intervention into the governments and lives of people in other countries.

Although it's a potentially boundless subject, the specific topics that have emerged as campus political organizing issues, that will be addressed here are:

reduced financial aid for students; the farm crisis; union organizing on campus; environmental movements; the homeless and the hungry; and PIRGs.

Any actions to reverse the cutbacks in financial aid for students are linked to elected officials. The budget tug-of-war pits segments of society against each other, and college students are seen as a "special interest" not as a crucial investment in the country's future. Previously enacted programs, designed to remove impediments to college have been systematically attacked during the Reagan years. The proposed '87 budget would cut $6.5 billion, or 26% from these programs[1] at a time when more than 70 percent of full-time undergraduate students rely on some form of financial aid to continue their education.[2] Student government representatives have lobbied Congress to oppose these cuts, often led by the USSA, which provides detailed data on the dollar amounts involved, the impact on all types of students and universities, and suggests strategies for combatting the assault.

For many children of farmers, the economy has assaulted not only their family life, but also has damaged prospects for attending college. They often find that the market value of their parents' land makes them ineligible for financial aid. This problem, and the escalating loss of family farms to corporations or bank foreclosures, have prompted students in farm states to create support service organizations.

Alliances between students and campus workers have developed at several schools. While media attention centered on Yale's protracted strike involving District Local 34 (it lasted from September 26 to December 4, 1984), students also provided solidarity with workers at Cornell and Columbia among other campuses. At Columbia a strike lasting for five days in the fall of 1986 brought students together with the clerical workers' union, District 65. Classes were moved off campus, and students joined picket lines to back the workers' contract demands. And when New York University narrowly averted a similar strike the following January, some looked to the example of solidarity at Columbia as one reason the administration agreed to a settlement.

Students also lent support, food, supplies and money to various labor struggles off campus, notably in the strike at the Austin, Minnesota, Hormel plant and to the long cannery workers' labor dispute in Watsonville, California.

One ongoing student effort was the Coors boycott campaign. Pulling this effort together was Frontlash, a union-sponsored training and education organization which has involved college students in union drives in Nevada, voter registration drives in several states, and in a rally at the US Department of Labor opposing proposals for a subminimum wage.

The Coors boycott stemmed from widespread resistance to that company's hiring and employment practices, including lie detector tests and questions about sexual preference during job interviews. The company had a record of union-busting, and William Coors had been cited widely for anti-black statements.[3] Gay activists and women's groups also backed the boycott and campus employees' union publications urged their members not to buy the beer. Student governments, fraternity councils, third world students groups and a wide spectrum of other groups conducted education sessions to explain the boycott and its history. Coors boycott campus organizers visited local bar owners to explain the boycott.

Other types of boycotts channel student buying power away from targeted companies and corporations, such as General Electric, for its nuclear weapons research, and Coca-Cola for its presence in South Africa. And the United Farmworkers of America's Cesar Chavez has been invited to speak at more than 100 campuses in the last two years about a new grape boycott prompted by the alarming health conditions for workers exposed to pesticides—as well as the effects of those pesticides on ground water and agricultural land, and on consumers who eat the sprayed food.

Farmworkers staffer Arturo Rodriguez reports, "a tremendous amount of support for us on college campuses. I think it's bullshit to think that there's no activism on college campuses."[4] The UFW has initiated a coordinated effort to urge student governments to ban affected products from their campuses. Rodriguez, who works in the northeast, says requests for appearances by Chavez in the region will jump from eight in 1986 to about 50 in 1988; sponsoring groups include campus labor centers and student government committees, as well as latino groups.[5]

Students join others in showing concern, and alarm, at the growing environmental threats the planet faces. In a February 1987 statement, Worldwatch Institute president Dr. Lester R. Brown noted that "Since 1950, world population has doubled, food production has nearly tripled, and fossil fuel use has more than quadrupled." Referring to the 1987 State of the World report, Brown added that the resulting pressures on the earth's resources have surpassed many natural threshholds, including the capacity of forests to tolerate pollution, of the atmosphere to absorb waste gases, and of cropland to sustain intensive cultivation. Brown concluded that "no generation has ever faced such a complex set of issues requiring immediate attention. Preceding generations have always been concerned about the future, but ours is the first to be faced with decisions that will determine whether the earth our children inherit will be habitable."[6]

Younger environmentalists, a large number of them college students, have turned away from the old-line environmentalist organizations which they view as too conservative, too compromising and not activist enough. Of the older groups only Friends of the Earth, founded by David Brower, enjoys support from young people. A new breed, termed the "New Ecologists," has been willing to employ ecological sabotage ("ecotage") to disrupt or reverse the actions of corporations guilty of environmental damage.[7]

Boycotts have also been employed in this area—against, for example, Burger King. This action stems from revelations that the company found it cheaper to use beef raised on cleared rainforest land in Central America. According to Rainforest Action Network, half of Central America's tropical rainforest has been destroyed in the last 25 years. Activists have urged Congressional legislation banning the import of beef products from cattle raised on such land. Students have also joined in Earth First! actions directed at preservation of endangered species, protesting unsound logging practices, and pushing for a program of national forest planning.

The plight of Navajo (traditional name: Dineh) and Hopi peoples in the Big Mountain area of the Southwest also attracts college supporters. Plans call for the removal of native peoples to open the land for the mining of coal, uranium and other minerals. The response includes concern over loss of spiritual lands, the racism involved in imposing such a decision on indigenous peoples, and the significant environmental impact. Activists have launched broad educational campaigns and lobbying efforts aimed at Congress. At UC Santa Cruz, the Big Mountain Education Committee distributes detailed handouts explaining the situation, listing other sources for more details, and explaining how to lobby Congress. The group's actions range from tabling in the parking lot in front of the bookstore to staging guerrilla theatre pieces on the subject.

An even more direct involvement with the political structure comes out of the Green Party, inspired by the West German party. Greens have founded chapters in several US cities and towns, many with college affiliations. One of the strongest is at the University of Vermont at Burlington, where activities include campus-wide recycling, education on energy issues, political organizing to create pressure for reducing the pollution in Lake Champlain and a better regional toxic waste program. The Greens are evolving into a political party, with candidates for elected office.

Campus Green, a national volunteer action organization aimed at educating students about environmental issues, operates from a small office in Durham, N.C. With affiliations on 82 campuses in 29 states, Campus Green stresses local control; coordinator David Lakin emphasizes the importance of groups "feeling the ownership of their programs" in explaining why they use an affiliate rather than a chapter structure. "We're building a coalition and network of people who believe very strongly that action needs to be taken on environmental issues,"[8] including toxic dumps, radioactive waste, acid rain and coastal erosion.

Two model programs demonstrate the diversity of the group's concerns and approaches. In North Carolina, the students of Warren Wilson College administer the Swannanoa River Project, monitoring pollution, testing the water and developing programs for recreational uses of the river. And at the University of Colorado at Boulder, students manage an extensive recycling program, which produces enough revenue to fund other environmental programs on campus.

The Campus Outreach Opportunity League (COOL) also symbolizes a growing interest among college students to attack social problems directly on the local level, which many see as a bridge to long-range political solutions. Students pull together local projects to address illiteracy, homelessness, problems of the elderly and the disabled, hunger, juvenile justice and other issues. COOL provides background information and networking capabilities, as well as training in fund-raising, public relations, organizational management and volunteer recruitment. Founded in 1985, COOL attracted 350 delegates from 80 schools to its 1986 convention. At Southern Methodist University, David Lawrence points out that their COOL chapter has been involved in neighborhood clean-up work, tutoring young students, soup kitchens and helping the homeless. "I think people underestimate the power of volunteer groups to do as much as we can to help those living now. You can't help think about what causes it, an analysis of the problem." Lawrence sees that, among student volunteeer groups, "They are attracting a larger and larger membership. If it's not a movement yet, it's the beginnings of one."[9] The sharp increase in volunteer service—at Harvard, for example, 56% of its 1986 class had participated in some form of volunteer community service, compared to 35% in 1983—has led to the institutionalization of this type of activity on campuses. According to Catherine H. Milton, assistant to the president at Stanford, who oversees this activity on her campus, "Every year more and more students are participating." She continues, "Students are sick of reading polls and surveys about what they are supposed to be like. They are showing just what they can do."[10]

Spending time on the problems of hunger and homelessness accounts for a large portion of this activity. Many channel their work through chapters of national groups, such as Oxfam or Bread for the World, while others create their own. At Vanderbilt University, Scott Givhan founded "First Step" to provide shelter, job placement assistance and recreational outlets for homeless families. At Columbia, Kate Stoia, Sarah Block and Michael Herman run "Friends," patterned after the Big Brothers model, matching students with the children of homeless families for recreation or outings.

The task of finding a permanent place for these efforts within the university system has begun on many campuses: hiring a coordinator or staff may insure the continuity often hard to guarantee in campus organizations. Some of these centers use school resources, such as the Community Volunteer Service Center at Columbia, while others, like Yale's Dwight Hall, are independently funded. Many operate under the auspices of campus ministries. An organization of college and university presidents called Campus Compact, founded in 1985, serves a clearinghouse function among administrators with volunteer service on their campuses.

The National Student Campaign Against Hunger (NSCAH), based in Boston, serves as a strong resource for many groups; its annual Hunger Cleanup project attracts the most attention. Students provide their labor to improve housing in poor neighborhoods and solicit individual and corporate sponsors for their hours of work. Some campaigns involve several campuses. For example, groups from SUNY Albany, Canius College, Buffalo State and Dameon College joined to clean up Buffalo's Broadway Park-Riverwalk neighborhood, and raised $5000 for local hunger work. According to Bill Hoogterp, NSCAH staffer who developed the Hunger Cleanup concept while a student at Aquinas College, "We're really into doing what we can about hunger rather than feeling guilty about it. People need to see that they have made a difference."[11]

Finding ways for students to make a difference motivated Ralph Nader to found the Public Interest Research Group (PIRG) program in 1971. Funded on each campus by a per student donation, PIRGs initially confronted consumer and environmental issues, and have broadened their agenda to include other issues, even involvement in divestment. Because they have championed consumer issues such as bottle bill legislation, PIRGs have found themselves the target of organized business associations, and the College Republicans (CR) have carried on a sustained campaign to remove PIRGs from campuses. During the spring '87 semester alone, challenges, often backed by CR groups, were levelled at PIRG chapters on twenty campuses, including Bunker Hill Community College, Merrimack Community College, UCLA and BU—but succeeded only at Duke, passing the proposal to place the refundable PIRG fee on the student bill. PIRG chapters follow the direction of their local organizers, often concentrating on issues within their own region. This work has enmeshed students in battles with public service commissions, and with state and local politicians.

Willingness to link electoral politics to economic issues varies from group to group. Some incorporate political education; others purposely separate political action for those who do not wish to spend their time with it. The political impact however, increases, as more students learn about the connections between these problems, their causes and the sources of their permanent solution.

SCENE

Money Matters

"It's the only basis of power," Paco assures me, finishing dinner in the hotel dining room the first night of the 1987 USSA Conference in Washington. Francisco Duarte, who represents the student association at SUNY-Albany, is talking about money, a topic that permeates almost every workshop, discussion and caucus at the three-day event.

People are buzzing about the Reagan adminstration's proposed elimination of the College Work Study Program, which would knock out nearly 800,000 jobs for needy students, and the loss of an estimated 325,000 loans to students from reduced federal commitment to higher education. The weekend also brings in economic subjects such as boycotts, foreign policy and personal rights, which connect students to the larger society. The 500 delegates from student governments across the country can pick topics that range from no-nonsense lobbying on "The Federal Budget Process" and "The New Tax Bill," to down-home sessions such as "Student Control of Fees," and "Student Employment on Campus."

Jackie Kendall of the Midwest Academy assures participants that political activism is on the move, stating, "It feels like 1962. Things are bubbling right below the surface." And Jesse Jackson exhorts them to recognize "the contradiction in marching to free Mandela, to get the right to vote, and to have the right to vote and not use it."

After watching "The Wrath of Grapes," a documentary updating the plight of farmworkers, students hear Cesar Chavez remind them they can initiate boycotts. "Get the word out at your colleges and universities," Chavez urges, "and let people know that one-third of pesticides used on grapes cause cancer. Virtually everyone is now exposed to pesticides through food and water supplies."

Monday is Lobby Day, the focal point of the event. The front desk area bustles with neatly-dressed collegians, ready to confront their legislators, who have the power to channel money into higher education, to reestablish it as a national priority. Paco looks smart, ready for the confrontation. "We've got to let them know we're watching," he smiles, heading off to the Hill.

INTERVIEW

Jerry Farelli, St. John's University   *May 1, 1987*

Jerry Farelli, a student at St. John's University in Staten Island, New York, works as an organizer to spread the boycott of Coors Beer on campuses and travels throughout the state for Frontlash.

TV—*Which schools have you been to?*

JF—Bronx Community College, Lehman College, Queens, York, Hunter College, and I had a conference at New York University on the Coors boycott where representatives from 30 schools came. There were about a hundred students. On a three-week tour, I worked with Syracuse University for a week, with the University of Rochester, Rochester Institute of Technology and Monroe Community College. In Buffalo, I primarily worked with SUNY, Buffalo. I've also been in touch with Erie Community College. St. John's was the focus of the starting off of the boycott. We had a boycott resolution passed by the student government.

TV—*Are there campaigns like this in other parts of the country?*

JF—It's a nationwide campaign. It's in 36 states now. The boycott started in '77-'78, when they went on strike. Coors was kicked off the University of Massachusetts at Amherst then. People are going to drink their own beer. With college kids, it often comes down to what beer is cheapest, what beer tastes better. We're hoping that they think about what Coors is connected with, and what they really stand for.

TV—*What do you say to students?*

JF—I try to emphasize to them that I'm only one person, and that it doesn't take a lot to care about an issue. It's very easy not to care, to be apathetic. I try to stress to them that it's going to be a difficult task if they want to take on a boycott. I tell them don't pass a resolution that doesn't have any backbone behind it. Really do something: go out and let the people in your neighborhood know, see the store owners, give them the information and tell them not to sell the beer. It's worked at Columbia, and it's worked at our first campus Frontlash chapter in New York, at Cornell. I try to target my message to the group. If it's a black group, I'll try to emphasize Coors discriminatory practices. Coors comes in and says they've increased their hiring of blacks, hispanics and women, but it's not because they've seen the light of day. They were charged by the Equal Employment Opportunity Commission. A lot of people don't know that.

TV—*What role have students played in the boycott?*

JF—In California, Coors was the bestselling beer in the market, and they're down to about 14% now. The Stanford CAL-PIRG did exhaustive research for about a year and a half on the whole issue. They were very influential. They usually go to student governments and try to get an outright ban then try to get support from other campus groups. With a united voice the students can go into their communities and into the bars near campus and tell them, don't sell it—we patronize this establishment and we don't want you to sell it. Usually a bar or restaurant owner, if he sees that a college group really patronizes his place, he's going to accommodate them. It hasn't worked so well in commuter schools, where you don't really have a strong sense of community, where your impact on bars surrounding the school may be minimal. If the owner wants to continue to sell, we have a program of informational picketing, during prime hours, with leaflets and fliers that say please don't buy Coors beer. It's tricky—you can't say don't go into such-and-such a bar, because that's a secondary boycott. It is illegal. You have to say please don't buy Coors. Your whole aim is to get them to not buy Coors. You might go into a bar and just not buy it. If people don't buy the beer, the owner is going to say it's not selling, so I'm not going to keep it. Coors is a non-pasteurized beer, it has to be refrigerated constantly. There's only a certain amount of storage space in these bars, and they can't keep it without selling it quick. So if it doesn't sell quick, the chances of people buying it are going to be slimmed down. Usually when you get a new product, you have to put in storage space. The distributors here have had to put in refrigerated space for this beer. They have to keep it cold.

TV—*What do you tell students about the connection between Coors and cutbacks in student aid funds?*

JF—I tell college students, and even high school students, that this is a crucial time. Reagan has proposed more financial aid cuts. The Heritage Foundation has been the prime sponsor of these aid cuts. There are people who are part of the Heritage Foundation and part of the administration. Joe Coors supports the Heritage Foundation, and sits on the board. While other companies like GM support the Heritage Foundation, you're not going to see any money made from a GM plant that's supposed to be given as a dividend to stockholders taken as a chunk and given to the Heritage Foundation. But with the Coors company, it's a private company, 90% owned by that family. There's no board of directors. William and Joseph Coors have given over control of the company to their sons, Jeffrey and Peter. If you buy their beer, the money goes into their pocket. Like divestment, this is a corporation that has to be held accountable for its actions. They touch a lot of people's lives. I say, you have a choice. If you don't care, that's your choice. But if you do care, know that if you're buying this beer, this is where the money is going. You may think it doesn't matter, but it does add up. I've wanted to debate them, but they won't debate anybody from Frontlash, or the unions.

TV—*Do you talk to fraternities?*

JF—If I know someone on the campus in a fraternity, I try to speak to them, but usually we try to start off in the Greek system with the interfraternity council or the panhellenic league.

TV—*And gay and lesbian groups?*

JF—Yes. At NYU, for instance, we spoke to the Gay and Lesbian Student Union, and the law school association.

TV—*As a practice, how do students react to the idea of a boycott?*

JF—It's hard to boycott, because you have to be constantly on the alert.

INTERVIEW

Six students, Iowa   *March 15, 1987*

For students from farm families, economic problems relate not only to student loan rates, and job possibilities but to the crisis of the family farm. Steve King, Julianne Marley and Cheryl Johnson are from Iowa State University at Ames; Connie Esberg, Mary Pepper and John Atwell are from the University of Northern Iowa (UNI) at Cedar Falls.

TV—*Do you work on farm issues through your student government, or other groups?*

JM—At Iowa State, we have the University Rural Concerns Group, just formed this last fall, that is funded through the student government. They've been working on raising money for scholarships for people affected by the farm crisis. They're hoping to give three scholarships; they got 60 applications so far.

CE—At UNI, we have a Rural Crisis Group. It was modelled after the Iowa City Rural Crisis Group. Ours is fairly small so far. The Rural Crisis Center in Iowa City is a highly motivated group. It's been involved in planning the Farm Aid concerts and the Farm Aid conferences. Now they're going to combine the two.

JM—Students who are affected by the farm crisis apply for financial aid, and there's no distinction made between liquid assets and material assets. This land that their family has isn't worth what it says it's worth on paper. The same is true of the machinery. Because of that, the financial aid forms essentially by-pass a lot of these kids that would otherwise be considered, in their real wealth terms. There's still a lot of misinformation and misunderstanding about the issue, right in Iowa.

TV—*What kind of events have you done?*

MP—We adopted the USSA farm policy platform, and our senate ratified that. And we've also had a series of farm crisis workshops done through our student government.

TV—*What can the universities do to help the farm crisis?*

JM—The student government at Iowa State just passed a Biotechnology Bill. It pointed out the universities in our state are doing research on farm issues that can't be used by moderate or family-sized farms. The research is all geared toward corporate-sized farms. That's ludicrous when the students are overwhelmingly from farm communities.

TV—*Do you make connections between farm issues and the rest of the world?*

SK—There's a link between all third world countries and the farm crisis: American corporations are going into those countries and using that land to grow crops for export to the United States, which doesn't really help the economies of those small countries, and doesn't help the economy of our country. Doing this has undermined a lot of the farm economy. Right now, we import four times the amount of red meat that we produce in this country. Grain that's produced in this country is not used to produce that red meat, so demand for grain in this country is reduced.

CE—A lot of people perceive the farm crisis as similar to a drought, that it's going to go away. It's been a major downfall. It's not something that you can fix with a good rain.

MP—The implications are just beginning to be felt, with the closing of the Caterpillar factory in our state. As the dominoes fall, more and more people are going to be aware of it. Now they don't hear anything unless it's the guy who shoots his banker; then it's in the headlines. And people are scared to talk about it.

JM—There's a coalition of groups on the Iowa State campus titled Progressive Action Coalition—the Central America groups, anti-apartheid groups, six or seven groups. They organized a nuclear madness week and had a rally which was quite successful. A third of the money they raised, they gave to the farm crisis scholarships. So they're supportive, but not to the extent that they go out and educate on the issue. I think the support is going to grow, because the campuses I see are getting more and more active on the issue. Some people stay out of it, because the rural crisis groups have gotten support from progressive groups on campus.

If you analyze the situation real closely, the land that farmers have lost and stand to lose will either wind up with large corporate farms or back into the hands of the farmer. That starts sounding a lot like the redistribution of this land, and that starts sounding like a socialist sort of theory. People don't quite understand what that means, so they shy away from that kind of tactic or idea.

SK—We really haven't allied ourselves yet. We really should—with the third world groups.

INTERVIEW

Chris Ruge, New Mexico PIRG   *December 16, 1986*

A small two-room apartment, tucked away off a modest courtyard behind a neighborhood restaurant, houses one of the most committed student organizations in New Mexico: the Albuquerque office of NM-PIRG, the New Mexico Public Interest Research Group. Chris Ruge, a nursing student at University of New Mexico, talks about his work.

TV—*What has been the effect of the PIRG on this campus on state legislative issues?*

CR—First of all, it is the most vocal and the most obvious student group in the state, they are constantly up in Santa Fe lobbying different legislators. Last year they were trying to push two or three bills and were successful on one. It was a law about damage deposits for tenants. And they've also been trying to push through a bottle bill every year now for the past three years. It's really needed in New Mexico. There's actually quite a lot of support for it. It's hard to get it through the legislature, where one of the most powerful lobbies is the Coors Brewery, and the people who run it in the state of New Mexico belong to one of the three richest families here in the state, one of the family members being on the Board of Regents.

TV—*Is there a Coors boycott on campus?*

CR—It's not real obvious. The main push against Coors was once again through the Central America group. After Mr. Coors was tied in to sending aid to the contras and to the right-wing in Central America, the Central America groups carried placards and protested outside of numerous dealerships. That's about as far as it went. But as for an ongoing Coors boycott, it is more or less a personal thing—people do it on their own. But in the state legislature, some people obviously considered PIRG, as small as it is, with a budget of $18,000 this last year, a threat. Students actually had the nerve to come up and try to talk to legislators, and they tried to pass a bill which basically would have outlawed lobbying by any student group receiving funds on a university campus. Even the Student Veterans Association gets a set amount to help them do their thing. And this would have outlawed every single group, whether it's a fraternity, a veterans' association, a PIRG or anybody else, from going up there and lobbying or trying to introduce new bills to legislators. The College Republicans national office has brochures on how to create PIRG-free zones on your campus. They send plaques out from the east coast to any local chapter that effectively eliminates PIRGs on campus as a legislative force. College Republican manuals suggest efforts to eliminate their funding base, to effectively deny them access to the legislature through these type of bills, and to carry on a constant campaign to discredit them on any controversial issue. We had a person in the College Republicans who gave us all the things that came in the mail, it's just amazing how much of their mail is dedicated to bashing PIRGs on campuses. The College Republicans are not the Republican Party, but rather a conservative fringe group that is backed by very major business interests out East, and they basically consider PIRGs anti-business, so we've been attacked by them—which is totally ridiculous because the vast majority of our time and money goes to service the landlord-tenant hotline, which has nothing to do with business.

TV—*So your work continues.*

CR—It is definitely the most controversial group on campus. We play very straightforward politics, using diplomacy, lobbying student senators, talking with them all, individually, really playing the political game to the hilt. They keep as many people as happy as possible, doing favors for everybody, avoiding anything controversial, any causes which may make them appear too radical. Like Central America issues, they really ignored that completely. It's all just straightforward local issues. They're going after three bills in the state legislature, none of which are all that controversial: one allows a tenant with a serious problem that is ignored by the landlord to repair the problem himself, after giving legal notice to the landlord, and then deduct it from rent—nothing radical about it. Then there's a bottle bill that we're pushing once again, which we think this time has a pretty good chance. We're linked up with the Sierra Club and other environmental groups. Another one is rental referral agencies, a real major problem in this state. They take money, like a $50 fee; if they don't find you a place in 30 days, you're guaranteed your money back, but you never get it. We're just trying to introduce some legislation that safeguards people. We're also working on sub-metering. There's apartment units where tenants pay for all the shared areas, where you'll have an "eight-plex," and all the electricity goes through one meter for that whole eight-plex, for the swimming pool, the laundromat, the outside lighting, as well as the apartments, and the landlord just divides by eight. You can be gone for two months, come back and your electric bill has been $100 each month. We're trying to introduce legislation that would basically outlaw that. Those are some of the things that PIRG does. Also voter registration, which I'm sure will be a massive effort again. And we stay on top of most student issues like tuition raises. The legislature came up with a proposal last year to raise tuition, I believe, over 30%. The student government went up to the capital. We introduce them to legislators that we know, and let them use networks we have set up, helping set up press conferences, stuff like that. New Mexico has a lot of money invested in oil, and is losing lots and lots of money, and unfortunately, higher education is the first budget item to go, because they don't have much else here in the state.

It Touches Everyone

In the late eighties and the nineties, as Reagan's policies exacerbate economic problems, these issues will attract more support from college students.

And it will attract those students who find themselves caught between the desire to act on the conditions they see, and a reluctance to join political organizations which employ tactics they do not condone. As Janet Ng, who is active in housing and homeless work at Columbia stated, "I don't see 'activism' of that kind—deliberate civil disobedience—as solving any of the problems we deal with. At least it hasn't solved any problems so far. Our activities do not change things, but it is important in keeping people alive."[12]

The use of boycotts to protest a corporation's activities may grow in popularity, because divestment campaigns have shown students that economic actions can make an impression. They are hard to carry off, but provide students with a personal type action that demonstrates their beliefs.

Despite the mounting pressures against them, campus PIRGs have legitimized their positions; because they receive support, especially in research and information, from non-campus environmental and consumer groups, they offer students a chance to work with substantive, well-documented campaigns that make a difference locally.

Economic issues offer a chance for real connections among students and groups, but this will not happen without considerable effort on the part of someone or some group. For example, there are clear common interests that are shared by those opposing American intervention in Central America, by those affected by the displacement of cattle production from the midwest to the cleared rainforests of Central America, by those alarmed by the environmental impact of that agricultural shift and by those opposed to the CIA's role in creating and executing the United States' Central American foreign policy. But too often, these objectives are pursued independently of each other.

The issue most ripe for exploitation as a mass movement will be the reduction of financial aid to students, because it will touch the largest number, and because it is a clearly explained issue—more money for the military means less money for education. In the drive to establish state student associations, this issue offers the greatest opportunity for mass student organizing in the next decade.

CHAPTER NINE

Women's Issues

When women from all over the country gathered in Washington, DC in 1970 to celebrate the fiftieth anniversary of getting the right to vote, they were commemorating a victory that, with the passage of the 19th Amendment in 1920, had taken ninety years to achieve.

From the earliest women's rights convention in July 1848, and throughout most of the nineteenth century, women suffragists worked for equality for the sexes. Slowed by the Civil War and its aftermath, the drive took on new momentum in the latter half of the century. (Wyoming was the first to grant women the vote, in 1869.) Around the turn of the century, women challenged barriers to economic opportunity, fought for access to birth control and organized against World War I. Women's role in the workplace shifted considerably during World War II, with wives, sisters, mothers and daughters holding down factory jobs while the men went overseas. But after the war, women were quickly sent home or into lower paying jobs where their work was no longer valued as part of the war effort but devalued and considered a transgression of the new fifties' definition of womanhood.

In 1961, President John F. Kennedy, at the behest of Esther Petersen, the director of the Women's Bureau, created the President's Commission on the Status of Women. Three years later, the Civil Rights Act was extended to include sex as well as race, creed or national origin. And in 1966, the National Organization for Women (NOW) was founded, giving a national focus to women's equality issues.

The "second wave" of feminism was not free of historic divisions in the ranks of women, along race, class and age lines. Liberal-minded working- and middle-class women got their "training" from work in governmental commissions and lobbying groups, so they tended to look to governmental solutions. Others who were schooled in the radical, grassroots organizing tradition of the early and mid-sixties used more creative, countercultural and non-establishment modes of political challenge. They also sought solutions that were more sweeping, wanting to change the entire structure of society, not simply the laws that dealt with economic and political access.

Many college women worked with SDS and SNCC, but they soon learned that the men of the progressive movement were just as likely to exhibit male chauvinist traits as men outside. In 1968, women were booed off the stage at an SDS convention for demanding that women's liberation become part of the organization's national agenda. Women began to caucus separately, identifying their shared experiences and turning them into political objectives. Reproductive freedom emerged as an extremely important issue to college-aged women, but was not embraced by the NOW generation as a top priority. Younger women also insisted on calling attention to the problems of child care, the image of women in the media, and the place of lesbian relationships in society.

When both houses of Congress approved the Equal Rights Amendment in 1973, differences were put aside as women from all backgrounds, including college women, joined the effort to get it passed in three-fourths of the state houses. For the next several years, the ERA battle, which would eventually be lost, took a leading position on the liberal feminist agenda.

It was during these years that changes on the college campus, which are now institutionalized, first surfaced. The ongoing ERA debate called all aspects of the place of women in American society into question. Previously unchallenged treatment, restrictions and limitations were confronted. On university campuses, women's centers were established to ensure women would have access to information, energy, resources and political organizing concentrated in one place. Not all centers encompassed all these aspects—some were limited to health and counselling services—but many offered literature, self-defense information, career advice and legal assistance.

Other changes, such as co-ed dormitories, absence of special curfew hours for women, women's history and women's studies courses, birth control information and lesbian support groups became familiar features at many, but certainly not all campuses. In most cases, these followed political organizing and pressures from coalitions of women students, faculty and staff members. Personal safety issues, rape prevention and sexual harassment grew in importance, and joined reproductive rights as the principal areas of concern for feminist students. Furthermore, as movements for divestment in South Africa and against intervention in Central America grew, women participating in these struggles began to identify and fight male domination as it manifested itself in those organizations' internal workings.

In recent years, while working women have focused their energy on campaigns to correct the imbalance in the pay scales between women and men, college women have continued to address reproductive rights issues, especially after passage of laws prohibiting or limiting federal funding for abortions and the recent jump in violent attacks on abortion clinics around the country.

Cooperation among the generations helped defeat an anti-abortion referendum in Massachusetts in 1986, when members of NOW and NARAL (the National Abortion Rights Action League) joined ranks with activists advocating a broader, more radical reproductive rights agenda, such as Boston's chapter of Reproductive Rights National Network.

One large-scale political action involving college women with women of other ages and backgrounds came in the spring of 1986, when a national March for Women's Lives brought 80,000 to the capital. The marchers shouted their opposition to intervention by the state, the church and the corporations into their personal lives, and served to empower college women with the sense of history and continuity they had not yet experienced.

A Battlefield With Too Many Targets

The women's movement at colleges and universities, finds itself comprised of groups reacting to half a dozen different unrealized objectives. Women have made great advances in the last two decades, but the direction of the future is uncertain. For college women today, even the label "feminist" has become problematic. Twenty years after the beginning of the modern women's movement, popular culture has associated feminism, once a badge of honor among progressive women and men, with a variey of undesirable images, including "man-hater" (usually a homophobic code for lesbian), a yuppie-type woman who is only out for herself, and the now legendary "Superwoman" who is able to masterfully juggle an impossible schedule that includes a home, a husband, babies and a career.

During the last several years, college women have identified specific concerns which can be divided into six loose categories: (1) personal safety; (2) reproductive rights; (3) women's studies; (4) economic equality; (5) administration policies, and (6) empowerment and leadership.

Rape on campus captures the most attention. Outrage at poor security and the growing awareness of "date rape" or "acquaintance rape" ensures widespread support. Women cool to the need for a women's studies department or uncertain about abortion all identify with sexual harassment, whether it involves simple innuendo, a man's refusal to accept "No," or rape. The Berkeley Women's Liberation Front marked locations of rapes on campus with large red paper "X"s and staged protests at football games. At Ann Arbor, the Sexual Assault Prevention and Awareness Center holds peer education workshops on sexual assault and coercion, led by a female and a male facilitator.

On many campuses, the most dramatic and popular public activity is the annual "Take Back the Night" march. Usually it culminates days of workshops, films and panels on all apsects of sexual harassment and intimidation. At many schools the march involves women only; at Boulder, a workshop for men has been conducted while the march takes place and at some schools, fraternity members have shown support by standing along the parade route with lighted candles.

Reproductive rights has always been a strong concern of younger women. Mimi Adler, who works with Columbia-Barnard's Student Health Advocate Program, believes the right to an abortion hits closer to home than other issues for college women. "Many college women who haven't had an abortion but who are sexually active have probably had a pregnancy scare, or they recognize that pregnancy is always possible. They may have had to have an abortion at some point, or at least had to think about it."[1] Some women's groups use January 22, the anniversary of the Supreme Court's 1973 *Roe v. Wade* decision decriminalizing abortion, to call attention to the overall picture of reproductive rights, which extends to adequate prenatal care, affordable child care, maternity leave, freedom from sterilization abuse and access to safe contraception methods. In the absence of any national college organization covering these issues, college women often work with the National Organization for Women (NOW), the National Abortion Rights Action League (NARAL) or Planned Parenthood on these topics.

Some are reluctant to consider NOW as a model. Stephanie Berger of Hampshire College, who helped pull together a weekend conference for college women in reproductive rights issues, faults the organization. "I have a problem with their ideology. NOW is a hierarchy. It has a president-vice-president-treasurer kind of structure. I don't work well with that. It's liberal feminism—comparable worth stuff. My politics are more radical. I find their analysis limiting because I don't feel it touches the personal experience of the majority of women in this country."[2]

Laura Wiede, who attended the Washington march organized by NOW, criticized the event because "there wasn't enough emphasis on women who can't afford to have an abortion. The majority of the women who die from failed abortions are poor and non-white."[3]

Some campus chapters of DSA adopted reproductive rights as a priority for the 1986-1987 school year, using DSA literature coordinated by Lisa Laufer including a how-to guide on planning a reproductive rights project with a reasonable goal, such as gathering signatures on a petition or sponsoring an event. Other recommended activities include protesting "fake clinics" that advertise themselves as counselling services but in actuality attempt to dissuade women from having abortions, and escorting women safely to and from abortion clinics.[4] The PSN's Reproductive Rights paper also provides support.[5]

One creative tactic is the "Speak-Out on Abortion." At Hampshire, faculty members who had illegal abortions told their stories to students in an open forum. Students who had abortions more recently contrast their feelings and experiences with the older women. Sarah Buttenweiser, who helped coordinate the event, affirms that "the program was incredibly moving and effective. Everything became very real. In the 1960s, abortion was an issue of survival. If one could find someone to do it, one still had to ask: what if I die?" She feels that today's college women need to accept the protection of this right as their responsibility.[6]

Though stories about sexually transmitted diseases fill the media, college students, with the exception of gay men, are not making serious changes in their sexual practices.[7] At Wesleyan College, reproductive rights activists led a week-long petition drive to force radio and television stations to carry condom ads, and attracted

1200 signers. Generally, however, efforts to link publicity about AIDS to larger matters have proven ineffective.

Though they have been characterized, often far too sweepingly, as a generation interested only in career advancement, women in college are relatively inactive in political organizing connected with economic equality. Many activists who belong to multi-issue organizations such as PSN or DSA will support local labor struggles, especially those involving contract negotiations for campus workers, the majority of whom are women. But the most visible strategy in the women's movement at large, the push for comparable worth statutes, does not count college women among its regular advocates.

When coalition work does occur, it is usually focused on the university policy-making apparatus. For example, reporting procedures for women who have been assaulted fall between the cracks—some women believe this highlights a university's insensitivity, or is a conscious attempt to minimize this problem. At Madison, the PSN chapter charged that the school's sexual harassment policies do not point out where to go with a sexual harassment complaint, do not specify what punishment (if any) may apply to faculty members, do not describe the formal procedures that follow a complaint. There is no policy on student-to-student sexual harassment. Furthermore, campus administrators tell students and employees that the process of answering a complaint will be long and cumbersome and may be fruitless—even if the responsible office makes recommendations regarding a known sexual harasser, the administration is not obligated to take any actions. PSN adds that, under Title IX (US Department of Education), institutions must have a grievance procedure which is "capable of prompt and equitable resolution of sexual harassment complaints."[8]

However, Title IX—originally designed to withhold federal funds from universities guilty of sex discrimination—was severely limited in 1984 when the Supreme Court, in the Grove City College case, ruled that only directly funded campus activity had to swear to be non-discriminatory. As a result, women's groups, such as the Project on the Status and Education of Women, a research and monitoring division of the Association of American Colleges, charge that the Department of Education has chosen to enforce Title IX in a very limited manner. Along with the drive for equality in athletic programs, women's groups had used Title IX to force colleges to adopt mechanisms for women to appeal sexual harassment cases and to increase the number of tenured women faculty. Some have taken to state courts for redress, but only 12 states have laws prohibiting sexual discrimination in education.[9]

Even within the realm of economic equality, activist women point to universities' low number of tenured women faculty members and to contracts that keep female employees in lower-paying jobs.

In the area of reproductive rights, campus policies dictate the availability of birth control information and materials, the establishment of child care facilities and access to abortion referrals. Organized efforts to challenge unsatisfactory policies take the form of candlelight vigils, dormitory meetings to explain the issues to students directly and campus rallies.

The debate over women's studies programs at schools where none exist can pit those who want a separate field of study against those who would incorporate women's contributions in every field in every department's course of study. Many also press for at least one mandatory course in women's issues for all incoming first-year students.

Only a direct commitment from a university administration can create new departments, or mandate expanded emphases within existing departments—the steps needed to launch or expand women's studies within the curriculum. Some women's centers house women's studies programs. The center at Barnard, for example, has a collection of feminist literature, and regularly arranges women's issues luncheons, seminars and lectures by guest speakers. But the center at the University of New Mexico emphasizes health counselling, stress management, weight control and nutrition assistance.

The most common problem facing all activist college women is the problem of access to leadership and decision-making positions. Men in many organizations still show patronizing attitudes; women often fight back through women's caucuses. These efforts to bring women's concerns into the full sweep of political efforts unite college women who see as the heart of their political agenda their unquestioned acceptance as equals in any arena.

SCENE

Take Back the Fight

A little more than a year ago, students angry with their school's failure to divest built shanties on the Dartmouth Green—later sledgehammered by conservative classmates. Today, two couples are preparing to build the traditional January snow sculptures. The air is New England hard apple crisp.

Inside Collis Center, the "air" is 1950s, everyone-in-their-place proper. Two young women leaf through the most recent edition of *Womyn's Re\view*, the campus radical feminist paper.

Dartmouth College presents a challenge for anyone who wishes to foster feminist consciousness. Although this school has been officially co-ed for 15 years, and is now 40% female, there is still no women's center. Kanani Kauka, a senior, says that a number of women who spoke out during the divestment incidents "were physically attacked." She feels this made many women turn their attention from apartheid to feminist issues.

There is particular concern about rape. "More often than not, when rapes occur on campus, they're date rapes. They don't get reported. First of all because the woman doesn't view it as rape, and secondly because this is a very small campus." The case of a student raped on campus last year, its handling by the school and its coverage in the school paper, stirred new attention. "There is no centralized area where women can go for counselling in a crisis situation." Junior Ginnie Martin says women have pushed for a center, but the administration's responses parallels the reaction to the demands for divestment. "In 1978, they took a vote and 82% of the students wanted divestment. So what the students want is not important."

Campus women drew up a concrete proposal to convert an existing building, into a women's resource center, for research, health services information, legal and psychological support, and cultural presentations. The administration, according to activist Kristin Breiseth, said it must decide if the Center "will be beneficial for the undergraduate population as a whole," a criterion not applied, she feels, when Afro-American, native American and International houses were established.

But it is not only the administration that fails to act on these concerns. "In terms of everyone working together in a kind of coalition, it's not really there," Kanani continues. "There's been a lot of factionalization in the women's movement here, in terms of who's willing to do what, who is perceived as too moderate, or too radical, or not radical enough. There's a lot of frustration, and it's understandable. For years, people have been talking and trying to educate, and getting the feeling that nobody out there is listening. So a lot of people have gotten to the point that they don't care if anybody else is listening any more. The whole education process is bogus. So actions take place that alienate a large community, and nobody cares."

Alienation at best and sometimes outright hostility. At the homecoming last fall, as the college president spoke, a handful of women rushed up to him and threw 300 red-stained tampons at his feet.

Ginnie and Kakani hand me the *Womyn's Re\view,* another bold reaction to the pallid atmosphere. Filled with entries such as a quiz titled "Match the Misogynists!" and treatises on women's socialization and objectification, the tabloid partly reflects some women's dissatisfaction with the campus daily's handling of their views. As I leaf through the issue, it reminds me of early underground press publications, two decades ago also judged radical, more often than not for their eclectic style and content rather than their political positions. Kakani, mindful to temper any assessment with caution, points out that after the highly publicized rape, attendance at the moderate Women's Issues League shot up from 20 to 100.

On the first floor of stately Robinson Hall, offices of *The Dartmouth* ("The oldest college newspaper in America - Founded 1799"), are neat and trim, as are its new editors, Sarah Jackson and Jack Steinberg. Sarah agrees that the tampon incident was a response to the rape case. A reporter at the time, she also confides her view that "the paper really sensationalized that issue. Yes, it should have been our lead story, but," she questions, confirming that the decision-making editorial group was heavily male-dominated, "banner headlines and big photographs on the front page, day after day?"

While some of the radical women may feel that no one is noticing, Jack is paying at least enough attention to judge that the maverick publication is "very, very radical. Very, very angry. Put out by, as far as I'm concerned, a small, minority position on campus, but a very vocal minority position."

Support, however limited, is growing slowly. Jack's assessment is that "the women's movement, I don't think they're done being heard yet. I think the strength of their message hasn't diminished from the first issue of that paper." Kristen works with a core of nearly thirty women who vow to carry on the struggle until the center is established.

And Dartmouth's small town serenity, from the classic imposing library, to Lou's homey Main Street restaurant, has started to be broken. Phrases like "sisterhood," "body sanctity," "phallocentric" and "date rape" are beginning to replace conversations about skiing.

INTERVIEW

Joy Wallin, University of Wisconsin   *March 10, 1987*

Joy Wallin is director of The Women's Center in Madison, a comfortable, airy second-floor space in a coverted wood-frame house, a relief from the more than 400 institutional buildings that spread over the vast campus.

TV—*I heard the center has a lead role in day care here.*

JW—Two new programs grew out of this Women's Center. One was a child care tuition assistance program in which student fees money goes to students who are parents, and directly to their child care provider. Another is an actual day care facility, an alternative-type program that opened last fall. Both programs were started by a small group of women students in the center who started their own committee in order to be recognized by the university as independent groups.

TV—*What do you see as the most pressing women's issue on this campus right now?*

JW—I would put it under the umbrella term of sexual harassment, including classroom harassment, and the whole spectrum of sexual assault—be it verbal, be it the subtle assault going on in social interaction that students themselves aren't naming as sexual assault. And then the definite cases of rape, gang rape and those types of things that are going on. We're doing a lot of work on acquaintance rape issues. A new program has been started throughout the system called STAAR, which is Students Taking Action Against Rape, a direct service program. A lot of work went on this year about classroom sexual harassment—between professors and students, TA's and students, TA's and professors, all those interactions where there is some kind of inequality in the power relationships, where women are frequently victims.

TV—*What are the components of your approach?*

JW—We do workshops in the dorms and fraternities and cooperatives—any living situation where there are a lot of students. We go with two men and two women facilitators and give a program to a mixed-sex audience. We open the meeting by reading poems and that sets the mood, lets them know this is serious stuff and that we're going to be talking about it as adults. Then we do some activities to get people talking about their own feelings—we don't try to make it so serious that people feel intimidated to talk. We talk about socialization and some of the behaviors and attitudes that we tend not to question, not realizing that we're part of the rape culture and need to own up to that. Then we show a very powerful videotape called

"Tell Someone You Know." Afterward we talk about the message, which is that sexual violence is happening to people we know. Eighty-five percent of the time, the perpetrator of the violence is someone we know—and that's a heavy message for people to think about. They don't want to know that. It's much easier to just go blindly along and pretend it's not happening. After that, we talk about the services provided for people to deal with these feelings in case they have redefined their past, and realize that maybe they were a victim or a perpetrator. We tell about Men Stopping Rape, a program for men to call in and talk about their feelings. We also provide the Women's Counselling Service here with about 30 counsellors trained in women's issues and other services in the community.

TV—What effects have you seen?

JW—Trying to get this thing off the ground has been a two-year process. Until this past fall, when the Women's Center took it on it sort of floundered but we've really been able to get out there. We've done about 10 or 12 workshops already, and there are more scheduled.

TV— How are they set up? Do people invite you?

JW—We sent out a series of letters to the housefellows in the dorms. The Center has a speakers bureau on acquaintance rape. Men Stopping Rape has done workshops for male audiences, and they were beginning to be asked to talk to mixed-sex groups so they contacted the women's center to get women facilitators. Now, we have our own group, and we work with them. We've had a lot of trouble getting into the fraternities and sororities.

TV—How do you address sexual harassment between students and teachers?

JW—The Center has the only sexual harassment counsellor advocates on campus. The university does not provide that at all for victims of sexual harassment. The affirmative action office—that's where you go if you decide to file an official grievance—will treat you as a number. There's no one to deal with what you're feeling as a victim. That's what we provide. Right now, the PSN is really putting pressure on the university to make the policy more student-friendly. We're trying to provide a service for victims. One problem is that it's hard to get people to use it, to get women or men to feel justified in identifying their experience as sexual harassment. It's a symptom of the victimization: you blame yourself for what's happened. Or it's such a power thing, that there is nothing you can do: "This professor has my grade on the line; he's in control. I better not make a big deal or I could fail." Especially for graduate students, it's more difficult.

TV—The university sees it as a legal issue?

JW—Right. Basically, the policy is set up to protect the university, and to protect their prize researchers who aren't quite behaving themselves, not to help students at all. They have "intake" people, one or two in each department, that you go to first, to discuss what's happened. That person would deliberate with you a bit, and then send you on to Affirmative Action. And nobody even knows that that's all part of the system—which makes the whole thing that much more difficult, because if you're the victim of sexual harassment, your power has been taken away from you, and the last thing you need is to approach a system which you can't be successful with unless you have a lot of power. We try to be that powerful person, to go in and say, "Has so-and-so's file been processed?"

TV—*At some schools I've visited, women's centers are predominantly white. Is that the case here?*

JW—Yes. A few years ago women realized that it was a white women's center, and they weren't satisfied. They started a support group here for women of color, and then the women of color left and started their own thing. One time I saw some graffitti that said "UW = University of Whites," and I think, unfortunately, that's very true. The Black Students Union has a women's caucus but I'm not even sure what their priority issues are. I know they worked to bring Angela Davis to the campus. It's an issue that I'm really concerned about, and I think it's time white women realize that it's our responsibility to become educated. The attitude here has been we should welcome them, they should take their place here, but I think it's more that we have to educate ourselves as white women, about the racism in our own lives, in the feminism we talk about.

TV—*How do you look at the issue of women moving into leadership positions in other areas?*

JW—Part of what we talk about here is empowerment, and the center serves as a real growing space for women. We have support groups that talk a lot about self-esteem and empowerment.

TV—*Should it be the university's job to deal with these issues?*

JW—Our society has devalued women's experience, and personal experience, honest gut feelings. Women's studies classes deal with those kind of issues. I've seen a lot of people turn around after going through one of those classes, but not everybody turns around after going through math. I would like to see some kind of program that deals with some of the issues we deal with. I have problems saying it should be institutionalized by the university, but I think it can be valuable.

TV—*Where do you see things going in the next few years?*

JW—Women realize these issues are out there, there's a generally higher consciousness among women, and a lot more emphasis on letting men realize the same things. To make change, to create the kind of society I envision, that has to start with women exploring their own personal power, and taking that, grasping that, going with that. I think a lot of women then say, "Gosh, I wish my boyfriend understood this." I'm starting to see more men at the women's studies classes. My energies will go into educating and empowering women, but what I would really, really love to see is men taking that initiative. Men Stopping Rape is a wonderful group. They've realized that something's gone wrong in their own lives, that the society isn't real healthy right now, and they're taking responsibility.

Ann Scarritt, University of Colorado   *December 18, 1986*

Ann Scarritt sits in one corner of the sofa in the Feminist Alliance office on the second floor of the sprawling University Memorial Center, University of Colorado at Boulder, and talks about the nine-year-old group's current state.

TV—*What is the biggest women's issue here?*

AS—Our biggest issue is the Take Back the Night March. We have a whole week. This year we focused on rape awareness and also pornography, how pornography fits into that. But all the newspapers focused on was the fact that it was all women who marched. Because it's all women, it's seen as really radical. I consider myself radical, but a lot of the women just coming to college don't. So we're doing educational things. We have an abortion rights booth.

TV—*What's the attitude on campus about that issue?*

AS—I think most people on campus definitely think it's pretty insane not to have contraceptives available. And not many people support the anti-abortion people.

TV—*Is there a problem with lack of availability of contraceptives?*

AS—It's more of a problem of accepting. It's more of a social attitude—there's still that whole good girl\bad girl syndrome. Women are almost always the ones who are responsible for birth control. And a lot of what's available isn't necessarily very good, and you don't get information on what's wrong with the pill, the IUD.

TV—*What's the role of the health services?*

AS—They're not doing anything; we're working with groups in Boulder.

TV—*What are some of the other concerns women have?*

AS—There are so few women professors here, and there are pay discrepancies. In the past, we've made information available about what exactly is going on, the percentage of women faculty, how much they're being paid, the recruitment policy. This takes a lot of energy, because people generally have a very negative attitude toward feminists. Especially the student population. It's kind of scary.

TV—*Is it getting worse?*

AS—I wouldn't say that. More women are considering themselves feminists, in a more liberal, safer sense, where they would support the ERA, where they believe in equal pay. But the whole idea of being women-identified is very scary, especially in a university. A lot of women come in when they're 18 and just getting their identity, really being able to have real constant social interactions with members of the opposite sex. We take a real critical look at that, and that's the kind of stuff that makes people not like feminism. Also, there's such a big Greek system here. And some fraternities got burned down.

TV—*Burned down?*

AS—Yeah. There were arsonists. Two frats were burned here, and there were some in Denver and some in Ashland. Ann Arbor, too. It was the week before the Take Back the Night March last year. And the Feminist Alliance position—we didn't condone or condemn it.

A Renewed Movement on Campuses

More than racism, more than homophobia, more than economic pressures levelled directly at students, sexism affects the greatest number of people on college campuses. However unfocused or diffuse the concerns, strategies and constituencies may be, women's issues have the potential to generate a renewed round of feminist activity on college campuses.

This generation of women, children of a post-liberation age, grew up seeing women—if not at home, certainly in the media—confronting barriers to equality. Many who do not assert themselves as political activists on women's issues seem to do so out of choice, not because they believe it is not their "place" to do so. They know they have the option, and the right, to act.

In the short run, strategies will vary from school to school, region to region. Conferences of students who share views about reproductive rights will continue to plan attacks against recalcitrant administrations, and to develop methods of reaching complacent young women who view themselves as untouched by these issues. Also, many women make the connections between sexism and militarism, and are reaching out to those concerned about the arms race, the war economy and nuclear proliferation.

Allies are found primarily amoung men on campus rather than women off campus. The remarkable impact of a group such as Men Stopping Rape at Madison, easy to duplicate and clearly effective, offers the likelihood that other such efforts will become regular fixtures in university life. But differences in agenda, strategy and organizational structure keeps college women and the national organizations from achieving much more than a businesslike working arrangement.

The greatest controversy facing this movement is the attempt to redress the low level of participation among women of color. The women's movement has often diminished the role of non-white women. At the turn of the century, for example, many white feminists were willing to drop black suffrage from their list of demands if it meant that their own struggle for the vote would be advanced. Today, many young women of color believe that white women do not understand their experiences and concerns; attempts to bring them together will come as they identify more areas of common interest and as white women begin to take seriously the problem of racism in the movement.

University and college policies affecting women will change as women move into positions of authority in administrations, but this is still a slow process. Similarly, alumnae may press trustees by tying donations to demands for more female tenured faculty, department heads, deans and administrators.

At this point, activists in women's issues believe they have an uphill fight ahead of them. While many on campus may agree with the basic principles of equality, there remains the challenge to convert that first level of acceptance into actions that result in institutionalized changes.

CHAPTER TEN

Gay, Lesbian and Bisexual Rights

The Stonewall riots changed everything.

While homosexual men and women had quietly begun to group themselves together in the 1950s, in organizations like the Mattachine Society and the Daughters of Bilitis, the drive for open, equal recognition marks its beginning on June 28, 1969.

The Stonewall Inn, one of many gay bars in New York City's Greenwich Village, frequently weathered harassment and raids by the police. On that warm early summer night, young gays joined hands with older drag queens and bulldykes and fought back. Many had marched to end the war in Vietnam; many had marched to support equality for blacks and women. Now, it was time to stand up for themselves. The Gay Liberation Front (GLF) was born.

Within six months, "young homosexual radicals, many of whom had worked with Students for a Democratic Society throughout the country," constructed an alliance with gays from New York City to create the Gay Activists Alliance (GAA).[1]

Two years earlier, the world's first campus homosexual organization, the Student Homophile League at Columbia University, had made the front page of the *New York Times* when they were granted official status by the university. But the conservative climate of the times dictated that students' names (including heterosexuals who supported the movement) be kept secret. The SHL, founded in October of 1966 and chartered in April 1967, set a precedent for other campus groups in the next few years. They began by picketing a symposium on homosexuality at Columbia in the spring of 1968.[2]

The youth culture and the sharpening confrontational climate throughout society dominated these early years. College gay men and lesbians found more in common with young political activists from other movements than with the older men and women who had pioneered the civil rights and social organizations of the previous decade. Older gays were categorized as too conservative, too afraid to offend, too worried about losing status—the same charges young heterosexuals made of the previous leaders of their movements. The difference was that there was no "history" of campus activism in this movement. This was new territory.

By 1969, "Coming Out" dances, first held at New York's Alternate University, were held at Temple, Berkeley, City College of New York and Minnesota. By the following year, gay organizations, including GLF chapters, sprung up at nearly a dozen campuses around the country. And in the spring of 1971, the first Midwest Regional Gay Liberation convention drew more than 100 delegates from 14 schools in six states to Northern Illinois University.

Organizing continued as students from existing groups visited campuses to lend support to help young gay men and lesbians confront obstacles to recognition. "By the beginning of 1972 student homophile groups were organized on some 70 American campuses, half of these organizations being chartered by their institutions."[3] Thirty-six states boasted some type of homosexual rights organization, and groups were operating on college campuses in 21 states. Three years later, an estimated 200 of the nation's approximately 1,000 gay groups were student-run; by the spring of 1987, various estimates calculated the number at between 300 and 500.[4]

"The homosexual has a fundamental human right to live and work with his fellow man [sic] as an equal in their common quest for the betterment of human society." This phrase, part of the Columbia SHL founding resolution, formed the basis for what gay students were, and are, seeking. The resolution claimed the rights of all gay men and lesbians to "develop and achieve full potential and dignity as a human being."[5]

Achieving such a position has required gays to learn to believe that they, in fact, deserved that dignity. Conditioned by a culture to think they were mentally ill, criminal, sinful and willfully aberrant, young gay men and lesbians have confronted each segment of that culture to learn why and how these beliefs developed. Learning from the Black Power Movement to confront the dominant culture's view of them as inferior, gays, in defiant marches, chanted "Gay is good," "Out of the closets and into the streets," and "2-4-6-8, gay is just as good as straight." Building self-esteem, they discovered, was the first step in being strong enough to claim all the other rights they sought.

In 1970, Michael Brown of the National Gay Task Force declared that gays had to stop hiding, and spoke of "an affirmation and declaration of our new pride." Rap groups, discussions and consciousness-raising sessions led to requests for gay studies courses at universities. The University of Nebraska provided the first in 1970, with others following. New York University's School of Continuing Education offered

"Homosexuality: A Contemporary View," while Kent State's curriculum included "Politics of Gay Liberation" and "The Sociology of Deviancy." A dozen campuses had added 30 similar courses by the following year.

Following several years of cases involving the rights of gay employees to hold on to their jobs, the US Civil Service Commission Bulletin, in December 1973, issued a policy to all job supervisors decreeing that the commission could not find unsuitable for civil service employment anyone who is homosexual or engages in homosexual activity. This policy institutionalized the criterion that an employee's sexuality can be considered grounds for dismissal only if their behavior directly interferes with their work, or the work of their agency or place of employment.

Major corporations, including NBC, the Bank of America, AT&T and IBM, announced they would not reject openly gay job applicants on the basis of their sexuality. In December of 1973, following three years of protests, the American Psychiatric Association's board of trustees voted to remove homosexuality from the APA's list of mental disorders and passed a resolution deploring "all public and private discrimination against homosexuals" and urged "the repeal of all legislation making criminal offenses of sexual acts performed by consenting adults in private."[6] Throughout the decade, with the assistance of national organizations dealing with gay rights issues, gay caucuses were established in professional and trade organizations.

Through the 1970s and early 1980s, students struggled to gain the ability to socialize and learn about their hidden heritage. In 1970, after groups at New York University had successfully sponsored three gay dances, the school attempted to prevent the fourth. A large crowd demonstrating at the hall where the dance was scheduled persuaded the administration to reverse its opposition. But University of Maine administrators refused to grant a campus group permission to hold a statewide conference that same year. For the next fifteen years, battles over simple recognition kept lesbians and gay men on campuses from developing as a political constituency involved with other issues. When in 1981 the administration at Georgetown University denied recognition to that school's gay student organization, the students sued and the DC Court of Appeals ruled the school could not legally deny funding to its gay student organization. (Georgetown fought the ruling until 1987 when its appeals were finally exhausted.) In 1982, similar court rulings prevented university officials from withholding recognition to gay student groups in Florida and Oklahoma.

But such cases continue in all parts of the country, as conservative student governments or school administrators attempt to block official status to gay student groups. Paula Ettelbrick of Lambda Legal Defense, a national gay and lesbian legal rights organization, says her office knows of about 10 other cases involving the rights of gay college students, all won by the students.[7]

On September 8, 1975, Sargent Leonard Matlovich became the first openly gay person to make the cover of *Time* magazine. In a sense, he embodied the state of gay rights in America in mid-decade. Matlovich, dismissed from the Air Force when he confirmed his homosexuality, brought suit. The case forced those not familiar with homophobia to confront the issue. Matlovich was an exemplary serviceman,

recipient of awards, trusted by co-workers. When a Federal court ruled he should
be reinstated with back pay, Americans in general, and gay college students in particular, understood more of how society translates the fear of homosexuals into its
behavior toward them. The stereotypical, media-generated images of gay men and
lesbians as people fixated on gender role-reversal, as untrustworthy, as seducers,
weak-willed, emotionally unstable were all challenged by the Matlovich case.

As dramatic, confrontational approaches gave way to more systematic, formalized strategies of the late seventies, the gay and lesbian movement fell victim to two
powerful forces: the Reagan adminstration and the onset of AIDS.

Liberal and progressive politics of all varieties suffered setbacks and defeats
in the early 1980s, as Americans voted an avowedly conservative administration into
office. Attitudes toward basic civil and human rights may have changed little, but
there was a pervasive climate of intolerance toward diversity. Gains made by all
minorities over 25 years slipped away, and the momentum which had built up in
creating openly gay college groups slowed—new groups were formed, but they
faced hostile, public opposition.

Gay students discovered that their mere existence qualified them for arrest.
Before 1961, when Illinois repealed its sodomy laws (statutes which outlaw a wide
range of sexual acts in private between consenting adults of any gender), gay men
and lesbians were "unapprehended felons" in every state. By 1987, sodomy laws
had been repealed in 26 states and in dozens of cities and towns across the country.

In 1986, the United States Supreme Court, in *Bowers v. Hardwick*, upheld the
right of the state of Georgia to classify sodomy between consenting adults in private
as a crime, overturning, in a 5-4 vote, an Appeals Court finding that the Georgia
statute violated the defendant's fundamental rights. Michael Hardwick was charged
when a policeman, who came to his home at night to deliver a summons for carrying an open container of alcohol on the street, was directed by a sleepy houseguest
to an upstairs bedroom. The policeman walked unannounced into Hardwick's
bedroom, and witnessed him engaging in sexual activity with another man. The
Court rejected claims that the case violated rights to privacy, Fourth Amendment
rights to be secure "against all unreasonable searches and seizures," referring to
traditional Judeo-Christian beliefs and asserting that "the Constitution does not con-
fer a fundamental right upon homosexuals to engage in sodomy."[8]

In dissent, Justice Harry Blackmun stated, "This case is about the most comprehensive of rights and the right most valued by civilized men, namely the right to
be left alone." He noted that "only the most willful blindness could obscure the fact
that sexual intimacy is a sensitive, key relationship of human existence, central to
family life, community welfare and the development of human personality. The fact
that individuals define themselves in a significant way through their intimate sexual
relationships with others suggests, in a nation as diverse as ours, that there may be
many 'right' ways of conducting those relationships, and that much of the richness
of a relationship will come from the freedom an individual has to *choose* the form
and nature of these intensely personal bonds," and later added, "The makers of our
Constitution undertook to secure conditions favorable to the pursuit of happiness.
They recognized the significance of man's spiritual nature, of his feelings and of his

intellect. They knew that only a part of the pain, pleasure and satisfactions of life are to be found in material things. They sought to protect Americans' beliefs, their thoughts, their emotions and their sensations."[9]

The setback from the Hardwick case chilled legal advances that had been made, but some observed that the close vote signalled the possibility that a future case might strike down the legality of sodomy laws.

When the AIDS epidemic first drew widespread public attention in 1982, it was labelled the "gay plague," and was, in the US, for the most part confined to and linked with the sexual practices of gay men. The press was filled with theories that the condition stemmed from particular sexual practices. Others wrote that AIDS was a punishment from God. Old prejudices resurfaced: Gays were beaten, evicted from their homes, dismissed from their jobs, denied custody of their children and blamed for introducing a deadly syndrome into American society, especially when it reached "the general population." Educating people that AIDS and homosexuality had only a coincidental connection, and fighting vigorously against the prejudices that were resurfacing emerged as principal strategies.

To combat monumental discrimination, gay students learned to support each other, to hold on to the gains they had achieved, and to work with students at other schools. In 1984, a small group of students from a handful of eastern universities held a weekend conference to exchange information and share experiences. Coordinated by the Boston Intercollegiate Lesbian and Gay Association, the students agreed to make the conference an annual event. At the second conference, sponsored by a Cornell group, students founded the Northeast Lesbian and Gay Student Union (NELGSU). Within four years, the group's annual weekend conferences grew from about 70 participants to nearly 500. At the 1987 event, held at Columbia University to commemorate the twentieth anniversary of the creation of the Student Homophile League, now called the Columbia Gay and Lesbian Alliance, representatives from more than 60 schools attended 110 workshops, classes, forums, films and speeches.[10]

The agenda for that conference, like those of similar conferences around the country, represents the new directions these organizations are taking—from parenting and job discrimination to health care and equal recognition for domestic partners. Despite the challenges, gay, lesbian and bisexual students assume they have a right to an equal place on their college campuses, to share fully in the college experience, and they recognize that political activism is the route to achieve and to maintain that place.

The Pink Triangle

When the Nazis rounded up "offending segments" of German society in the 1930s and forced them to wear insignias to designate their category, homosexuals were assigned the pink triangle. Gay college students today have adopted this as a symbol of their demand for equal rights in all areas, wearing it openly to proclaim knowledge of the extermination of gay people throughout history and a willingness to confront anyone who would return to those days.

Being gay in college today means benefitting from an openness about diversity on the part of many fellow students, and suffering from an increase in homophobia which is often tolerated more readily than even racism or sexism would be. "Coming out," the process of confirming one's homosexuality to others, itself makes a political statement in a hostile or unfriendly environment. College students, already under great pressures to conform and adopt lasting "grown up" behavior patterns, frequently suffer tremendous personal anguish when they discover and decide to deal with their sexuality, especially when it puts them at odds with the majority of their peers and with the larger society they are supposedly in college to gain access to.

The emergence of recognized campus organizations for lesbian, gay and bisexual students has moderated that anguish. It takes more than willingness to establish a group, however. At Lehigh, one of the country's most conservative non-religious colleges, the Human Diversity League had to wait nearly three years to be granted official recognition.

Before the political side of gay issues can be dealt with, the personal side needs attention. At the beginning of each semester, the University of Maryland's Outreach brings together small discussion groups of six to ten, each with a trained facilitator. Matthew Alexander of Madison's Ten Percent Society states, "Mostly, the group addresses the issue that there is no place on campus for lesbian and gay students to meet, just to socialize. Not to find a relationship, just friendships, to have somebody to communicate with. And when you show a film about [assassinated San Francisco gay politician] Harvey Milk, you give people a sense of history, where the gay movement has been—a sense of history, a sense of self, and a sense of self-worth, also."[11]

At Millersville State University in rural Pennsylvania, Darryl Brown has tried to launch a gay students' organization, and has looked to the nearby Franklin and Marshall group for guidance. In the past, gays at Millersville "would publicize where the meetings were, and people would come and harass them. That's why it never got off the ground: it was too open to start with."[12]

Prejudice still surfaces when conservative or religious students or groups try to remove these organizations. The Rutgers University Lesbian\Gay Alliance, concerned about Christian propaganda against gays, published a two-page pamphlet: the cover, in Old Roman-style script, proclaims "What Jesus Christ said about homosexuality"; inside, the pages are blank. Sometimes hostility comes directly from the institution itself. At Notre Dame, a collection of courageous gay students has been attempting to gain official recognition for years. When the administration instructed the college radio station not to run the group's public service announcements, station managers resigned in protest. Although they regularly involve 50 students in their activities, the school's student senate has repeatedly denied them access to campus facilities.

Gay students want to enjoy the range of experiences open to other students— from the academic and intellectual pursuit of relevant topics to the personal and social activities including the everyday spontaneity of taking the hand of a boyfriend or girlfriend. And they believe the university has a responsibility to make these experiences equally available to them, and to move strongly against people or policies that try to prevent them. These include not only overt acts, such as beatings and physical assaults ("gay-bashing"), vandalism and discrimination in housing, but also the failure to have information about homosexuality in the library, banning of gay social events, and so on. Gay students also ask that schools schedule speakers who address gay issues, and create an orientation program for all students that confronts homophobia.

Some schools have made efforts to overcome discrimination. The University of Michigan Affirmative Action Office has produced a pamphlet "Preventing Discrimination Based on Sexual Orientation," which outlines the school's policy and explains where and how to find confidential help. However, even seemingly simple efforts often fail: at the University of Maine, student Mary Kay Kaster, a resident director, ran into opposition from superiors when she proposed homophobia workshops in dormitories.[13]

Making even modest gains requires action. And while most gay students, like most straight students, are not activists, a growing number are willing to put themselves on the line by organizing to force necessary changes. One popular method is the legal approach, forcing the university to issue a written statement outlawing discrimination based on sexual orientation or sexual preference. Model nondiscrimination clauses are available from the National Gay and Lesbian Task Force to groups trying that route.

Establishing a presence in any arena where there is potential for discrimination against gay students has also achieved results. By creating formally-recognized campus organizations—as valid and accepted as a debating society or a glee club—gay students legitimize their place as people within the university community with a worthy special interest. Openly gay students holding positions in student government can make the point that their sexuality does not disqualify them from helping run the campus community. When Matthew Alexander ran for student government co-president at Madison, he recalls, "people were smart enough to keep their mouths shut and not use any real neat epithets, but when I went to some of the Greek houses and some other places, you could tell some of the people were snickering, and not very supportive at all. And were antagonistic." Still, he thinks his successful campaign drew some support from fraternities. "There are a lot of gay men in fraternities."[14]

Some groups sponsor other activities to benefit the community, most frequently telephone counselling hotlines. At Columbia University, some proceeds from the Gay and Lesbian Alliance's monthly dances, which attract at least 400, support a weekly Study Group founded by Gary Lucek. Open to students and non-students, discuss such subjects such as the Church and Sexuality, Gays and the Media, Erotic Behavior and the Law, and the Politics of Gay Liberation. Madison's Ten Percent Society annually contributes money to help run the Take Back the Night March, which draws attention to women's issues.

Gay Awareness Weeks have become an institution on campuses with strong gay student organizations. Speakers, films, discussion sessions and even lighter approaches like "Kiss A Dyke" booths seek to demystify gays. At the University of Massachusetts, the 1987 Awareness Week included more than 30 free events: cultural offerings mirrored serious and satirical views, from lesbian poetry readings to a coffeehouse performance by the comedy act United Fruit Company. Workshops and panels included "Politics of Prejudice: Institutional Responsibility," a session on taking leadership roles ("The Future Belongs to the Fearless") and "Being Better Allies: Strategies for Heterosexuals on Ending Heterosexism." And on many campuses, gay activists post flyers urging students to "Wear Blue Jeans on Friday—Show Your Support for Gay and Lesbian Rights."

But hostility, fed by misinformation about AIDS, does exist and still requires strong action. Marches and rallies confront both students and administration members unwilling to challenge that hostility, making the connections that failure to confront it transmits a message of tacit support. At the University of Chicago, Gay and Lesbian Alliance (GALA) member Erwin Keller relates, "There have been bumper stickers saying 'Clean Up Hyde Park—Stop AIDS—Castrate Gays.' There were death threats to known gay students, to anti-apartheid activists and to known liberal faculty members. And that's when the university first decided to take some kind of a stand and get involved in the investigation, although clearly the policy of the university appears to be: Let's hope it all blows over."

It did not blow over. Keller explains, "People responding to a personal ad found that their employers and neighbors were contacted, informing them that this person is homosexual and a probable carrier of AIDS. It seems now parents have gotten letters saying that if their children don't renounce their deviant sexual behavior, further action will be taken against them. I am very concerned, because there are people on campus who have written letters to the editor, but who aren't out to their parents, to employers, etc. In Chicago, this can be a real threat. People can be fired in Chicago for being gay. We have no protection at all. So the FBI has been called in, because we do have mail fraud and threats through the mail."[15]

When the lesbian information bulletin board was defaced and vandalized at Mount Holyoke in the winter of 1986, several women, including Carolyn Breen, organized a meeting on heterosexism. "So many women showed up, straight and lesbians, that the room in which the meeting was to be held was too small." The following week, the bulletin board was defaced again, coinciding with racial incidents at the nearby University of Massachusetts. When the administration called an all-campus meeting, the focus was racism, although the most recent incidents of harassment on that campus were against lesbians. Carolyn remembers that "at this meeting, heterosexism was mentioned only once. The morning after the meeting, a banner was found hanging from an academic building in the center of campus. This banner had batiked on it a double women's symbol, with a slash through it. It took a lot of time and effort to make, meaning to me that it was done with a lot of hatred."[16]

In response, lesbian activists mounted a tabling campaign on campus, and distributed pink felt triangles, asking students to wear them in protest. As a result of that protest, the student government openly condemned the acts of violence, the college president wrote a letter, printed in the newspaper, condemning heterosexism, and the Dean of Students' Office offered money to help cover the groups' expenses for the protest. Most significantly, the effort resulted in the addition of "sexual preference" to the college's anti-discrimination clause.

Even progressive students active in other political issues often fail to confront their own heterosexual prejudices. Ricardo Velasquez, a leader in chicano rights issues, confirms that "if somebody were openly gay, and ran for the presidency of MECHA [a national chicano students' group], it would be ridiculously hard. Those are part of the restraints of this culture." When asked if the inconsistency, asking others to support their rights as a minority but refusing to deal with gay rights, is openly discussed, he answers, "No. They're openly ridiculed. People are homophobic, largely."[17]

But gay students have continued to organize. When one campus develops a strong, stable organization, it assists nearby schools. And nationally, plans have been drafted for a national gay students' association. Students have been working with the National Gay and Lesbian Task Force in Washington to launch a national gay students association sometime in 1988. When the national gay rights organizations staged a march on Washington in October of 1987, thousands of students from all over the country provided visible evidence that they are joining the battle for equal rights, both in their universities and beyond the campus gates.

SCENE

Choosing not to Pass

"They don't realize how significant it is that they're here." Congressman Gerry Studds is standing off to the side, in the chilly March evening, telling me how impressed he is. He has just finished addressing the 1986 conference of lesbian, gay and bisexual students from colleges in the northeast. Now the more than 500 participants are marching through the streets and walkways of Brown University, singing, chanting, celebrating not the conference, but themselves.

Throughout the weekend, they have challenged the myths they have been taught about themselves. They hear stories from students about being active—gays are not passive; about lesbians and gays working together to win political gains—gays do not dislike people of the opposite gender. They hear stories about being a gay parent, a gay teacher, a gay counsellor, and from Gerry Studds, a gay Congressman.

The march is not somber, but more like the spontaneous outpouring that follows a victorious football game. A 25-piece band, led by an exuberant drum major, blazes the route as paraders shout, "2-4-6-8, how do you know your roommate's straight?" or "2-4-6-8, how do you know the faculty's straight?" The bubbly, almost electric energy pulls them along, holding hands, almost dancing at times through the quiet Rhode Island streets. From an upstairs window, one woman student holds out a cardboard pink triangle, and waves. One marcher carries a sign with a pink triangle in one corner, a Nazi insignia in the other, and the words "Never Again." They fill the campus, chants echoing back from stately structures that symbolize an historical link to the traditions of a past intolerant of personal differences.

At Manning Chapel, they receive a warm salute from the four students fasting inside the church to protest the school's failure to divest South Africa holdings. The connection is real; these marchers, however lively, carry a message as political, serious and urgent as the message of the fasters.

On the campus green, the group stops. Within minutes, nearly five hundred candles are distributed, and a circle of light, like a lambent necklace, rings the green in a silent tribute to gays who have been killed through legal oppression, personal assault or societal indifference.

One thoughtful dark-haired young man confides "You know, it's easy for me to keep it a secret." Indeed, he looks like anyone's image of the average boy next door. "But from now on, I'm choosing not to pass."

INTERVIEW

Phil Ault, University of New Mexico   *December 17, 1986*

At the Albuquerque campus of the University of New Mexico, the average age is 27 and the student body numbers 20,000. Phil Ault was head of the Gay and Lesbian Student Union for four semesters.

TV—*What is the history of the group?*

PA—Way back in the early 1970s there was a group called the gay co-op. It was very, very, very politically active about being openly gay. And then in the mid-70s it went underground, and was more of a closeted organization—first names only, never never give your last name type of thing—called Juniper. They had counselling groups, and met at the mental health center for a while. They had a gay hotline, the first one in Albuquerque. And then around '80-'81, Juniper decided it was going to come out of the closet. So it changed its name to the Gay and Lesbian Student Union GLSU.

TV—*Is it recognized by the student government and the school?*

PA—Yes. It's a student-chartered organization. We've received funding from the student senate and outside grant money, also. We write up a budget and apply to the student senate finance committee in the spring for the next year. They review our budget just as they would any other organization. It's put on a ballot and voted on by the entire student body. Most of the time it has failed. It passed a couple of times, most recently last spring.

TV—*What happens then?*

PA—You can go back to the student senate and apply for 75% of what you had originally applied for, and they can allocate that. It's like an override of the student general vote.

TV—*So organizations learn to draw up budgets larger than they really need?*

PA—Those that generally fail have done that. But this last time around the groups that always fail, the minority groups like GLSU, Black Students Union, Arab Student Union, Chicano Student Organizations, all those groups networked together, and everybody passed for the first time in history.

TV—*So the result was a political coalition that achieved something?*

PA—Yes. I also ran for the student senate, and won. I received support not just from GLSU and the minority student groups, but from the fraternities and sororities, which is a wide spectrum, and the business student organizations, too.

TV—*Any signs of homophobia when you were running?*

PA—Oh, yes, yes, of course. No one ever said anything specifically to me, although my two years as coordinator of GLSU were brought up as part of my qualifications, to show I knew student government, roots up, from being a leader of a student-chartered organization. I didn't make an issue of the fact that I was gay, but it was there. Some of my campaign workers had people come up to them and say, "Isn't that the faggot that's running for senate?" And in most cases, someone campaigning for somebody else would hear that, and step in and say, "And who are you, some kind of macho asshole?" or something to that effect, and the issue died right there. There is homophobia. There's a multitude of Christian student organizations on campus, from moderate to very severe fundamentalists, who obviously don't support GLSU's existence, but the general mood of the campus is that GLSU is just another organization.

TV—*What kinds of activities have you sponsored?*

PA—We have speakers on different topics. A doctor comes in at least once a semester and talks about AIDS, an AIDS update. Counsellors come in and talk about positive self-image. Marriage counsellors come in who do couple therapy and talk about relationships, not just heterosexual, but gay relationships, too. One thing I was really proud of last semester, we had two women come in who had travelled in Central America, and they talked about women's issues and gay issues in Central America.

TV—*What other events have you held?*

PA—Last spring, we had a rap group, that was really, really good. We haven't had any dances this semester yet, but we had potluck dinners and movies.

TV—*Do most students usually wait a couple of years before they come out and get active?*

PA—GLSU is basically a coming-out support network. The vast majority of gays at UNM don't really do much with GLSU. It's the ones who are just leaving home, or even those who are a little older but are in the process of coming out, and build their support network of friends.

TV—*Have you seen any changes in the last year or two?*

PA—We've done a lot of work with high school students, and it's different this semester. In the past, they fit the traditional "nellie," effeminate stereotype of what it was to be gay. They thought it was a game—anything political was beyond their conception. The ones that are involved this semester are younger, but more concerned about what it is to be gay. The level of political awareness is much higher.

TV—*Is their behavior less stereotypical?*

PA—They're just general students who happen to be gay. They don't feel they have to act a certain way to be gay, whereas in the past, fulfilling the "nellie" image was part of the game. I think there's also more desire to be somebody that happens to be gay and not automatically be identified as gay, so they may be prejudiced against the stereotypes. That isn't necessarily good either, because with some men, being themselves happens to fulfill the stereotype. And there may be problems in the future with individuals who fill that role model not feeling welcome.

TV—*Has this topic come up in discussions?*

PA—We've discussed it, because a lot of people feel uncomfortable around drag queens and transvestites. Most everyone says that's fine, but it's like heterosexuals talking about gays in general: it's okay, but they don't understand it.

TV—*Does the university have any kind of anti-discrimination clause dealing with sexual orientation?*

PA—The hiring policy anti-discrimination clause includes race, sex, everything, and then it does say sexual orientation.

TV—*What about in admissions?*

PA—I don't think it's ever been an issue. Any teacher, any professor, even if they're tenured, would be hard-pressed to support a prejudice against a gay student. I don't think they'd find support within the administration. The administration may not be comfortable with having GLSU on campus, as individuals, but I think as a whole they would support a student's right if the issue came up.

TV—*Was the recent coalition on student government funding the first coalition?*

PA—There was coalition-building between the minority groups and PIRG when PIRG had a referendum about changing the funding process. Also one year there was an extremely conservative student senator who built a coalition around himself of senators, including his sister; and whichever way he voted, they voted. When GLSU went before the full senate in the budget process he moved to have GLSU's charter revoked. And only one of his other senators voted with him. His sister even voted for GLSU. Several senators got up and stated for the record that he was an idiot.

TV—*Does the group involve lesbians as much as it does gay men?*

PA—No. That's one thing that I've been working on. The majority has always been men. The Women's Center on campus is very strong; the Full Circle Bookstore right next to campus is the gay, lesbian and feminist bookstore, but mainly women congregate there and have social gatherings. There's a lot of networking outside of GLSU and outside of UNM for women.

TV—*Is there a mixed attendance at social events?*

PA—There is, but still the majority is male. I would like to see more intermingling; it feeds stereotype that gay men are uncomfortable around women, or don't like women. Those are two different issues: being uncomfortable and not liking. And then the women not being comfortable around men. I'd like to see that broken down some more.

TV—*Is your organization networked with others in the state or the southwest?*

PA—In the spring of 1986, we started going to the Desert States Conferences, which is for Arizona, New Mexico, Colorado, Utah and Nevada, for general gay and lesbian organizations. We used grant money to pay for our hotel accommodations and student fees from student government to pay for registration. And we learned a lot.

TV—*Does GLSU take positions on issues that other groups are involved in?*

PA—PIRG always comes to our meetings at the beginning of the year and explains what they are, and I've told other groups that they're more than welcome. Most organizations really haven't actually come to a meeting, but we do mention what other groups are doing and give them time to talk about their activities. As for specifically endorsing other activities—no. GLSU doesn't do that. We try to stay within the guidelines of gay and lesbian issues. But most of the core is fairly progressive and does help when others need help. When the Black Student Union is having speakers and they're only allowed so many flyers within the Student Union Building, but the GLSU is not included in that, so we normally put up flyers inside and outside the office. So we lend support.

TV—*Is it reciprocal?*

PA—Right.

TV—*Is there some political motivation that you think people don't see?*

PA—In New Mexico, there aren't so many attacks for being gay, except for just general prejudice and discomfort about being around gays. I think that generally it would be wise for gay men and lesbians to be more open, and GLSU could be helpful in that. Working in the wings at present are people like LaRouche and Falwell and Robertson; people laugh at them right now, but people laughed at Hitler in his early stages. It may be paranoia on my part, I think it's wise to have a little bit of that. Unless people are willing to come out now, they're going to have a hard time if things get worse.

TV—*Is there a potential AIDS backlash here?*

PA—Because of the strong organization of New Mexico AIDS Services and because gay men have changed their lifestyles considerably in New Mexico, even though they've been touched only marginally by the crisis, AIDS is not going to become the big issue in New Mexico, that it's become in other states. Estimates are that only 20% of all gay men in New Mexico are carrying the virus, and that number is not increasing. Although some estimates have been pretty astounding as to the possibility of AIDS in New Mexico, I don't think it's going to grow. If it does, it could become an issue, because it's a poor state in general, so funding for the health care will become an issue.

TV—*Is there a noticeable relationship between coming out, being visibly active and ethnic background?*

PA—I've been told that it is a lot harder for the hispanics to come out because of the strong Catholic background and a real close family network; but I haven't seen an overwhelming predominance of anglos coming through GLSU just because it's "easier" to be gay and anglo.

TV—*And native Americans?*

PA—Indians are a different culture altogether. For the Navajos, being gay was recognized, and was part of the tribe. It served a function for some of the pueblos. It wasn't something that everyone wished their son to grow up to be—the tribal faggot basically—it wasn't something a mother would hope for, but it wasn't as big an issue as anglos and traditional western culture have made it out to be.

TV—*And you, personally?*

PA—When I first came here as a student in the fall of '81, I was very closeted. I was active in the Mormon Church. I stayed on campus for a year and a half, then I took a leave of absence from the Navy ROTC program to serve as a missionary in Spain. When I came back, I immediately checked in with GLSU because my mission was the pits. I loved Spain, but I hated being a missionary. I learned a lot about myself, and a lot about the stupidity of religion in general—the games people play. And I decided I was the biggest games-player of all, trying to be a missionary in this conservative church when I was gay. So I checked into GLSU and within six months, I was excommunicated from the church, I was discharged from the Navy ROTC program, and I was the coordinator for GLSU. Two years ago at this time, I was coming out, being excommunicated, and notifying the Navy that I wanted to stay in the Navy and be a Naval officer, but that I was gay, and that that was something they needed to deal with, and it wasn't my problem, it was theirs.

TV—*And they dealt with it?*

PA—They dealt with it by giving me a discharge "at the convenience of the government under honorable conditions." They gave me that because they knew I had a lawyer, and they would have a fight on their hands if they gave me anything but an honorable one.

TV—*How do you see the future of GLSU?*

PA—I see a continuing need for GLSU, no matter how things go in the future. It's always going to be somewhat traumatic for someone to come out as being gay, and they're going to need the support network of GLSU, the ability to find friends at that time. It was important to me, in that I was able to build that base, so that when I decided to come out to the Navy, to the church and to my parents, I had that network to fall back on.

TV—*So there will be a need for GLSU for a while?*

PA—Forever.

INTERVIEW

Kirsten af Klinteberg, University of Lowell   *March 28, 1987*

Lowell is 30 miles northwest of Boston, and draws heavily from Massachusetts public high schools. Student Kirsten af Klinteberg has been active in gay issues on campus for many years and has served in leadership roles for the Northeast Lesbian and Gay Student Union (NELGSU).

TV—*You've been to how many of these conferences?*

KK—I've gone to all four. It's probably doubled every time, and it's gotten more and more involved in various issues, reaching out to different people. I think you're going to see it get executive staff people. I think the people behind this are going to become very powerful.

TV—*Do you think that's a good thing?*

KK—In some ways yes, in some ways no. I kind of like the way it is right now—it's more down-to-earth, it's rooted into the students. If we get too much involved in centralizing it all, with staff people, it's going to become detached from the students, and I wouldn't like to see that.

TV—*Is this partly because there are some non-students on the board?*

KK—That's not so bad, because they have recently been students. It seems like you have to choose between being in school and being a gay activist, and I don't like to see that either. A lot of people are quitting school for a year, or diminishing their load, just to be an activist.

TV—*Does that say something about the amount of work they feel needs to be done?*

KK—Yeah. There's a huge amount of work to be done, and I think, rather than have a few people do a lot of work and quit school for it, they should stay in school and try to network out to other people to get more people involved in doing the work.

TV—*What about the possibility that this will grow into a national conference, or a national organization?*

KK—I think that's great. The northeast is a pretty progressive area, and the sooner we get down into Florida, to Texas, to the midwest, the better—that can only help. And starting to organize on college campuses is the first step—it's where you get a lot of energy. Gay student activism is going to become a very powerful force in gay politics, very powerful. We have a lot of energy and time and resources through our schools. In Lowell, we service the entire community. We're the only group in the community. We run a gay hotline, and membership is open to non-students; we've produced a radio show for about four years now.

TV—*Do you feel that a lot of political activity on campus ignores gay people?*

KK—On and off campus, that's definitely true.

TV—*Do many openly gay college students get involved in non-gay issues?*

KK—I think so. Being a gay activist myself, I tend to focus everything on that because it's a very important issue to me, and that's all I want to work for. I don't think that's a good idea. I basically quit school to do this, but I've recently come to my senses. Instead of quitting school, I find about five other people and say, "Look guys, I need help." They get more power, too, and I have more time for other things that I'm interested in—I'm on student government, I've become involved with the Women's Center and some other things, too. Also, being an "out" lesbian—being on the radio and other things is about as "out" as you can be—I think I've educated people.

TV—*And you got elected to student government?*

KK—Yes, it's not hard.

TV—*Was sexual orientation an issue?*

KK—No, no. Student elections at my school are not a big deal. But once you're in there, there's a great deal of power. I was able to educate people by being in something other than my gay ghetto. Letting other people see you as a person is very important, because you're never going to educate people otherwise.

TV—*Are you seeing an increase in activity generally in gay student work?*

KK—Definitely. Actually, we've been sort of a parent group to a few organizations. We're starting a youth group. Merrimack College has come to us for help, and also another college. We help other groups to start, but they go up and down like waves; every group goes through their strong times and their weak times.

TV—*Where does the opposition come from?*

KK—At my school, the opposition is very subtle. Other than tearing down posters, it's sending back a purchase order, saying, "How long is this subscription for?" Of course, it's for a year. It's like dragging feet. Also, with articles in the newspaper, they say, "Oh, we misplaced that." Basically what I do now, I use strong-arm tactics. I take my purchase order and go to the committee, and put it down, and I sit there, and wait for them to pass it, then I take it to the next committee, and that's what you have to do. On my newspaper things, I put "carbon copy: Dean King." And if they don't publish it, then he comes down on them.

TV—*How do you assess gay college students' willingness to be more aggressive, in coming out, or in political areas?*

KK—In terms of coming out, I think they're just afraid of the unknown. We had a meeting the other day where people were saying, "Coming out wasn't as bad as I thought it was going to be." They were even more upset than the people they were coming out to. It's just that fear. "Oh, my God, what's going to happen if I kiss my girlfriend in the middle of the quad?! What's going to happen if I'm an out lesbian?! Are people going to come down with machine-guns?" You have to keep yourself safe, but there's also a point where you have to say, "Enough of this bullshit! It's time to go out and do something outside." There are a lot of gays who are out, but they're apolitical. Being out is a political statement in itself, but there's a lot of people who don't want to get involved, they think it's too much trouble, it's not going to work. I don't think people feel threatened enough right now, but if something real threatening happened, they could.

TV—*Where did all this energy came from in the last few years?*

KK—I think it's through organizations like NELGSU, but also I think it's visibility in general. The AIDS epidemic has really given a lot of visibility to gays in general, and kids are seeing gays on television. When I was a kid, I never, never saw anyone gay on television. But just seeing them, they start thinking, and by the time they go to college, they want to do something about it, and they come out. More and more kids are coming out so much younger. Sexuality in general is coming on to kids younger and younger, and part of sexuality is dealing with what kind of sexuality.

TV—*At last year's conference, there was some talk about the issue of male-dominated leadership. What do you think about that? Is it changing?*

KK—I think people need to have their own groups—lesbians need to go to their own group of lesbians and draw strength from that. But I don't think that's the be-all and end-all. I think they have to go outside of that and form an alliance with gay men, and the other way around, to understand each other's issues. Let's face it: nobody has less in common than gay men and lesbians—they're on totally opposite sides except for the fact that they're gay. So, often times, there's a lot of misunderstanding between them. Lesbians are very feminist, and a lot of gay men can be very chauvinist.

TV—*Have you seen any improvement in the last year?*

KK—Actually, yes. I think the gay male leaders are a lot more sensitive as far as trying to increase the number of women involved in NELGSU. I think they've been educated.

TV—*What about students of color?*

KK—I haven't seen that many students of color and that's really disappointing be-cause I know they're out there and I think they feel alienated by the predominant-ly white gay culture—that we're not addressing their issues, and we won't unless more and more people become involved. I think their cultures are not as accepting of the gay lifestyle.

TV—*How do you see the next year or two—will things keep growing?*

KK—Definitely. The momentum is too much right now to even think of slowing down. But we need to do a lot of thinking about how we're going to grow before we start growing some more.

TV—*There were several references at the conference to the idea of Virginia Apuzzo, an outstanding gay activist, conducting a presidential campaign.*

KK—I think people are dying for this, waiting for this, something so tangible to work for, so focused. I'm sending my resumé to Virginia right now.

TV—*What would the implications be?*

KK—It's obvious that she won't win. I don't think that even an unmarried white male could win. But it would poll how many gay people are out there, or how many are willing to vote for a gay candidate. We really think it's an important issue and will really throw it in the Democratic Party's faces and say, "You have to deal with this now. You can't shrug us off any more. We have so many thousands, so many millions of voters." I see big things for this. I hope she runs. She better. If she doesn't, I will.

INTERVIEW

Robin Sweeney, University of Pennsylvania   *March 28, 1987*

Penn is a very urban campus and, with three out of four students coming from outside the state, offers a cosmopolitan diversity. Robin Sweeney is co-chair of the Northeast Lesbian and Gay Student Union.

TV—*What is the gay student group at Penn like?*

RS—At Penn, the LGAP—Lesbians and Gays at Penn—has about fifteen core mem-bers. We get about 45 at meetings, and between 300 and 400 at dances.

TV—*Do revenues from the dances make you self-sufficient?*

RS—The Student Activities Council gives us a budget each year, but a lot of our outside fundraising is through programs and the dances. Running Gay and Lesbian Awareness Week gets very expensive, because we bring in big speakers, and do big stuff, so we have some outside fundraising.

TV—*How would you characterize the situation at Penn?*

RS—There's been an enormous increase in homophobia at Penn in the last two years. AIDS-phobia has really given people a lot of excuse to be out-and-out disgusting with their homophobia. People who before might have been upset but polite, quiet, now react homophobically. LGAP has done more than talk about it. We've been more open. There's been more in-service training for the RAs. I wrote a column last spring about my life as a lesbian woman and about homophobia at Penn. That really let loose the lid off a lot of icky stuff people had been holding on to. Having my face in the paper with a column gave people a chance to personalize it, so it wasn't just "those fags," or "those dykes," or "those perverts" or "those sickos." It was "Robin, that queer." When they painted over the wall we had painted for Lesbian and Gay Awareness Week, they painted "Robin is an ugly bull-dyke" instead of "LGAP sucks." It really gave people a chance to focus their anger, which was something I took into consideration when I decided to write the column.

TV—*Are there other examples of homophobic behavior?*

RS—It's more omission than real commission. People forget to include LGAP in the activities. People forget to say the words lesbians and gays. They forget to include sexual minority issues when they talk about issues of oppression, definitely with the Black Student League and a couple of other racial minority support groups. Our BSL president this year is a Farrakhan follower, who is very sexist and very homophobic. Before, we had a good dialogue going with the BSL chairperson; now, we have a lot of conflicts. He won't announce LGAP things at BSL meetings because it's against his religion. The fraternities are a whole other matter. They range from being just sort of generally stupid to very offensive. One of them, Sigma Chi, is selling boxer shorts with "Do Not Enter" written on the rear. Most other student groups on campus, when you point it out to them, they apologize and try to make an effort but the frats are a totally wasted case, even though there are so many gay men in them.

TV—*Has there been any public demonstration at Penn?*

RS—Last March, when things started to get really hairy with homophobia on campus, we had a March Against Homophobia, where about 50 to 75 of us marched through the campus and had a rally. It was very impressive.

TV—*What prompted this?*

RS—Two weeks earlier two friends of mine who were on a trolley got beaten up, one very badly. It was definitely gay-bashing. If it'd been a woman who'd been assaulted that way, or a black assault on straight white people, the university would have been totally, totally supportive of them. And they didn't, because they don't have ways of coping with gay violence and anti-gay sentiment on campus.

TV—*Did the university react differently after the rally?*

RS—They sent me back to the sexual harassment chapter of the policy book of the sexual harassment committee, saying, "Of course we're inclusive of gay and lesbian issues." To be inclusive is one thing. To institute a study on it, to give it the same weight and importance as ethnic bigotry and racial bigotry and sexual discrimination would be another.

TV—*Do you believe it's better to have more than one organization on a campus that deals with gay issues?*

RS—I think it's wise for there to be a coalition, to be more inclusive—to have a lesbian women's rap group, to have a bisexual\questioning circle, to have a people of color discussion, to have a writers' workshop, to have people willing to do political action and to work under a whole broad title. So when they meet, if and when they want, they can pull together and throw one dance or one rally.

TV—*Is it a problem having both men and women in the same primary group?*

RS—A real problem with including women in a group is, men come out when they're sixteen or seventeen. They're on campus, they've been out for a little while, they're involved, and the group just sort of self-perpetuates being male-dominated. And if women don't come out until they're 20 or 21, they show up, they want to meet lesbian women, and there's only two or three in the room. It's very off-putting for lesbians who are just coming out. It happens at every school.

TV—*What are your principle goals for NELGSU?*

RS—There are three: administrative issues, increasing people of color and women in the organization, and throwing a really well-organized conference.

INTERVIEW

Ethan Felson, Lehigh University   *March 29, 1987*

Ethan Felson, a Lehigh University senior, is working to create a national gay student organization.

TV—*How do you see this national organization shaping up?*

EF—It's going to be a very long process. An organization like this cannot survive like NELGSU does by having a conference once a year—a big bang; it needs constant work. We need to target money from a lot of different sources, build up a small endowment, and get some kind of guarantee from the National Gay Task Force and a couple of other organizations to sponsor something that is one of the most important parts of the gay rights movement right now.

TV—*What's the situation with the National Gay Task Force?*

EF—We're hoping at the very least to use them for an address, for a computer to keep a mailing list on and to serve as a clearinghouse. They already do a lot of organizing for student groups in the student organizing packet they send out.

TV—*What's the intent of a national organization?*

EF—It's manyfold, I think. At a time when there are many setbacks, when a lot of groups are having difficulty and a lot of people are going into the closet, gay and lesbian student groups are getting bigger and bigger, and the number is increasing every day. The emphasis on awareness weeks and non-discrimination clauses is tremendous. If we can facilitate that process, we can serve Jane Doe, the fresh-woman who's in a residence hall and doesn't know anyone, in a number of ways: we can educate her non-gay friends and make them more accepting of her, we can create a social environment for her, we can create outreach for her, we can do AIDS awareness on a national level, and non-violence. If we're going to do it in one area, if the University of Massachusetts is doing an anti-violence project, it's going to make some recommendations and we can distribute that to the deans across the country. Then it serves more than the University of Massachusetts. It serves Jane Doe who's in a college in Cincinnati.

TV—*What other issues can gay organizations be connected to?*

EF—A myriad of issues. When you're talking about a social movement, you must divorce that from what is being talked about here—a political movement. In the political movement, we're part of the progressive movement, and within that there are issues from apartheid to Central America, and much more closely related issues of right to privacy and body sovereignty, such as birth control, contraception and abortion.

TV—*Is there a place for traditional political organizing, like demonstrations or ral-lies, in gay campus work?*

EF—Yes. It's a tremendous opportunity. When a university takes away your office, or refuses to respond to something in the AIDS crisis, that's usually the same univer-sity that does not want the outside world to know there are gay students there. And even if it's a small group, it's just a couple of phone calls to get other groups over there and embarrass the hell out of them. They do not want 20 or 30 or 100 gay students picketing the administration building. They'll react very negatively at first, but turn around a little bit later and do whatever the hell you want, just to shut you up.

The Newest Battleground

In the ongoing war for equal rights, this is the newest battleground. And those doing the fighting are often society's most vulnerable—not only because of the in-tense negative feelings about them generally, but because college students are them-selves at the most vulnerable point in their lives. It's hard not to be struck by the courage of these students. Their adversaries unapologetically condemn them, harass them, assault them, and still they rebound. This reserve of inner strength will push their movement forward.

These activists project continued growth. From nothing about two decades ago, there are now hundreds of campus groups. They inject themselves into politi-cal situations, registering their needs and their presence. In this first step, they will work toward formal acceptance as organizations, with all the benefits that bestows. Legal anti-discrimination clauses will be added to more school constitutions. Gay and Lesbian students will demand, not request, protection from harassment.

Like any group defined in terms set by the white, male, heterosexual "norm," they still sort themselves out into smaller categories. The most favored direction seems to be distinct subgroupings, working together in political and social coalition. Students who discover they are bisexual, or who are still questioning their true sexuality, find themselves facing the toughest time, because even enlightened students are uncomfortable with ambiguous or unresolved sexuality.

The drive to form a national organization of gay, lesbian and bisexual students will further legitimize this movement, and it can succeed if the national gay rights organizations recognize its potential value. With AIDS bringing both greater visibility and greater harassment, support for college-aged gays can only strengthen the larger human rights issues the nationals address.

Students know that gains may be temporary, that a society with the ability to show tolerance retains the ability to withdraw it. They are realistic about the struggle, but see it as something they will fight for the rest of their lives. Like other minorities, they live this cause. It is not an area of concern; it is a daily reality.

Notre Dame: Where the Administration is God

Student activists confront parents, teachers, administrators and the government. At religiously-affiliated schools, God is often not only on that list, but at the top of it.

Notre Dame's wooded acres shelter a school founded in 1842, and a student body 92% Catholic. But a progressive opposition is forming, and those students who sought to start a gay and lesbian organization, who question Notre Dame's refusal to divest its South Africa-related stocks, or who see the school as racist, have a new voice: *Common Sense*. Named to honor Thomas Paine, the independent monthly newspaper published its first edition in spring of 1987, with articles on homophobia at Notre Dame, on anti-nuclear activism and on divestment. The front page featured an essay on "Catholicism in Crisis" and a Statement of Purpose which charged that, "many students, faculty and even alumni have learned through painful firsthand experience that no adequate forum exists at Notre Dame for the dissemination of a wide variety of viewpoints on controversial issues." It adds: "The University is not a seminary."

What struck me first, meeting Notre Dame activists Sophia Taurog and Scott Zachary in the LaFortune Student Union, were the surroundings. An imposing semi-circular wooden reception desk presided over the serene lobby. In a side lounge we sat down just as the chimes rang out five o'clock. Through the doorway arch, I could see students hurrying off to mass. The scene was strikingly genteel and orderly.

Common Sense's first issue met with trouble. Several hundred copies disappeared, discovered later in a dumpster. The paper's independence, Scott explains, frees them to discuss issues the administration would rather not see in print, including racism. One charge against the university is that minorities are underrepresented. Scott adds, "It's also discriminating in its hiring policies. Unfortunately it seems that a lot of people who are racist and who inhabit this campus exert a lot of pressure to keep that kind of rhetoric out of the general language of the university, because it starts to question the image that the university is attempting to foster. And it might threaten some of its revenues." Scott, who writes for the paper, believes it has survived its early stage because it generated a fair amount of local press coverage, and because nearly 50 people have committed themselves to help with production. They hold planning meetings off-campus, in private homes.

On religious grounds, the school has refused to grant official status to a gay students organization, or to permit the school paper to advertise its meetings. The restrictions offended many students, regardless of their sexual orientation. *Common Sense* printed thoughtful challenges to standard theological rhetoric against homosexuality.

Other issues are also percolating, Sophia says, as people take a closer look at the relationship between student and school. "This is a weird campus. It's sort of like the university and the administration are the adults, and we're just kids who don't know any better." Female and male students in the same room past a certain hour, even with the door open, results in students being kicked out. Scott confirms this, "You cannot live in the same domicile with someone of the opposite sex, if you're not married, even off campus. Even if you're a graduate student, 37 years old, you can be ejected. Two law students were ejected—they took the school to court, and lost."

Sophia introduced a chapter of the Overseas Development Network onto the campus, hosting fundraisers "to sponsor grassroots development projects in the third world. We just sent $300 to Chile to build three bread ovens in the shantytown on the outskirts of Santiago." A week of anti-intervention in Central America and anti-contra education is also planned. Sophia believes Notre Dame provides the largest number of CIA recruits of any campus.

Every Friday at 12:15 p.m., students opposed to the school's position on constructive engagement with South Africa hold a vigil on the steps of the administration building. Scott almost apologetically says, "If it's really cold and obnoxious weather, there may be only 15 or 20 people," not realizing that a weekly public action on a campus like this is remarkable. Warm weather triples the crowd; a major event attracts a few hundred. The school paper does not cover these events.

Publishing *Common Sense*, raising money for use in third world countries and steady agitation for divestment do not add up to a mass progressive movement. But in its first edition, Notre Dame's independent monthly set out its initial objective, "On a campus strewn and cluttered with icons, too many of them gathering cobwebs, we pledge to do our best to stir an occasional breeze of fresh thought." It may not be a cyclone, but it is certainly more than an occasional breeze.

CHAPTER ELEVEN

Student Empowerment

A 19-year-old standing on a street corner handing out anti-war leaflets enjoys the constitutional guarantees of free speech. A 19-year-old standing on the campus of a private university handing out the same leaflets does not.

The relationship between student and university, forged through more than a century of confrontations, is basically a legal one. In a sometimes muddled mix of contractual agreements, the *in loco parentis* principle, corporate and consumer law and private property rights, the courts have handed down decisions which grant students some rights, grant universities certain authority and often fail to define the boundaries between the two.

Nineteenth century courts treated the student-university relationship as similar to that of the relationship between any corporation and one of its members, which led to the support of the right of a student to redress grievances, such as suspension without a hearing. In this concept, a student, like a member of a corporation, cannot be dismissed without being informed of the charges and given an opportunity to rebut them.

Early in this century, courts accepted the university's contention that it stood in place of a student's parents *(in loco parentis)*, and bore the responsibility of overseeing student conduct. Under this concept, widely held until the 1960s, all types of school-initated regulations were sanctioned. Administrators decided where students could and could not eat, what they could and could not wear, what time they had to go to bed and with (or more correctly without) whom.

In the sixties, challenges to the *in loco parentis* principle emerged in both public and private schools. Students in state colleges or universities argued their institutions were an extension of the state, and therefore bound by the constitutional restraints on all governmental authority: if you're handing out leaflets, the steps of the student union at a state school are the same as a street corner. But in private schools, the courts say, students enter into a contractual agreement with a private entity. By paying their tuition, they implicitly consent to its regulations: the steps of the student union at a private university are owned by the university. If you disobey the rules you are subject to arrest.

In a landmark decision, *Tinker v. Des Moines Independent Community School District* (1969), the Supreme Court ruled that a public school can abridge a student's right to free speech only if the student's activity causes "material disruption of the educational process," or if a school official can "forecast," not simply fear, that disruption will occur. Schools can, however, impose reasonable time, place or manner restrictions on freedom of expression.[1]

Applying this principle, the University of Texas has designated "free speech areas" where demonstrations or rallies are permitted. At the University of Michigan, the common area known as the "diag" at the heart of the campus, can host demonstrations only at specified times, to prevent nearby classes from being disrupted. And the efforts of students to exert their rights extend to student life issues— dormitory regulations, library hours, social events rules—the daily "bread and butter" issues that affect all students. More and more, students want to have power over these decisions and the organizing that these issues generates often serves as an entry into political activism. Today students use any avenue open to them to gain or retain their rights as students, as consumers and as citizens. Pressure to affect regulations governing use of student fees has spread across the country. Pressure to define, refine or refute student disciplinary procedures viewed as arbitrary, too harsh or too closed often overshadow other objectives as students learn how they will be disciplined.

While some students have long exercised influence—especially those with well-organized student lobbies in their state capitals, or well-run, well-financed state student associations—others have just discovered this subject. Many first realized student pressure could affect investment policies during a divestment campaign. Now, they are asking for or demanding seats on university policy committees and on boards of trustees. They are asking for or demanding representation by legal counsel in disciplinary hearings. And they are learning that winning these requests, or demands, may require a long-term, dedicated campaign.

Politics and Everyday Life

"I'll spend time in jail, but I don't want to get kicked out of school."

Most campus political activists would agree with these sentiments, expressed by University of Texas at Austin student Marc Salomon.[2] And university administrations, mindful of this, are readjusting their disciplinary procedures to capitalize on this most common of student fears.

Seeking power always brings a certain degree of risk. Students seeking power within the university community risk facing all the consequences the university has authority to administer. In trying to gain more control over their lives as students, activists are concerned with both the operation of the university and with regulations imposed on them as citizens of the university community.

Since they realize their fees, contributions and tax dollars run their university, college students have injected themselves into its decision-making process in a number of areas: granting tenure to professors, creating new classes and courses, investments in the school's portfolio, admissions policies, grants and loans procedures, labor conditions of campus employees, government and corporate research contracts executed on campus, and the selection of the businesses patronized by the university in its purchase of goods and services. In the realm of university regulations governing student conduct, areas to challenge include restrictions on enrolling in certain courses, mandatory drug testing, freedom to express opinions, access to library and research facilities, dormitory and dining hall regulations, and rules on social activity.

To mount their challenges—and there are more every year—students must choose the mechanisms available to them, often reflecting the particular grievance. For instance, students who erect a shanty to protest investments in South Africa may find themselves embroiled in a freedom of speech controversy instead of one dealing with South African investments and then move to sue the university for denying First Amendment rights. Or a chapter of UCAM may stage an action to protest acceptance of government contracts to do weapons research on campus, only to find the discussion shifting to one involving the university's right to accept any contractual agreements it chooses. Moves to start a gay and lesbian students association, or to protest mandatory drug testing for athletes, would likely evolve into issues of freedom of association and the right to privacy. In each of these instances, the issue would surface through the actions of a student group dedicated to a particular cause or activity.

On many campuses, student governments—working with, or sometimes in opposition to, the administration—increasingly see themselves as advocates for full rights for students in areas such as free speech, policy decisions, disciplinary proceedings and a role in the conduct of the university's business. They usually seek a voice for students in the overall decision-making process, rather than taking a confrontational stance.

Chris Cabaldan, vice-president of Associated Students, University of California at Berkeley, believes it is the place of student government to work for change, but that it must be done carefully. "There were times during the South African protests that the student senate went down to the University Administration Building and sat down as a senate to try and make a statement on behalf of the student government. But that's been the only time. People in the student government tend to participate in student actions, and may be involved in organizing them as members of the student groups, but I don't think any of us are real comfortable about having student government organizing them. As a student, I wouldn't be very interested in a protest that was being organized by the establishment, the student government."[3]

In some states, such as New York and Wisconsin, students or student governments have allied themselves into associations to increase the flow of information on subjects of mutual interest and to increase the potential political impact whenever needed. And a few universities and a few state systems, bowing to student activism of the sixties and eighties have created student trustee or student regent positions.

Wherever an action originates, if it violates university rules, civil or criminal law, proceedings can be brought against the students involved. Generally, charges are for trespass or disorderly conduct. Most students would rather avoid expulsion than jail, but more and more universities are moving to keep these matters on campus. The advantages are considerable: much less publicity, much more control—and a much greater threat to the students, both those involved, and those looking on, perhaps planning to become involved in future. Bringing in the courts, and certainly bringing in the police, always tend to radicalize students who were mere participants or observers previously.

On campus, the disciplinary process may change from school to school, year to year. In court, things are a little more stable, but not much. Student rights cases and rulings are binding only in the jurisdictions involved—state decisions in the particular states, federal district court cases only in that district, etc.—only Supreme Court decisions apply nationally. Attorney Jack Lester, a ten-year-veteran of students' rights cases, cautions, "Each situation is fact-based. So you can't say that there is one formula to follow. Some courts are more restrictive than others, some more liberal. It's hard to say uniformly what the student's rights are. It depends on the facts of the case."[4]

A student rarely has the right to an attorney when an infraction is being dealt with on campus, though some schools permit an attorney to be present as an advisor. Use of student fees to hire an attorney to defend students in legal actions against the university has been challenged or forbidden by several administrations.

Most cases fall into two broad categories: those involving some element of free speech and First Amendment rights, and those involving discipline and due process guarantees. For students, the right to express an opinion or a political position may indeed emerge as something very conditional. Students exercise this right through demonstrations, symbolic expression and the student press; and by distributing literature, inviting speakers on campus and working to gain official recognition of student organizations.

As in all areas relating to students' rights, distinctions between public and private institutions weigh heavily. In public schools, the Tinker case mentioned above upheld students' rights to free expression, but interpretation of "expression" varies from case to case.[5] In a 1980 case, the US Court of Appeals sided with Jackson State University (Miss.) students disciplined for violating rules that required three days' notice of a demonstration, and a limit to activities of a "wholesome nature," finding the restrictions arbitrary.[6] In 1976, a court ruled University of Oregon students were not protected by First Amendment claims for erecting a tent on campus,[7] but a decade later, shanties on the University of Utah campus were found to be a legitimate expression of free speech.[8]

In private institutions, Jack Lester points out, "The courts have ruled that public, common areas are open to free expression. Even if they are private universities, by virtue of the fact that these are common, public areas, such as the common green or square, the university cannot restrict time, place or manner in an arbitrary, capricious manner. They can restrict it insofar as demonstrations may disrupt the overall educational purpose of the institution, such as disrupting classes, and the university has the burden of proof in showing that the demonstration is somehow disruptive."[9]

For example, a Princeton University student found guilty of trespassing, in 1980, for engaging in political activity on the campus had his conviction overturned in the New Jersey Supreme Court applying the doctrine that the campus was a public place and a legal site for public debate.[10] As Lester points out, however, the inside of a classroom does not enjoy the same protection that public areas do. When two MIT students entered ongoing classes in 1978 and refused to leave, they were found guilty of trespassing by the Supreme Judicial Court of Massachusetts.[11]

In one of the most celebrated recent cases, in the spring of 1986, Yosef Abramowitz sued Boston University for entering his room repeatedly to take down banners stating "Divest Now" which he continued to hang from his window. He was expelled from BU, took his case to court, and argued that the university was acting arbitrarily since it never bothered to enforce a rule against banners when they were exhorting athletic teams to win. Abramowitz won not only the right to hang the banners but the right to return to classes—the court forbade the university to institute disciplinary proceedings against him.[12]

Student newspapers' rights as legitimate vehicles of expression for student opinion separate from the university were established in several cases in the early seventies. From time to time, a zealous administrator will try to interfere with the editing of a campus publication; students, when they resist, rarely have difficulty proving their rights. A 1987 case at San Diego State University overturned the suspension of the college newspaper editor who had challenged a school regulation banning political endorsements in the paper.[13] Students have also generally kept the right to book the speakers they want on campus.

The ability to grant or withhold official status to an organization still gives administrations the chance to limit certain activities on campus. Ten or fifteen years ago, this was used to counter the "threat" of politically radical groups: students at Central Connecticut State College in 1972 had to appeal up to the Supreme Court to win the right to establish a chapter of the Students for a Democratic Society.[14] Recently, cases are more likely to center around the creation of a gay and lesbian students' organization. According to Mark Schulte, the president of Gay People at Georgetown University, when gay students were denied the right to organize a group, they appealed to the mayor of Washington, DC, pointing out that District of Columbia law forbids discrimination based on sexual orientation. The mayor agreed, froze financing for the student union building under construction, and halted work with the building partially completed. Students subsequently took their case to court and won a ruling ensuring they would be treated like other student groups—able to apply for funds and use school facilities. Following this victory, Georgetown students created two gay organizations, one for undergraduates, another for law students.[15]

Prevailing public school disciplinary law stems from a 1961 civil rights sit-in case. Alabama State College students were dismissed without a hearing for participating in a lunch counter action. The students sued, citing the Fourteenth Amendment, and won, setting a precedent that student disciplinary hearings must include notice of charges and the grounds which would result in expulsion, access to a hearing that is more than an informal interview, and an opportunity to present testimony and the right to respond fully to charges.[16] A 1967 Central Missouri State case further protected students.[17]

For private school students, the picture is still hazy, though courts have been willing to find in favor of students when a school violates its own rules. In 1980, a Wagner College student was expelled without a hearing and got the expulsion overturned in court on such grounds.[18]

Marc Salomon's case exemplifies how one type of action can lead to another. In the spring of 1986, UT students erupted in a series of protests to push the university to divest. School regulations permitted demonstrations in a designated "free speech" area only between noon and 1 p.m., and only with approval from the student activities office; groups that violated these rules could lose official status and the individuals involved could be suspended. On April 11, when students extended their protest past 1 p.m., police were called; 42 were arrested. Two days later a rally protesting the bombing of Libya resulted in 4 arrests. On April 18, another rally on divestment and free speech ended with 182 arrests. On April 25, more than one thousand people showed up to protest the free speech regulations—and the police did not attempt any arrests.[19] Brian East, head of the National Lawyers Guild-sponsored Legal Defense Team, proclaimed, "I think it's a sort of victory for the students. It has established their right to assemble."[20] In Marc Salomon's view, "We've won the battle, but the war isn't won yet—apartheid being the war, free speech was the battle."[21]

The school subsequently established a 24-hour free speech zone, with limits only on amplification. Still, students brought a class action suit against the university, claiming false arrest, and sought an injunction prohibiting similar arrests in the future, a declaratory judgment that under the Texas constitution the arrests were illegal, and monetary damages. When students returned to the business of agitating for divestment, they changed their tactics.

According to Elena Manitzas, "After eight or nine years of people and organizations working for divestment, UT was not doing anything. The Steve Biko Committee had met with the Board of Regents quite a few times, showing them alternative portfolios and presenting petitions. Every time, they were received by the Board as if they already had made their minds up. We tried every avenue. The faculty senate, the student body and the union had all voted for divestment, and the regents were still not budging. So a bunch of individuals who had worked for divestment for a long time decided that we had a legitimate right to create a scenario where we could sit down and really talk to these people."[22]

The scenario played out this way: on October 20, 1986, students occupied the president's office, barricaded themselves in, and presented a list of demands for the regents. Within half an hour, police stormed the office. At least three students charged excessive, brutal force had been used against them. Thirteen were jailed. In the following weeks, students refused to participate in separate university hearings, prior to the court case, fearing they would prejudice their trial; the court accepted their arguments and issued a restraining order blocking the university hearings. Yet unresolved, the developments illustrate the role of creating and exercising definitive legal rights in political actions and how the absence of such rights can prevent the substance of a protest from being heard.

Students are reacting to the realization that their rights may be either tenuous or non-existent by mobilizing legal assistance, reshaping campus regulations in all instances where they have the ability, and taking these considerations into account whenever actions of any kind are planned.

SCENE

Meeting the Board

Kevin Harris uses red and black magic markers to sketch a quick floor plan of the room where the Colorado Board of Regents will be meeting. Christine Smock checks to see if her camera is loaded. José Morales checks the supply of blank poster paper. One by one, Boulder students drift in for the early morning strategy session, preparing to assert the view that they deserve a voice in shaping university decisions.

Some are suspicious that the regents have chosen to meet during final exams. Less than six weeks earlier, these students openly challenged the regents to forbid CIA recruiting on campus, an action that garnered national television news coverage as hundreds surged from behind a police-installed fence to rush the building where the regents were in session. The previous May, 478 were arrested in a similar protest that put the school on notice that students were insisting on having their position heard.

In case police confiscate posters and placards, everyone makes a "collapsible sign," a folded sheet tucked into jeans and shirts. Kevin holds up the floor plan, indicating where the "twelve white men" will be seated. At 10:15 a.m., the 16 students, members of CISPES, student government and other groups, get ready to walk the two blocks across campus. As they gather coats and scarves, a woman who works in the student union building strides in, offers everyone cookies and instructs the students to "give 'em hell."

In the hallway outside the meeting room, a large breakfast buffet table has been arranged: formal silver urns of coffee and tea, styrofoam cups, silver trays of pastry, muffins and rolls. Slowly, the students file in, climb the risers until they reach the back of the room, raise their signs and turn to face the regents. No one speaks. The regents pause, interrupting their commendation of the Ensemble Band, and take note. The elaborate system hooked up to tape the proceedings will have no record of the reason for this momentary silence. The 27 other men and women in the room, most in blue or gray suits, whisper to each other. The regents exchange glances and continue.

Perched on chair backs or on table tops the students remain still—silent, but not somber. Regents look up expectantly, studying the signs aimed directly at them. "No Way CIA." "Stop CIA Terrorism." A warning, "See You In The Spring." Another admonishes, "Remember Nuremberg."

After half an hour, Kevin leans his sign against the side wall, consults in whispers with each protestor, slips into the hallway and, after a few minutes, returns smiling with one of the formal silver trays, delivering coffee, tea and pastry.

Forty minutes pass before the police chief arrives. On a signal, the students descend, and leave the room and the building in an orderly manner. José pauses to hear the regents tell someone in the audience, "We don't want to exclude anybody." They schedule their next session on Martin Luther King Day.

INTERVIEW

Jane McAlevey, Boulder   *December 19, 1986*

Organizing students into a voting, lobbying constituency has been a major objective of Jane McAlevey who has served as president of the New York Student Association of State Universities (SASU), on the board of the USSA, and as an advisor to students in Boulder.

TV—*Is it true that students are now moving into electoral politics actively?*

JM—In Albany, a number of students have been taking the Democratic ward seats, the liberal wards within the county. Taking over the ward seats is important because that decides who's going to be running in the primaries. Basically it's a fight for control of the Democratic Party. Three students won really key races in ward seats this year, and those campaigns began last year. In Buffalo, the student government vice-president last year ran for town council, but he was defeated. And I've heard about campaigns in Madison, and in northern California.

TV—*Is there a town backlash?*

JM—In Albany, there's no backlash at all, expect for the Democratic leadership, and they, of course, try to make it a town-gown issue. But Albany is fairly young liberals, at least in registration.

TV—*What do you think is the future of this kind of effort?*

JM—I think it's pretty good, because students have more skills to organize now than they did in the past. And they're becoming more aware of their electoral power. In New York, it's very difficult because, outside of New York City, residence requirements mean students don't have the right to vote in their college communities, so it's virtually impossible for us to take communities. We've been litigating in and out of courts since 1978 to get students the right to vote. We have tons of documentation from all the court proceedings and the litigation: it was very specifically done because New York has the largest student population in the country. *If* we had the right to vote, we could control half the legislature.

TV—*If they were at home, wouldn't they be voting?*

JM—Right, and they would be able to form blocs. In Buffalo, we won the right to vote when I was student body president, after we sued the county. That was the first year students got the local vote. There are 55,000 students just from the state university in Buffalo—55,000 is an incredible number. So the first thing we did was form a coalition with the community college, Buffalo City College, and the University of Buffalo. Right then, there was this huge statewide voter registration coalition organized by mainly labor unions and civil rights groups, the New York Voter Registration Network. Because we got the right to vote and made ourselves very visible, they had a student co-chair of the citywide network. I think that once students in New York get the right to vote, there'll be an incredible amount of students getting involved in electoral action.

TV—*In other states, is it a question of them not exercising the right they have?*

JM—They're not being organized. If you look at the places where it's happening, most of them have had state student associations for a while. New York and Wisconsin are the two oldest student associations, and definitely the most sophisticated in terms of staff people and programs. The California State Student Association is probably third. Those are the major places where students have been organizing electorally. It goes hand in hand with having a state student organization that's actually doing something on their behalf, and has continuity and full-time organizers for developing strategies and plans. I never really appreciated SASU until I came to Colorado and realized what they don't have. They wanted to launch a CIA campaign and focus it on the board of regents, but it couldn't be done because there's no state organization for students. That's just one example. They wanted to launch a statewide tuition campaign and they don't even know how to contact the other schools. I'm a real believer at this point in state student associations. Students here in Boulder, the most radical part of Colorado, don't think they're capable of, or even should challenge the power of the board of regents or the university. They still think they should be sort of polite, even the leftists at Boulder still think that—people involved in the CIA work have been negotiating with the police for two years, holding these very preplanned arrests, where if you walk over a line, you get arrested. And that shit's just not happening in New York at all, and hasn't been for a long time. The Colorado board of regents every single month makes a major violation of student rights and the student government still thinks they have to negotiate with the regents. They get all decked out and dressed up and go to meetings and have coffee and tea. Now I'm not saying you have to be really rude—I dressed up to go to board of regents meetings, too. But that didn't mean that I didn't walk in there with 300 students behind me and take over a meeting if they were doing something which really violated students' rights. So it doesn't mean that you're irresponsible and an idiot; it means you're responsible, and you really know your shit, but if the board is doing something bad, then it's your responsibility to do something about it. Tuition in Colorado has been increasing every year since 1978, but they never waged a formal campaign against tuition. New York had a huge increase one year—Cuomo's first year—and when he proposed another one the next year students went absolutely berserk, the average state university student in New York went berserk—and we stopped the increase. Every year since, Cuomo proposes it and every year we stop it, and that's part of becoming organized. Here, when I started working with them on this tuition increase, I'd say, "What's been the percentage increase since, say, 1970?" They wouldn't know. And I'd say "What's been the percentage increase since 1980, and what was the tuition in 1980?" They don't know. It's going to take them a year to do the research on tuition in Colorado before they can wage a campaign. That's the problem with not having an organization where you can just call up and get the information over the phone.

TV—Are they accepting that idea, rather than just having a demonstration?

JM—It's pretty split. Some people have been convinced of the need for a state organization, the need to be able to get historical data about student actions or tuition or room rent or dormitory policies or whatever. They're slowly making that decision. That's a result of them holding the USSA conference here in 1986 when Boulder was kind of bombarded by USSA. Students here had this attitude that they had this huge budget and they control all their money, that they had more control over student fees than any other student government in the country. In reality, they have no control over their money at all. It was very delicate for me, being new in this area, to figure out a diplomatic way to tell these people that they were light years behind, but it worked. They are starting to devote their energies to building a statewide organization. There was some real, real resistance to it. They view groups like SASU in New York as incredibly radical, left-wing—"how can you ever tell off the board of regents?" They can't accept groups which do that.

TV—Do you think women now, as compared to the sixties, are more involved as decision-makers in campaigns for student empowerment?

JM—I don't think it's changed greatly. In New York in my year, two out of 64 campuses had female student body presidents; the rest were all white men. Our state organization, in its 16 years, has had only three female presidents, me being one.

TV—Why do you think that's the case?

JM—Student government in most areas is like any government: it's kind of bureaucratic and it deals with money. There's been such a stronghold from the '50s and '60s, when student governments were created by people who are traditionally involved in government—which is white men—that it's a very unattractive thing for a woman or a third world person to get involved with. I had to deal with some really serious shit the years I was student council president, not just from the administration—you know, the first floor in the administration building was all white men who treated me like a complete moron until we took over the building. Rochester's student government was predominantly white male at the beginning, and at the end we had successfully run a mini-Rainbow ticket. But student government is an unappealing thing, I think, for most students on campus. If a woman's an activist she'll most likely get involved with a women's group on campus, and the same for third world people—especially third world people, because it's still true that third world people are in an incredible minority, and when they have a chance to get involved, they're going to get involved with a group related to that.

TV—*Do you think it's getting better or worse?*

JM—I guess it has to be getting better, because it was almost non-existent in the sixties. I think it might have changed the most in the late seventies. I did a lot of writing about women in student government and in state student associations, and it seemed that all the student governments in the country and all the state organizations were having their first women leaders in the late seventies. It hasn't gotten much better since then. In Buffalo, the university is decades old and I was the first female student body president ever. I don't think that's so atypical.

TV—*What issues besides tuition can student government affect?*

JM—I don't know if I want to say just student government. SASU isn't a collection of student governments—most people think it is. It's a state organization which operates like a union. The whole campus votes whether or not to be a member. If we were just student governments, we'd be a lot less activist-oriented. It's rank-and-file students who want to get involved in activist things as part of the SASU. I think that's the flaw with the Wisconsin state organization, that it's a collective of student governments, and student legislative bodies vote whether to join for a whole campus, and that's a radical difference. The main thing is, don't let it be a collective of student governments. It's got to be the whole campus voting yes or no in a referendum, because that gets the average student involved, so they know what their state organization is. Our dues come directly from each student. Each student in New York pays $2 a semester to SASU directly. It's the best structure.

TV—*And students elect an at-large representative?*

JM—Right.

TV—*Can you explain to students that working for control over their funds and in making decisions is worth the work? What do they need to understand?*

JM—The commitment to the long haul, and that you can't win something overnight. I think that's a real myth. So many people come in and they think they can win overnight and the leadership is telling them, "Yeah! We can win! Just one more protest!" You have to win little teeny victories to build up to the big ones. That's the fear of people my age—we don't want to be labelled the way people in the sixties were and it's almost the other direction. We try to convince people that we can protest, and just not smash windows, that we can do CD non-violently and combine it with using democratic and diplomatic channels first. The point is always legitimizing our protests, but using our democratic channels first. In New York during my first year, we had over 6,000 students march on the capital, which totally freaked Cuomo out. He was just astounded. We were only able to do that after we had spent four months doing letter-writing campaigns, and petitioning, and phone calls. With the whole trial and arrest that happened with us, we had five years of being very patient and diplomatic to justify it to the mainstream. When I'd go to a campus, they'd say, "Holy shit, you just got arrested. You're crazy. You're a radical. You don't respect the board of trustees." We'd say, "But wait. For five years, we've been really patiently, really nicely lobbying the board of trustees." I think if you legitimize yourself, almost any average mainstream student will support your cause. What happened in the sixties is that they often didn't have as much legitimacy, or they may have had it, but they didn't show it.

INTERVIEW

Jackie Ross, University of California   *February 26, 1987*

Jacqueline Ross, a student at the University of California at Davis, holds the student regent position on the California board of regents.

TV—*How does the student regent fit into the regents' governing structure?*

JR—The student regent has a really unusual position because the rest of the regents are not people who are associated with the school. They are gubernatorial appointments. There are seven *ex officio* members on the board, and 22 people appointed to 12-year terms by the governor—and I believe only one of those is an educator. The rest are people involved in business, politics and so forth. The UC president is also a regent, and there are representatives from the academic senate. But the student is the only person who is really immersed in the UC system every single day. The rest of the regents expect the student to express his or her own views, and not those of students. They seem a bit perturbed when the student expressed what students generally are concerned with, but it's hard not to do that. The student regent is expected, by the students at least, to make contacts with students on each of the nine campuses and find out their main concerns. The regents certainly deal with a lot of things and are really a board of trustees as far as the business goes, but I don't think there is a lot of knowledge about the educational system. They rely a lot on the president and people from the academic senate to provide information about what is happening educationally, on educational policy anywhere from faculty appointments to student issues. The student regent needs to pay a lot of attention to the educational area, but also external issues such as the investment policy. There is always surprise when students are interested in something outside the realm of the campus, such as divestment or weapons research. So the regents may expect one thing from the student regent, students expect quite another.

TV—*How can this balance be maintained?*

JR—It can be pretty dangerous for the student regent to get into an issue without support. It's usually brought to the regents' attention by student protest. Then it comes up as an agenda item, and the student regent can present anything such as petitions or statements from the students. Yet, the student still has to maintain an individuality to receive any validation from the rest of the regents. That creates a pretty interesting situation. Often there's a question of whether the student body will support the student regent at all, or whether they just regard the student regent as a mere token. The student regent has to clarify her position really quickly with all the student groups, or be in limbo and be completely ineffective. As to whether the person in this position feels effective or not, that really depends on how she starts. I'm the last to serve in a trial period. This coming spring, we will be voting on continuing the position of student regent, and if that regent should keep all its privileges, such as the right to vote. With the right to vote, it's not just an advisory position. My view is that the regents are a lot safer having a student regent on there, because whenever a student issue comes up, or students get riled about something, it's very easy to target the student regent and expect her to carry the ball through the meeting; without a student regent they would have to deal with the students as a whole more directly. But the feeling is that the regents may decide they don't want a student regent any more. If they do, they are going to be experiencing a lot more conflict than they currently do.

TV—*What's the student reaction generally to the student regent position?*

JR—It wavers. Some student regents have been extremely vocal in expressing student opinion; that's not highly regarded by the board, but it is highly regarded by the students. The thing is, there's not a lot of student input into the selection of the student regent. The UC Student Association (UCSA) has a rigorous interview process. It was the hardest interview of all, and rightly so: 16 student legislators essentially question one applicant. You certainly get a good feel for what they are concerned about. But that's the only time students can question the candidates for student regent. The final decision comes down to a committee of the regents. Because, the students as a whole don't have a lot of responsibility for choosing this person, the feeling is like a stepmother or stepfather coming into the family: the kids don't have a lot of say in it. But somebody wants them in there.

TV—*Where do the candidates come from?*

JR—This year there were 106 applicants; they divide the state into a northern and a southern region. A committee of students, including some who have been involved in this process before, pick nine finalists, four from one region and five from the other. Then the UCSA board—one undergraduate and one graduate representative from each of the nine campuses—interviews these nine semifinalists and chooses three finalists. The regent selection committee selects one—a UCSA representative sits in, to make sure that regents don't ask anything unconstitutional, and also to see if the candidates' stories have changed since the student interview. This year, it was very interesting; all three finalists were very, very similar on some of the harder issues. One student was a Nigerian, one was a chicano, and I'm native American. We've all been politically active on our campuses and in our communities. We're all interested in some of the same issues, such as including ethnic studies as a mandatory requirement, making sure that divestment goes through. On things like that, we were all very similar, but we were very different people: the other two were grad students, and I was the undergraduate; I might have more of an in on women's issues. But I think UCSA would have been happy with any one of us.

TV—What role do you see for student groups, especially activist-oriented groups, working with you? Do you believe that student protest, or very active organizing on campuses should be part of your role?

JR—Definitely. I feel student protests are real healthy. That's where I come from anyway—a grassroots political and cultural orientation. It's very comfortable for me. It's very uncomfortable, though, for the rest of the regents. I'm the only one there applauding that. A lot of times, that's the only way to get the media involved. The regents don't tend to publicize their actions so when the students get the media to focus on the regents, that's good; it holds them accountable. And the UC system enjoys a kind of autonomy from legislative action in California so it's good to let the taxpayers know what is done at UC. A lot of times, that's done chiefly through student protest attracting that attention. As for working with student groups, my first efforts are to call or write students. I need to find out who these people will be, since a lot of leadership changes hands at the end of the year. I'll be telling those people my office hours—this is where you can reach me, this is who has an agenda packet. Each UCSA person gets an agenda packet so they can see if any of their issues are coming up. You know, please come up here, or I'll fly down there and we can talk about this. I see myself as virtually useless if I have no support. I can't thrust myself on regents without that kind of support, and it will be hard for students to understand if an ethnic studies requirement goes through without their input. It's important for me to let them know what's going on.

TV—What kind of financial support do you get?

JR—My travel is paid for. I also had the option of getting six hours of secretarial service or a typewriter for the year. I got the typewriter. It's easier for me to work like that. The regents position isn't paid, but some of my educational fees are waived. It's really hard for the student regent to hit all nine campuses consistently. If they make it to each campus two or three times each year, that's considered an accomplishment. You have to be a full-time student throughout this process. Carrying those loads and doing whatever work you need to do to support yourself, and then being a student regent on top of that requires a lot of juggling and a lot of balance.

TV—How old is this position?

JR—I'm the thirteenth one. There was a lot of controversy at the beginning. They definitely felt threatened at having someone from a completely new element coming in. And a lot of those who dissented are still on the board, and a lot of the proponents of the position are off the board, which makes it interesting for this coming spring when we vote again. The faculty representatives from the academic senate do not have a vote, but the student does and that's a bone of contention for a lot of people. It's also interesting to see the difference in attitude of the student regent for each year. They come in with completely different issues from one year to the next. The most recent one, the youngest ever, was a sophomore, and I think he was a bit overwhelmed by the whole thing. But his main issue was student participation in university governance, being involved in policy decisions at every level. The year before was Jan Eberly, an Ag-Econ major. The regents loved her because she came up with an investment plan that was much better than they had originally. She kind of wowed them, and they actually adopted her policies. The year before, there was a real rowdy who brought up university divestment, and how many investments each regent had personally in South Africa. So each year, it changes. I'll be the affirmative action person, no doubt. The uppity woman, as far as they're concerned.

TV—*What happened to your predecessor's work?*

JR—His name is David Hoffman. He actually took an incredible amount of time to do research, to go way, way back through a lot of minutes from years ago to see if there was ever a point when students were involved and to see when that stopped. You know, there has never been an archive for student regents until David tried to put some stuff together for me. There's no training for a student regent. You sit and watch what's going on for a three-month period, but there's no formal instruction or any kind of training from one student regent to the next.

TV—*Do you think this is a strategy—to be able to point to the student regent position but to make it ineffective? Having to be a full-time student automatically cuts the time you have to see your constituents.*

JR—Well, sure. If the student wasn't full-time, he or she would be a regular regent, God forbid. Anyway, it's only for a year, out of the twelve the regular regents get. So it's a lot less powerful position from the beginning. And you can't call someone a student regent unless they are a student to begin with, right? If the person was not going to school, a person of my age would not have the connections and the prestige to be appointed by the governor. So I don't know if it's a conscious strategy—I think that's just the way it worked out—but if it was a strategy, it was a darned good one. It definitely hampers the student representative, but not enough to keep me from thinking it's worthwhile.

TV—*How often do they meet?*

JR—Nine times a year. One of the big challenges for me is summer contacts. A lot goes on during the summer. Again, I don't know if it's a conscious strategy or not, but it can be really detrimental to students if they don't know what went on over the summer. For instance, you come back from the summer and teachers have been denied tenure, and students aren't there to rally for them. It's a really tricky time.

TV—*How will you measure your success?*

JR—I'll measure it a lot by how much the opinions or at least the insights of the regents as a whole have changed. I'll measure it in terms of attitude difference. I'll certainly measure it in terms of how UCSA thinks I'm doing. I'll see how my relationships with the chancellors are by the end of the year. There are a lot of different components to pay attention to. And also, see how angry people are at me. Anger is a pretty effective measurement, one way or the other. If I go on to campus at the end of the year, and people do not know the student regent, and do not know some of the issues, then I have really failed. If they do know what the issues are, and they have been kept aware one way or the other, then I'll feel pretty good about it.

Organizing for Empowerment

The growth of student empowerment directly affects literally every single student on every campus. But its champions are scattered throughout the movement.

The primary center of organizing remains the USSA. With its line to student government representatives, it is able to make the connections between greater control over regulations and greater access to other changes in university business affecting expenditure of funds, channeling of resources, selection and retention of students, influence on the society and general conditions for everyone at the university. Student government is often the most logical and most legitimate means of giving students representation in university affairs. And training student government members in the politics of being a student continues to be a major USSA objective.

At Fairfield College in Connecticut, for instance, student legislator John Chiara helped organize a letter-writing campaign to members of Congress when student loan funds were threatened, a strategy mapped out after attending a USSA-sponsored training session. "The object of the letter-writing campaign was to have students whose opinions are not normally respected, because so few vote, to be heard. To let their Congressional representatives know they're going to vote, and this is how they feel." The other nationals treat student empowerment in one of two ways: either they deal with it in relation to a particular issue or cause, or else they consider it as an important subject, but treat it tangentially, almost like discussing another type of strategy.

The other nationals treat student empowerment in one of two ways: in relation to a particular cause (DSA, CISPES) or as an important subject to be considered as a tangent or as a strategy (ACOA, PSN).

The National Lawyers Guild, with chapters around the country, is an excellent resource for students seeking various kinds of legal information, including how to bring suits against their univeristies.

Some student groups whose publications do not represent the university, notably the *New Indicator* collective at the University of California at San Diego and the Union of Concerned Students at the University of Vermont, produce handbooks—"Disorientation Manuals"—which explain the real workings of the school and student government to incoming students, a process which also unearths much more information, relationships, facts and material for those students doing the organizing.

Progressive groups will continue working to place their candidates in influential positions within student government, on policy committees and in student regent posts. Perhaps someday a national organization will undertake the broad responsibility of gathering, sorting, coding, categorizing, analyzing and disseminating the mounting information about student empowerment issues. However successful these institutional and organizational efforts are, students' struggles for more power over the everyday questions of campus life will always remain vital. Indeed, of all the political campaigns happening on campuses today, this one is often the most spontaneous, the most inclusive of the whole student population, and the one that speaks most directly to the immediate needs of students. Because issues of student empowerment can provide such a spark of political activity on campus, it is an important goal for activists to try to link the struggle for student empowerment with the other, broader political campaigns for peace, divestment and anti-intervention, and against racism, sexism and homophobia.

CHAPTER TWELVE

The Role of the Media

In America, an event hasn't actually "happened" unless it has been covered in the press, and trivial events suddenly gain status when the media deems them newsworthy.

In many ways, student political activism is subject to this gospel. Student activists, like any activists, hope to use the press to reach others in their group or constituency, to reach those who can change the conditions they oppose and to reach the general population. What gets covered, how and how frequently is the end product of a complicated series of decisions that are roughly the same for print and broadcast media. Basically, reporters carry out an assignment given to them by someone else; that work is then shaped by an editor; another person decides whether and where it gets used. How long it runs, in inches or minutes, can depend on what else has happened that newsday.

One of the greatest myths of the last two decades has been that television news determines what people think and talk about in this country. The example most often used is the decline in public approval for US involvement in the Vietnam War. In fact, research by Dr. David Weaver, professor of journalism at Indiana University revealed that newspapers, not television coverage, led the process of framing public issues.[1] Since television coverage is confined to a fixed number of available minutes while a newspaper can always print more pages, television more often reflects rather than directs what has been covered in the print medium. When CBS News anchorman Walter Cronkite proclaimed, "We are mired in a stalemate" during a news special in 1968, he was reflecting a growing dissatisfaction with the war.[2] In comparing the curve of opinion between the Vietnam War and the Korean

War (barely covered by television), Professor John Mueller of the University of Rochester discovered a remarkable similarity: as American deaths increased, support decreased.[3] Thus, television *per se* was not the pivotal factor in the growth of opposition to the Vietnam War, but the growing realization, measured in lost lives, that the policy was a failure. It was the message, not the messenger.

Although television does not control people's dissent from war, print and television coverage remains a barometer for the effectiveness of an action or movement. For student activists, this means college print and broadcast outlets as well as mainstream media.

Major daily metropolitan newspapers exert tremendous influence in their regions. The *New York Times*, however, holds a unique position as the "newspaper of record" for the country. Every day, the Associated Press photographs the front page of the Times, and sends it over the wire to newspapers and newsrooms around the world. They look to it for some idea of what is the news of the day, and the relative importance of each story.

On Monday, April 27, 1987, more than 550 people, a large portion of them students, blockaded the entrances to the CIA headquarters in Langley, Virginia. The action was unprecedented. The *New York Times* chose to downplay the event, and to trivialize its participants by running a piece on page A-18, 16 inches long, with one photo.[4] In contrast, the *Washington Post* placed the story top center of page one, accompanied by a three-column photo;[5] it continued on page A-6 with three more photos, a map of the CIA headquarters area, and a sidebar piece on the general mood of the demonstration filling most of the page. Both papers ran down the basics in their opening paragraphs, such as the number of people arrested, and the action's connection to the April 25 Mobilization march.

The *Times'* treatment of the story illustrates the character of much of its coverage of student political activism. Quoting Daniel Ellsberg saying it "reminds me of the '70s" cast the event as a throwback, an echo from a previous era—a viewpoint reinforced by quoting Reverend Joseph Nagle, "It's kind of a '60s crowd."[6]

The *Post* also made the comparison, but with a difference: "The presence of Vietnam-era activists, as well as a profusion of tie-dyed garments, love beads and long hair, led to inevitable recollections of the protests of the 1960s and early 1970s. That comparison was resented by many of yesterday's protestors, who were trying to stake out an identity of their own."

The *Times* piece had the flavor of a society report. "Many were disappointed that Amy Carter…and Abbie Hoffman were not among them." In the absence of "Miss Carter, Mr. Ellsberg was clearly the star protestor of the event."

A paternalistic attitude generally colors reporting about student activism in the *Times*. Students are generally not considered credible sources. A February 22, 1987 front page article claimed that today's college students are looking to their administrators for more help in running their lives, quoting a Wesleyan dean who asserted that students are "expressing diminished confidence in their ability to shoulder the responsibilities of adulthood." Only one college student is quoted with an opposing point of view, one of only two students quoted at all.[7]

In December 1986, when four Boston University students won the right in court to hang "Divest" banners from their windows, the *Times* story devoted 15 lines to quotes from the university provost and president. The only defendant quoted, Yosef Abramowitz, was limited to a four-word excerpt.[8] A week later, a *Times* piece on the arrest of five Brandeis students protesting their school's investments in South Africa quotes the school's vice president for communications and public relations, but fails not only to quote the students, but to give any facts at all about them.[9] On the same day, a piece about the College Republicans, who issued a lapel button proclaiming Lt. Col. Oliver North an American hero, included ten lines of quotes from that group's chairman.[10]

In coverage of the CIA trial in Northampton, Massachusetts, nearly every headline and lead referred exclusively to Amy Carter and Abbie Hoffman. Little of the coverage indicated the breadth of the testimony, the issues under contention or the implications of the case. A few samples: "Carter defends anti-CIA protest" (*Philadelphia Inquirer*),[11] "Amy Carter's Trial Starts" (New York *Newsday*),[12] "Carter wants focus on CIA during her trial" (*Boston Globe*).[13] References to "her" trial continued though Carter herself in fact took great pains to discourage or prevent this sort of separation.

On the whole, sixties comparisons, personality emphasis and poor research mark most reporting of campus political activism. For example, a March 9, 1987 account in the *Times*,[14] running 49.5 inches about campus racial incidents, never mentions any of the commitments made in the early seventies to increased minority enrollment, minority representation on the faculty and the introduction of non-Eurocentric courses—though the failure to meet those commitments has been a source of deep resentment to students of color.

There are some publications, however, that students find useful, such as (in no particular order) the *Nation, In These Times*, the *Guardian* and the *Christian Science Monitor*. In addition, although students seldom see it, the *Chronicle of Higher Education* does a consistently thorough job of reporting on student political activism.

In a nation where 98% of the homes have television sets and the average adult watches five hours of television daily,[15] TV reporting clearly has an effect. In "Television and the Troubled Campus," Neil Hickey asserts that the influx of television news crews onto the Columbia University campus in 1968 gave protestors the impetus to continue, and that those crews, by selecting Mark Rudd to be interviewed, turned him from one of the organizers into the leader and a media figure.[16]

To develop some idea of how television reports on student political activism, 25 samples from commercial news programs[17] were surveyed, stretching from 1969 to 1987, from black-and-white to color, from film to videotape, from Walter Cronkite to Tom Brokaw.

During the 1969 Chicago Eight trial, CBS allotted 3 minutes 40 seconds (3:40) on October 9 to report that 200 "hardcore" students were demonstrating against the proceedings in which defendant Bobby Seale was bound and gagged. All reports were from police and Mayor Richard Daley.[18]

The following week, on October 15, Walter Cronkite reported on the nation-wide Vietnam Moratorium in which "perhaps a million people" participated, "most of them young," but added that "a couple of hundred million did not." Despite the observation that most of the million were young, no students were quoted in the 4:40 piece. While Cronkite pronounced the protest "dignified, responsible," the report noted "one brief moment in an otherwise peaceful day of protest" and viewers were shown that one brief (disruptive) moment. Senator Eugene McCarthy represented the students' views; Senator Barry Goldwater spoke for those they disagreed with.[19]

In the fall of 1984, some students supported striking employees at Yale University, but that support was almost invisible in the television coverage. On September 26, the "CBS Evening News'" 1:40 piece quoted only one student, who was opposed to the strike.[20] "NBC Nightly News" took longer, 2:10, to explain that some students supported the strike, but most did not, quoting two of them.[21]

NBC did offer more balance in coverage of the blockade at Columbia University for divestment the following spring. A 2:10 piece on April 8, covered by local reporter Jennifer McLogan, who had time to learn the facts, carefully compared the action to the 1969 shutdown of the university, but also quoted professor Eric Foner who noted this was not a replay, but an event of its own. Two students supporting the action were quoted; objections to the blockade voiced by a third were countered by a fourth student. The piece opened with a reference to a hunger strike students had staged when they were denied access to a trustees' meeting; the blockade did not begin until after this protest failed, a point which legitimized the blockade.[22]

A little more than a week later, a 40-second piece on NBC of a demonstration at Berkeley sought quick categorization rather than reporting, calling it "a replay of the sixties." The principal person quoted was Secretary of State George Shultz, restating administration policy in regard to South Africa.[23] By the following week, when actions had taken on a life of their own, a 25-second piece on the "CBS Evening News" did mention that 5,000 students were sitting-in at Sproul Plaza in Berkeley, that "thousands more" attended a forum in the gym, that 12 of the 28 regents were there to discuss the issue, and that $1.5 billion in investments was at stake.[24] In a round-up piece two nights later, CBS devoted 3:20 to growing dissatisfaction with US policy in South Africa, which included embassy protests in Washington and a reaction quote from Secretary Shultz, as well as protests at Berkeley and Columbia with a "sixties connection" shot showing Mario Savio, student activist leader in Berkeley during that era, encouraging students of today not to give in.[25]

When conservative students sledge-hammered a shanty built on the Dartmouth campus to protest that school's investments in South Africa, the CBS report on February 9, 1986 wove in a fair amount of information, including the net worth of Dartmouth's investments ($63 million).[26] But as divestment-related student activities grew, short-hand coverage returned: "NBC Nightly News," in a 30-second piece April 3, barely mentioned the issues, but did show a fair amount of pushing and shoving, and shots of the shanties being torn down by police;[27] "CBS Evening News" packed even more violence into a piece that ran ten seconds shorter.[28] The next night, Dan Rather reported that demonstrations had "fizzled" on some campuses, but mentioned that more than a thousand students had rallied in Boston.[29] Stories over the following weeks focused on the arrest of students at Purdue, Yale[30] and other schools, rather than issues.[31]

That fall, attention turned to racism and CIA protests. In a November 15 report[32] and a November 24 follow-up, NBC's Denise Baker clearly explained the issues and the situation at the Citadel, where a group of white students dressed in Ku Klux Klan robes had entered the room of a black student.[33] But the CIA protests were another matter. When students at the University of Colorado in Boulder called for CIA recruiters to be banned from campus, a 25-second report on "ABC World News Tonight" on November 17 showed students pushing down temporary fencing and described the action as student-induced, when in fact police forced students into an area where they had no room to move.[34] A 20-second story on NBC that same night barely dealt with issues, featured some of the most confrontational moments from the action and failed to explain the sequence of events that led to the use of police clubs and mace.[35]

The return of "famous people" provided an excuse for personality journalism in the spring of 1987. On April 14, covering the CIA trial in Northampton, NBC reporter Lisa Myers catalogued the "name" witnesses and Abbie Hoffman, but concentrated on defendant Amy Carter (who the report said "lives in a commune," using a '60s word to describe group housing, which is very common on college campuses today). Issues were barely mentioned; specifics of the trial were ignored.[36]

A notable exception came from Richard Roth of the Cable News Network, whose 1:45 piece April 16 did a fairly good job of giving the whole story of the trial. Although it inevitably used Amy as a spokesperson, and the reaction of her father, it seemed to strive for balance.[37] The next day's CNN report on the acquittal verdict however turned the news into an Amy story once again.[38]

Coverage of the spring March on Washington weekend followed this pattern. On April 25, 1987, CNN barely mentioned the issues which prompted the march, but did use one student inverview while flute music in the background suggested a sixties atmosphere.[39] NBC local news in New York that day featured a young man with a peace symbol painted on his face. Peter, Paul and Mary were shown; Holly Near was not.[40] Rita Braver on CBS described it as a "sixties-style march for eighties issues."[41]

In CNN coverage of the CIA headquarters action April 27, Bob Franklin pronounced the event was "as much a sixties museum piece as an eighties confrontation," and announced that many familiar sixties faces were present, a statement difficult to reconcile with the fact that, aside from Dan Ellsberg, no Vietnam era activist was present, and the thousands of students were infants during the height of the anti-Vietnam War movement.[42]

On the radio, coverage of student political activism falls into the routine of most radio news—short capsules at the top of the hour. Radio no longer constitutes a serious source of news, with the exception of broadcasts by the Pacifica affiliates and by National Public Radio, both non-profit enterprises.

The College Press

Press coverage on campus can attract or repel potential supporters, and legitimize or marginalize an issue in the eyes of administrators and trustees.

For "local," campus-based issues and in dealing with campus conditions, reporting is fairly straightforward. Broader concerns, such as racism or homophobia, however, require a more sensitive approach in gathering balanced data; coverage of campus reactions to national or international developments requires familiarity with the background of those developments. Many student activists express low expectations on how thoroughly issues can be covered by the campus press.[43]

Campus publications play a substantial role in university life. Many students read only their campus publication to learn about political developments. A 1986 Texas Tech readership survey discovered that half the students read only the campus paper, *The University Daily*.[44] According to the Directory of the College Student Press in America, "there may be as many as 10,000 student publications, resulting from burgeoning minority (ethnic, too), religious, feminist, political and residential college media..." Its sixth edition lists college media from more than 3,600 institutions. In all, college newspapers spend nearly $60,000,000 annually, 75% take ads, and fewer than half are supported by subsidies.[45]

Student editors do say they are concerned about national issues. In a survey (released in May, 1987 by *National On-Campus Report*) asking 541 college editors to name the most troubling national issue, 16% cited the federal deficit followed by education funding (14%), AIDS (13%), peace and nuclear war issues (11%), foreign relations (9%) and the Reagan administration (6%).[46]

Student activists often try to organize students who may know little about the issues. Political cartoonists understand this: such cartoons cannot be effective unless the reader is familiar with the subject. Mark Giaimo, whose cartoons in Madison's *Daily Cardinal* have received national attention, says, "The thing I've learned over the years is to go almost by headlines. You've gotta hit them on a real basic level, and be funny at the same time." He adds, "The CIA is something that's here in America, in a way, and so it's easier to grasp onto, kind of a focal point. People know a bit about Nicaragua, but I think they're confused. Progressives know it pretty well. We have a term 'P-C,' politically correct people here, and there's a pretty strong group who are pretty aware of what goes on. Your day-in-and-day-out student is against supporting the contras, but is not so pro-Sandinista, if they even know that much about it."[47]

How a college newspaper covers a campus political story depends on the size and professionalism of its staff, the degree of autonomy the paper has, and the political or social climate on campus. These factors can co-exist in many combinations with varying results.

Attempts to control news or editorials seldom occur, but it was discussed during the College Media Advisers Campus 1987 Student Press Day. Purvette Bryant, editor of Howard University's *The Hilltop* tells of meeting students from other schools who comment, "'On our campus, we don't get this type of coverage. The student newspaper is very passive. They just write anything basically the administration wants them to write, so there won't be any conflict.' I'm very adamant about freedom of the press, and if the press is passive, if the press is suppressed, then I would assume the student government is the same way. *The Hilltop* is the type of publication that will go out and get the story, regardless of whether the president says no or yes. We don't have those type of restraints."[48]

Though uncommon, lawsuits against student publications do occur. In March 1987, the Student Press Law Center, which monitors press and censorship developments, recorded 22 cases involving censorship and received enough inquiries for assistance in this area to publish "Law of the Student Press," a comprehensive 84-page book on the rights of student journalists.[49]

In a related area, in a recent case the California State University System was sued by the editor of the San Diego State University's *Daily Aztec* to overturn a ban on papers endorsing political candidates. A US District Judge ruled in favor of the paper, opening up the editorial pages of the 9-campus system.[50]

Paying close attention to professional standards can present the full story, and counteract rumors; failing to do so can inflame a sensitive situation. At the height of the racial tensions at Columbia during the spring of 1987, a group of white students called a meeting to discuss their opposition to racism; black student leaders urged those who convened the session not to start another organization, but to support existing, black-led efforts. The *Columbia Spectator* account gave the impression that no whites initially supported this position, when in fact, several had voiced similar views at the start of the session. This omission exacerbated an already tender situation, and may have contributed to the misconception that CBSC sees itself as a blacks-only group.[51]

At Dartmouth, the school paper in 1986 gave a lot of play to a rape case, but not to requests by radical feminists that their positions be represented. Jack Steinberg, a reporter at the time, recalls, "We got a lot of letters to the editor from the radical feminists. There are two women's groups; one is a little more radically feminist than the other—and they were constantly writing letters to us, asking us to have their issues heard, and why don't we print the words they like to use—why do we find the word "tampon" offensive when it's used 15 times. They can't understand that. We really didn't give them that much coverage."

Women concerned about feminist issues produced their own paper. Jack, now an editor, adds, "I don't think we're going to do a story on it, who's working for it, and what are they doing, because it's kind of our policy. We don't cover other publications, unless they do something terribly offensive."[52] The paper reflects the climate on the campus, which finds coverage of radical feminist ideas inappropriate, but does not find sensational the reporting about a rape case. Coverage, or lack of coverage, of a particular topic in turn contributes to the political climate on a campus.

And while publications such as the *Dartmouth Review* have piqued national attention as indicators of the so-called student swing to the right, at least an equal number of progressive alternative papers have been formed. Both types receive off-campus support—right-wing papers from the Institute for Educational Affairs, left-wing papers from the Center for National Policy. Most of the progressive alternatives feature campus angles on national and international subjects, local political reporting, extensive coverage of progressive views on foreign policy matters and a healthy letters section. Rick White, who writes for *The Gadfly,* at the University of Vermont in Burlington, thinks alternative newspapers are necessary "because mainstream campus newspapers, though they're important, tend to neglect how worldly issues affect us daily. And they fail to investigate the political and social patterns that affect us."[53] A network of alternative papers, begun during the winter of 1986-87, has now grown to include 26 publications. The Network of the Alternative Student Press provides support for promoting progressive student alternative publications and facilitates communication among existing papers. In an informal survey of student activists from more than 100 schools, one-third said an alternative newspaper was publishing on their campus.[54] News of progressive student activities also shows up in the pages of alternative papers printed in the towns and cities where universities are situated, such as the *Ann Arbor Agenda* and the *Santa Cruz Monthly Planet.*

College newspapers with an interest in expanding their coverage often employ campus news services to provide in-depth reporting; most widely used are *National On-Campus Reports, National Student News Service* and *College Press Service.* Most campuses also receive free magazines distributed nationally to attract the "college market." Their coverage of political issues remains marginal.

College Radio and Television

College radio stations do not only broadcast news and information, but also music, comedy, talk shows and other kinds of programming. But from WHCL's "Consider the Alternatives" (Hamilton College) and KALX's "Women Hold Up Half the Sky" (Berkeley) to WUSB's "Radio Lambda" (SUNY, Stony Brook) and WHUS's "In Black America," (University of Connecticut, Storrs), radio station managers break up the music with political programming. Unlike campus newspapers, where there may be limited space, competition for access to an audience is usually guaranteed, because time slots and host spots often go begging on college radio stations, which, according to the Intercollegiate Broadcasting System, number 650 nationally.[55] Beyond the talk show format, most political shows have little to draw from, but activists in foreign, domestic and personal rights issues all use available air time to present their message, directly, to students.

In 1987, a progressive news and features service began to offer programming for free. Radio Free New England, based at Goddard College in Plainfield, Vermont, packages news, documentaries, features and interviews, and makes them available to college stations throughout the country. According to director Michael Deacon, "We understand that many college stations just don't have the money. We want to reach those 10 watt and 100 watt stations that have no programming funds."[56] Backed by private contributions and user fees collected from those who can pay, the service combines domestic and foreign sources, and seeks to fill the gap for station managers who would like to present alternative programming.

Campus television stations also turn to programming services, such as Campus Network and Campus Satellite Network. Students find some political programming interspersed among the rock concerts, cartoons and syndicated old television shows.

INTERVIEW

Phil Levy, University of Michigan   *March 6, 1987*

Phil Levy is one of four news editors at *The Michigan Daily*.

TV—*On what basis do political activities get assigned and covered?*

PL—Sometimes we'll cover ongoing movements, but generally we try and cover any event going on on campus if we deem it important, which gets to be a judgment call. Racism is clearly the foremost issue. For a long time it was the issue of US involvement in Central America. There's an ongoing weekly protest by the Latin American Solidarity Committee.

TV—*Do you cover the weekly protest?*

PL—We do; we've actually gradually toned it down, but we do get it in the paper every week. I covered the first one of them, and it was our lead story. Two prominent campus activists, one of whom had been a Congressional candidate, got arrested and we gave that a lot of play. We don't give it as big a play now, because they're repeating the same thing every week. It makes it difficult, something we wonder about.

TV—*What makes the difference—the amount of other news on the same day?*

PL—That's part of it. And how important we judge it to be. We want to be a campus paper of record. We want to get it into the paper. However, its actual significance, the odds that it's going to change anything, enlighten anyone, diminishes as time goes on. But we like to record that it happens.

TV—*Has there been coverage of racism?*

PL—We have a minority reporter, and have had for years. So minority issues are examined.

TV—*During this recent series of incidents, has there been criticism of your coverage?*

PL—I've heard criticism from both sides. I've heard that we downplay racism stories, and that we take isolated incidents and blow them all out of proportion.

TV—*Asian students at the hearing said they were excluded in the racism analysis?*

PL—I don't think we've given that a lot of attention—it's not just the black students who suffer. I'm sure we've had coverage of anti-Semitism. I can't recall doing a story on the different aspects of racism.

TV—*How do you cover an important issue when there's no event going on in connection with it?*

PL—It's tough if we can't tie it to something else. We have one tool to check the mood of the campus, "inquiring photographer," where we go around and ask people what they think of a particular issue.

TV—*Is the fact that the paper's editorial board is composed overwhelmingly of white students an issue?*

PL—Yes. We had an incident that prompted a lot of introspection when a cartoon was run that was pretty widely judged to be racist. All the editors have said that we would really like to get more minority involvement on the paper. We've talked with professors, with groups. We don't have anywhere near the same problem with male-female ratios—on the opinion page, it's mostly male, but the news is half and half. On the next level down, it's more female than male. We make a real effort. We'd very much like to have a black editor, but you have to be thoroughly familiar with the workings of the paper. You have to have good writing abilites. If we picked somebody off the street and threw them in as a token black, it would be miserable for them, it would be a fiasco for everyone involved, and we would be accused of tokenism. It's a tough situation.

TV—*What influence does the national press have in what stories you choose to cover?*

PL—I'd say it has a lot. Every day you examine the *Detroit Free Press,* the *Detroit News,* the *Ann Arbor News,* the *Wall Street Journal,* the *New York Times* and the Associated Press wire, to see that stories they're running, and look to see if we can localize them, and examine what's going on here.

TV—*Do you look at the process that political organizations use to capture press attention—do you say, they're doing this just to get coverage?*

PL—That's a lot of what makes it hard. It is an event, but they are doing it to be in the news. They're sort of using you. They'll call up and say, "You guys are covering our event today, aren't you? There may be some people arrested." It's difficult.

TV—*What's the relationship between the paper and the administration?*

PL—*The Daily* is independent, although the university owns our stock. A board for student publications oversees us directly. We have pretty complete editorial freedom. In the past, there have been attempts to stifle that, and if I know my *Daily* history, that didn't work very well in the sixties. I've seen no influence by the administration where they've tried to force us to change our views, or to print something that they want printed.

TV—*When there are issues that somehow do not get covered, what are the reasons?*

PL—We have some real constraints. One is space. On a given night, we'll have three or four news pages, and sometimes the inside pages are half or more than half ads. We would like more space, but that's a business thing—they're not selling the ads to give us more space. And our other constraint is the staff. We're not able to pay very well. I make $100 a month, working 30 or 35 hours a week. Reporters are paid $50 a month.

TV—*On some papers they're not paid at all.*

PL—Right. But they're also full-time students. And there are only so many who can do the work. But, we realize that we don't always have the space or the ability to cover everything we'd like to. We really try and judge what's most important to students. Most national issues, almost every issue out there, since students are members of society and are going off into all walks of life—you could tie almost anything into students. When there are budget cuts, we cover that, for instance, and we pick it up where the budget cuts fit into higher education. We gave extensive coverage to local elections. We give very thorough coverage to Michigan Student Assembly elections. The closer it is to us, the more coverage we give it, because we recognize our limitations as a paper.

TV—*Are people involved in an issue disqualified from covering it?*

PL—We do have an ethics policy which says, for instance, that a reporter who is a member of the Michigan Student Assembly, could not cover it. People are not allowed to cover something that they are actively a part of.

Just What is a "Sixties-Style" Demonstration?

On June 13, 1987, a very vocal group of people staged a march to protest conditions they felt were unjust. Many carried signs, some were singing, most were chanting but in all the television and newspaper coverage of that event, there was not one reference to a "sixties-style protest"; perhaps because no "famous faces" were present, perhaps because they were in Aliquippa, Pennsylvania, and possibly because they were retirees protesting cutbacks in pensions.

The habitual use of "sixties-style" conveniently condenses much of what is wrong with the coverage of student political activism; it does not cover all the problems, but it certainly encapsulates many of them. Reporters, editors and news producers—in print and in broadcast journalism—still seem to view student activism as a phenomenon "invented" in the late sixties. They do not seem to realize that student political activism is a "political activism" story, rather than a "student" story; by comparison, union actions are not referred to as "thirties-style" actions.

To determine how seriously the media is treating an issue, observers often examine the length of a piece, in inches or in minutes and seconds, but this has no relation to balance or substance. In television, it more often has to do with the availability of attention-grabbing visuals, whether or not they are relevant to the story. In print, the ability to mention or quote a famous person will often lengthen an article. Students are still rarely quoted, although that has eased somewhat in the last two years. Activists may have become wary of dealing with the media, given what they have learned about some of its habits during the anti-war era. Today, they are more likely to insist that more than one person be interviewed, or that the spokesperson not be a white male.

One analysis of the downfall of SDS ties it to the media attention that it received. Quoted in Todd Gitlin's book "The Whole World Is Watching," Michael Klare, a member of the Columbia University SDS in 1968, comments, "The most destructive element of the 1968 uprising in the media was the sense of messianic power that the SDS chapter had: that it could skip intermediate steps; that because of its name and its prestige and its charisma, it could bring down the university. And several disastrous events happened afterwards because of that miscalculation, in which SDS crumbled...Mark Rudd was very involved in that. The media imagery was very much a part of the calculation."[57]

Significantly, none of the national student progressive organizations has a fulltime person dealing with press information. For most, this reflects a lack of money or an absence of someone who can do it as a volunteer. But it has reduced coverage of student activism, and definitely impacts the coverage it does receive.

Some student activists are aware of the importance of media coverage. Ricardo Velasquez, at Berkeley, finds the media "tremendously essential" in his political work.

RV—We saw the work of media with the Vietnam War. Now, we see that the media, with its far-reaching effects, like cable TV, can make or break things. We work to involve the media by inviting them to our events, keeping them abreast of what's happening, keeping good contacts.

TV—*Would you alter or shape an event because of media coverage?*

RV—A person without much integrity would say that you make more out of it than there really is. That person is wrong and short-sighted. Media people have bosses who say, "Where is the punch to this, what is the impact?" What you do is, with sincerity, take what is the bigger lesson, the moral of this issue. You show how this is a microcosm of a larger wrong. And you emphasize that, so the media people have an easier time developing the story for what it is.

TV—*And you think that isn't always done?*

RV—Sometimes we've had a sit-in somewhere, and it seems to be some specialized event for that particular issue, and people not involved with that find they are not able to sympathize or relate. And that's a tragic error. You win the battle and lose the war.

TV—*Do you deal differently between print coverage and broadcast coverage?*

RV—Broadcast coverage demands glossier presentations. You put it in a way that has immediate positive impact. It's the sort of thing they're willing to put on the six o'clock news. The sort of thing their editors will pat them on the head for. It's photogenic. It's a compromise you have to make, but not that much of a compromise as long as the issue isn't being changed in any way.[58]

During the CIA trial in Massachusetts, the challenge was to take advantage of the presence of two media personalities without letting that overshadow the substance of the cause. Students, particularly the other defendants, found themselves adapting to the pressures of the press as much as to the pressures of being on trial.

Defendant Mark Caldiera remembers, "We all decided to have one or two people as media contacts. If someone came up to you and asked what you think of something—to refer press to them. It didn't work. Why the caution was so great was because UPI or AP did a horrible story right before the trial." Mark adds that Abbie "was very much in our favor, saying, let these people talk to the press. The more people that talk, the better—the less it looks like a show of one or two people. He was giving us advice, saying don't go on for ten minutes, just say one or two sentences that really encapsulate, like, 'I'm learning more here than I would in school.' He really has the experience. As far as being a media person, I think he's great. He's still dealing with his sexism, but he's conscious of it. And contrary to what people think, he wasn't running the show at all."[59]

Roger Morey, another defendant, says, "I think it helped us to have Amy there. Sooner or later the press had to run out of saying how much her toothpaste costs. It was a problem because it divided her from the rest of us. After working with her, I find that she's a genuine human being who believes in what she's doing. She's not doing it for the press. I think she'd do a lot better working for the Democratic Party if that was what she wanted. And have a much better image for herself. I've gained some respect for her. Abbie's an interesting case, though."

TV—*Their personalities are very different.*

RM—I would say that, in one case, I don't think we would have got our feet off the ground without the initial money from Abbie to start. And I also think that we had a lot of divisions take place within the group because of a charismatic personality. People that follow him will work with him, and there are people that have a conflict of personalities, and don't want to deal with that. He'd rather listen to himself. You can work with a hawk—but you have to know what you're going to lose.

TV—*What did you gain?*

RM—First off, the press. He's also a good organizer. As much as he's a hierarchist, he's a good organizer. He's got us a lot of good contacts.

TV—*He has invited the sixties comparisons in press reporting.*

RM—I don't delude myself into thinking these are the sixties. The sixties happened because of events leading up to it and the same with the eighties. I don't think there's as much of a comparison between the fifties and the seventies as between the fifties and the eighties. In the press, it depends on what their focus is. If their focus is on what I'm doing, I try to put my ideas out, and they'll say one thing. If they focus on Abbie, then, yeah, Abbie does call up that symbolism."[60]

Most press coverage of student political activism falls victim to familiar styles of reporting—concentrating on events that involve large numbers of people or sensational visuals. Because contemporary student activism involves students working on a wide range of issues, the number of students involved in each particular issue, in most instances, is not large enough to attract press attention. And most activism does not include unusual visuals. When a particular cause or movement is finally identified by the press, reporting on it becomes the process of spotlighting a particular event in a particular place, like a CIA protest, without the accompanying information that students at dozens of other campuses have engaged in exactly the same kind of action in the last two months.

The problems associated with coverage by campus press can be resolved more easily. Most papers seek knowledgeable reporters to cover political issues, as long as they are not members of the organizations involved. Reporters already on staff usually welcome additional background for their stories. In cases where the editorial board proves disinterested, or hostile, students can target the paper for protest, or start an alternative publication. Most often, unsatisfactory campus reporting is the result of poorly informed or overworked staff reporters, not intentional misrepresentation or omission. Activists need to show campus reporters the relevance of the action to the campus itself. In broader actions, mainstream reporters need to be shown that student involvement is part of a larger picture.

CHAPTER THIRTEEN

The Outlook

It will not go away.

Whatever the economic, political, social or psychological climate, societies count on their young adults to identify and confront what has grown outdated, superfluous or hypocritical. In the United States, college students have been playing that role in one form or another for the past several generations—regardless of the evils they choose to attack.

In the late 1980s and early 1990s new issues will appear, and the shifting political climate, locally and nationally, will bring different influences into play. Other issues will remain relatively unchanged, and will continue to provoke steady protest.

When the campus cauldron started to heat up, and then boil over on some campuses in the mid-1980s, opposition to apartheid lit the flame. Students agitated on hundreds of campuses to force their universities to divest holdings in South Africa. Many succeeded. Now, the future of that movement depends on three separate but related factors.

First, the political climate and conditions within South Africa itself—worsening conditions prompt stronger reactions here though this factor is moderated by the nature of press coverage.

Second, the actual behavior of universities and corporations. Some institutions have been accused of sham divestments that only mask actual retention of investments. If enough of these are discovered, the reaction could generate new demonstrations.

Third, if students learn that the situation in South Africa represents a regional problem, one that extends throughout the southern half of that continent, this may lead to further actions. As students put more pieces together, and make political connections, actions on campuses could reflect their oppposition to the regional situation.

Of these three, the internal situation in South Africa is most likely to activate students—the other two factors require more education and a willingness to comprehend the nuances of the situation. Apartheid, in and of itself, represents a clear cut moral issue—students can choose to oppose it fairly simply. It does not require much investigation to understand what it is that people oppose. Learning about the internal and regional policies in southern Africa, and about the financial intricacies of stock transfers, may demand more time than some students have. However, ACOA is monitoring these issues closely and providing detailed information to campus organizations, and could play a pivotal role in determining how much activity there will be on this issue. Students from universities that have truly divested might well form coalitions with students from not-yet divested schools, to support them, and to act against coporations invested in South Africa.

Student political organizing on Central America will also be affected by internal politics within the countries. Direct US troop involvement in that region would catapult this issue to the top of the list, with outpourings on campus a reflection of general opposition to such a move. The degree of reporting about any political developments there also effects the level of interest on campuses. And, again, the knowledge that this is a regional, not a country-by-country situation will require more commitment from students to understand and sort out the whole picture.

Another facet is the federal government's surveillance of organizations opposed to US policy in Central America, and its attempts to deter activists from going to the region. Denying visas particularly would send a clear signal to campuses. The hundreds of students who have been there and returned to tell classmates about the situation would see this as an admission by the government that it had something to hide. And the increasing politically active population of students from latino backgrounds could also boost the presence of this issue on particular campuses.

Opposition to the CIA is a closely related issue. Since meaningful controls on this agency seem unlikely, the CIA as an issue will not weaken. Targeting of campus recruitment brings the issue home, and does limit somewhat the agency's ability to perpetuate its activities. To move beyond this, students will need to join with organizations willing to pressure Congress to enact strict, uncompromising legislation in regard to the CIA's activities.

Opposition to the war machine provides a most difficult challenge: the issue is multi-sided, often highly technical, and covers the widest possible range of projected outcomes, from limiting nuclear testing to outright disarmament. This makes pulling together coalitions problematic. The emotional appeal that characterized the freeze movement of the early 1980s has not carried over to opposition to Star Wars research, although that could easily change, especially on campuses where military research takes place, or whenever students link defense spending to the lack of funds for student loans and grants, or social welfare programs. One tactic, pinpointing specific scientists doing specialized research, may have unexpected results, because it is dependent on the role of a few individuals, and their possible defection leaves the research area very vulnerable.

The delicate, even raw climate that surrounds questions of racism prevents some of those best-intentioned from rationally proceeding with solutions. Racism is no longer a narrow matter of white over black, but encompasses discrimination against all students of color, and extends to those newly enrolled at American universities, such as Palestinians. In no other area does the university have such a serious, clear responsibility to help build and lend support. Expecting students to reverse overt or subconscious discriminatory feelings through student-generated volunteer orientation programs stretches the limits of their role.

Students of all races have moved to conduct forums, bring in speakers, show films, pressure for curriculum changes and a dozen other possible routes to an overall solution—and many have been implemented, some very creatively and successfully. Black students continue to fight for the legitimate place of black-led student programs. But at the end of every discussion, the same point is reached—why isn't the university playing more of a role? Energy which could be spent positively building a strong minority cultural and political presence on campus is instead spent trying to move the university beyond its unsatisfactory or non-existent attempts to defeat racism.

There is little chance that concern with the economy and the general welfare will diminish. The specifics may change, the emphasis may shift, but dissatisfaction with the allocation of public funds will not be resolved soon. Students in great numbers have been drawn to small-scale volunteer efforts to turn around large problems. If they begin to see this work as undervalued, or worse, defeated by official governmental policies, these students may become somewhat more radicalized. And escalating costs for higher education may trigger the kinds of student revolts that, in recent years, inflamed Paris and Mexico City where students theoretically guaranteed free access to college still found the financial pressures unacceptable.

Feminism on campuses seems to be passing through a crisis of identity. Young women do not have a solid women's movement with which they can feel comfortable. In the late 1980s, even the label "feminist" has negative connotations which cause women to shy away from women's rights issues. Older feminists are vexed by this younger generation of women who have little sense of recent feminist history, and who may not realize how easily these victories could be reversed. In matters such as right to an abortion and job equality, most college women come down strongly in the feminist camp, and can be moved to protest. Also, Take Back the Night Marches countering violence against women have a strong continued presence on college campuses. Except on campuses where blatant sexual oppression or discrimination occurs, however, organizing in this movement tends to focus on specific, local issues.

Among the most courageous of politically active college students today are those who are openly gay, lesbian and bisexual. Although they are assaulted by religious persecution, held back by legislative infringements, distorted by moralizing politicians and crippled by the tragic coincidence of the AIDS epidemic, they stand up on their campuses and demand equal treatment. Support for gay rights on campuses may crystalize the other common prejudices in society by forcing those holding these prejudices to confront them. Because, while students of color organize and protest regularly, it is rarely acceptable for someone to publicly air prejudices against them. Gay students regularly function in environments where prejudices against them are frequently tolerated and acted out violently. And gay students, who have often supported other groups' endeavors, may demand that progressive organizations begin to address *their own* homophobia. As more and more college students present themselves honestly as homosexual, and as other students learn about the links between their political struggles and the fight against homophobia, heterosexual students will be stronger allies when the rights of gay students are threatened.

Student empowerment is another permanent movement, though specifics change from campus to campus. Not all its advocates are members of student governments, but student governments do have a steady, revolving constituency that includes people willing to build on the past instead of challenging it. The next decade will likely see more statewide student associations or unions, which strengthen the political power of students. The increase in corporate-sponsored research programs, and its effect on University policies may prompt organized responses from students who object to the shifts in priorities this development brings. And as political rumblings on campus increase, administrations will react to stifle those rumblings. Already, the shift to on-campus disciplinary hearings, and the videotaping of participants in demonstrations have become familiar practices. And the resistance by administrations to change will only feed the drive of students to increase their power.

The Outlook on Strategies

Regardless of the issues, student activists' choice of strategy will be critical to their success or failure.

Public demonstrations and rallies serve a purpose, but most organizers have learned not to overuse this strategy by calling for a rally every few days. More and more campus speakers have learned that hyperbole does not play well among fellow students. Provocative rhetoric sounds contrived in a campus setting, and diminishes the impact of the message when employed there. Civil disobedience continues to be controversial, particularly in mixed race groups where blacks do not always see getting arrested as something political. But public defiance does generate support. Groups must discuss the issue of arrest as a serious strategy, not enter into it without preparation, or risk opening serious rifts within their membership. By and large, civil disobedience requires serious preparation and discussion—"planned arrests" continue to be used as a tactic. Students will come to accept the likelihood that videotaping equipment will be used, and adjust their planning efforts accordingly. Bringing a political issue to trial in court involves complicated procedures and runs many risks. Often, the process of the trial becomes the focus while the action itself is given less attention.

Getting the message out through tabling, postering, chalking, leafletting—these are mainstays that are not only effective in spreading information, but provide a concrete, entry-level task for new members. Hosting a national figure dramatizes a group's position and enhances their visibility. Putting together such an event not only has an energizing effect on one organization, but, when it is jointly sponsored, it strengthens the working relationship of a whole network of campus groups.

While large teach-ins occur infrequently, smaller teach-ins now crop up all the time. Their informal, almost spontaneous quality allows direct contact between participant and presenter. These could be used more, repeated several times in one day or one week. Making political changes by introducing new courses is a wide-open strategy, and represents a serious commitment to change that requires extensive research and a willingness to stay with the plan, sometimes for years.

Coverage of political issues by the campus press may be influenced by the Hazlewood Supreme Court case, even though it grew out of a high school incident, since the wording of the ruling is ambiguous. A rise in the number of alternative publications, now easy to produce with desk-top publishing, could be the result.

Using legal avenues to affect change will become more common. Students have learned from the divestment campaigns how to research the connections between their trustees and the controlling interests of the issue they are working on— which may soon lead to pressuring trustees with investments in Central America, in companies with discriminatory hiring policies, or ties to military or weapons research contractors. The Divestment Disk already provides some of the needed information; the process only needs to be refined.

Local and state laws that affect students and the legislative budgeting process also generate student input. The longer view is critical as students familiarize themselves with legislators and legislation and then lobby on their own behalf. Building coalitions is a difficult and long-term task that requires considerable coordination.

On the national level, electoral politics attracts different students for different reasons. Having grown up in an era of increasing cynicism about the effectiveness of politicians, students are wary of this process. Still, many view such campaigns as a vehicle for bringing certain issues to the public; for establishing the importance of student concerns; for meeting people from other groups, with an eye toward coalition-building that could pay off long after the campaign; and for learning personal electoral skills they can apply later, elsewhere.

Bringing a political issue to trial in court involves complicated procedures and runs many risks. Often, the process of the trial becomes the focus, while the subject of the action is given less attention.

Students are often willing to contribute money for a cause. This, too, provides activity for a new member—standing in front of the Union with a bucket asking for donations requires little skill, and offers concrete results. Material aid campaigns that collect items such as medical or school supplies rather than money involve greater coordination—arrangements for transportation, verification of receipt and an understanding of just what is needed on the receiving end, but the satisfaction for the sponsoring group can be greater. These efforts depend on the sort of contacts and international liaisons that national organizations can help supply.

Asking students to boycott specific products can prove difficult, because they are unusual consumers; many have their major food purchases made by the dining hall or food services. But boycotts are also an easy way to demonstrate political support. Successful efforts have combined public education, often involving student government, and popular acceptance on campus, along with the availability of alternatives. But it is important to remember that students often don't enjoy much mobility and may find it difficult to support a boycott by altering their buying patterns.

Because the labor force on campuses is changing—with more and more women of color holding down the support services jobs—the increase in union action on campuses will provide students with more opportunity to support efforts of this kind. For students to support a strike that may disrupt operation of the university is controversial but that itself serves to educate those unaware of the connections between labor negotiations and other political issues. The difficulty comes when unions need to figure out who on campus represents progressive students, and how to plug into that network. When no network exists, pulling together that student support can prove difficult.

Students volunteering to help the hungry and homeless will continue their work—the process has been institutionalized on many campuses, and the problems will persist. Similarily, students will continue to work in other countries, particularly Central America. Firsthand reports from returning students about conditions have proved so valuable that students will continue looking to them as an organizing resource once they return to their campuses.

From Boston to Berkeley, students interested in political organizing for any cause complain of one common, pervasive problem—poorly-run meetings. While this may be true of any volunteer activity, it tends to reduce participation at best; at its worst, it can divide an organization, misrepresent positions and sour students on the entire process of creating a political strategy.

Running meetings by consensus or some variation has become the norm, but there is still little understanding of how that process works. The simple but incorrect view that consensus equals assent creates huge stumbling blocks in meeting after meeting. Students who reject hierarchical governing structures seek alternatives, but when consensus is represented as a system in which everyone must agree, they shudder at the thought of endless meetings. In fact, consensus means consenting to permit a particular proposal to be accepted even if you are not in 100% agreement with it. Well-trained facilitators, who realize that their role is to clarify, to elicit reactions, to listen to individuals' concerns and try to carry the needs of the organization into the process while working continually toward a successful consensus, can help make meetings very productive.

All national student organizations have experienced growth, and every indication is that this will continue. ACOA has added staffpeople to do research, make connections and feed information onto campuses. CISPES has also expanded the attention it pays to the place of students in its overall campaign. COOL is tightly organized and will extend its reach into many more campuses in the next few years. DSA's Youth Section may benefit from election year activity in 1988, as students look toward the electoral arena as an outlet for political action. The National Chicano Students Association, if it can overcome internal differences, appears ready to make a strong national impact: both the level of interest of its members and existing issues will work for them. And the National Student Action Center, if it keeps that specific focus, need only increase what it does and by default, can play a pivotal coordinating role in the growth of the overall student movement. PSN offers the perfect home for students seeking a loose alliance of multi-issue activists. The only problem PSN may face is the difficulty of not having enough money to cover expenses, since its structure does not extract great financial requirements from affiliates. If its expenses grow beyond the present means to cover them, and the group moves to a more financially demanding relationship with its members, they may stand to lose some of their present constituency, who may not be able to afford greater required payment, or may not approve of this strategy as a way of covering the organization's financial obligations. UCAM also represents an issue that is broad enough to attract a range of students, particularly if engineering and science students are brought into its growing constituency. USSA's strong base can help it play a major role, especially if it focuses on the creation of new state student unions, and on skills training. Finally, the creation of a new national organization for gay, lesbian and bisexual students under the auspices of the National Gay and Lesbian Task Force in Washington will add another political force on college campuses.

Will the present wave of activism die out when these classes of undergraduates leave the campus? Not likely, if you look at the political activity among the college freshpersons of the next few years, the high school students of today.

High school students confront every major political issue of the times, using educational, direct action, volunteer and even legal means to express their opinions. Common subjects for their activity include world issues such as nuclear disarmament and support for Amnesty International; national issues such as US involvement in Central America and South Africa, as well as work in the major political parties; community concerns such as helping the homeless and feeding the hungry; school regulations issues such as grading policies and censorship of student publications; and personal rights issues such as women's rights, gay rights and racism. The January 1988 Supreme Court case limiting the freedom of high school journalists may chill one avenue of expression.[1] They sponsor speakers, conduct panels, engage in debates, work with nearby colleges, start chapters of national organizations, launch their own organizations, volunteer in their community, and even travel to Nicaragua.

The National Forum started by students at Milton Academy in Milton, Massachusetts, gathered thousands of signatures in a petition drive last year, and continues to work on educating students about nuclear war.[2] The Children of War Tour, sponsored by the Religious Task Force, introduces American high school students to counterparts from war-ravaged countries who visit schools and talk with students. High school students also organize "adoption groups" with Amnesty International.[3]

Speakers challenge high school students to learn more about the political situation. Mark Nelson, of the University of Utah Students Against Apartheid, spoke to classes at Alta High School in Sandy, Utah.[4] *Newsweek* reporter Richard Manning addressed students at the Groton School in Massachusetts about his experiences in South Africa.[5] Nuclear weapons expert Dr. Stephen Marks visited classes at the Lewiston High School in Lewiston, Indiana.[6] Throughout New England, high schools hear speakers and presentations from New England Students Against Apartheid, an ambitious program headed by Mark Lurie, who wants to link American and South African high school students.

And they put their understanding into practice. Students from Garfield High School in Seattle formed Teenagers Against Apartheid, and staged a protest outside the home of Joseph Swing, honorary consul of South Africa—and were arrested.[7] As part of their Awareness Days, students at Redwood High School in Larkspur, California invited two Salvadoran refugees who spoke about war in their region in a program that included films, slide presentations, panels and discussions about Central America. At Lincoln High in Lincoln, Nebraska, Nicaraguan activist David Moroga spoke to students about efforts to stop US intervention.

Students in Pittsburgh's Avonworth High School, displeased with faculty cuts, staged a sit-in at the cafeteria, boycotting all classes.

And personal rights issues also receive attention. Racism at a Washington, DC high school and homophobia at a Utah high school, reported in school papers, exemplify increased willingness to tackle sensitive subjects.

But perhaps the most striking indication of burgeoning political activism among high school students comes in the programs that assist students travelling to Central America. Fresh View, based in Boston, has sponsored dozens of students since 1985. Naomi Craine, a Detroit high school student, stated when she returned from Nicaragua that "I am really displeased by US support for the contras, to put it nicely. I think we have absolutely no right to disrupt the internal affairs of that country."[8] Ithaca high school student Noah Silverman commented, "In the United States, my political ideas are invalidated because I am young."[9]

The ideas of contemporary college students offer broad insights in every area of political thought. Among the people interviewed for this book, here are some who had significant observations about organizing, and the outlook for student activism:

Doug Calvin, CISPES, on starting a new political organization: "Do an event, like a film or something, then have a follow-up meeting or follow-up event for people who are interested. Everything you do should be multi-purpose: education, bringing people in, fund-raising, whatever. You should always have people sign their names on something. Call those people up and say there's another film going on, and we'll be having a discussion. Plan things that you know will be successful, knowing what you want to get out of an event, and what it will take to do it. A lot of new groups are coming out. Especially with campuses fighting isolation by linking together, and using the nationals as a resource is real important. What do you do if something happens in the news and 200 people come out for an event? Do you go back down to your 15-person group, or do you use it to build up?"[10]

Ethan Felson, NELGSU, on organizing gay students: "Beyond Gay Awareness Weeks, other activities that I see are the large residence halls' awareness raps, things like that. So much depends on the size of the group, whether it's urban or rural, whether there are a large number of women or minorities. The issue of gender parity is probably the thing I feel strongest about. I'm tremendously committed to creating women's outreach, because we're talking about training tomorrow's leaders today—not just leaders in the gay and lesbian movement, but leaders in corporate America. If we can increase the number of women and minorities in the pool of people we're drawing from, then our movement can become the model for many others. It's a political movement, part of the progressive movement, and we can connect to a myriad of issues from apartheid to Central America as well as much more closely related issues of right to privacy and body sovereignty, such as birth control, contraception, abortion. As for financing, it is important to have university funding, because the university has a responsibility to its gay and lesbian students, and to its non-gay and -lesbian students, for education and support. But I also think that it can be a liability, a trump card that the school can play. I've seen housing taken away, office space taken away, funding taken away as a means of punishing student groups for different things, and that has to be taken into consideration. So the group must plan their social events, like dances, so they are, indeed, fundraisers, and use that money for other programming. The biggest obstacle new groups face? Ignorance."[11]

Kim Paulis, director of the National Student Action Center, on how a new group starts on a campus: "With six people, you gotta pick an issue, then help them figure out what it is they want to do—bring in a speaker, show a film or a film series, or do a material aid drive. There's a whole range of fairly easily organized stuff. One suggestion would be to do a week of education on what's going on in Central America. If that's what they wanted to do, I would talk about how to use that week to build your group from six to twenty people. They'd need to brainstorm to figure out all the things they need—get a room, get a film, make banners, posters and flyers and put them around. If you have a mailing list, do a mailing. If you have a phone list, phone through it.There are groups like this. They're usually so ingrown, they don't have meetings, they don't ever recruit or do anything active other than hang up posters. And they've lost touch with the average student, which happens to a lot of left groups. Literally, people from every single campus I've ever come in contact with have said, "You don't understand—it's so conservative here." So I have a whole rap about conservatism and apathy and what those words really mean, and it's really just a vacuum of leadership. It's almost like, because people are apathetic, it's some kind of an excuse for things not happening. So I tell them, have once-a-week meetings. Get people focused on project-oriented stuff. Being oriented on a project in a month or six-week timeline, people can actually accomplish something. They can prove to themselves that they can do it. It takes work, but, if you figure out what you need to do, and put it on the timeline and do it, it does work.

To deal with the media we put together a two-pager on how to get media coverage. Write down the names of reporters you've talked to on cards, basic stuff. To use the fast as an example, we got virtually nothing on the national level, but we got big local coverage.

If a group has no source of money, there are free things you can do in connection with people in the community. Groups in the community have access to
speakers, films and information. Also campuses usually have speakers' bureaus or
they can go through an academic department. When I was in school, we brought
Ralph Nader, and we got the money from Poli Sci, from other departments, from
everywhere. And, of course, I tell them to pass around a sign-up sheet so they can
build up a mailing list. As for a next step, I think we need to set up institutions on
a local level, meaning states and\or regions. I think national is too big for students.
It's too expensive, it's too much time. We need to get networked and happening
on the local level before we do anything on the national level. And we need to get
all that stuff with racial balance and sexual balance worked out before we try anything national. Right now we're encouraging people to set up statewide networks,
so that all these issues can come out, and people can start putting out newsletters
and doing training and having regional meetings."[12]

Bruce Nestor, student at the University of Iowa in Iowa City, and steering
committee member of the Progressive Student Network, on new campus groups:
"We try to provide them with some materials. We encourage them by reminding
them that by raising a pole of opposition, even campaigns that seem entirely outrageous can succeed wonderfully well. The anti-CIA campaigns in Louisiana and
Florida and Kansas, three places where you'd think you wouldn't want to do such
things, did really well. You don't need to occupy buildings or break windows.
Leafletting at some places is a radical act. I think about activism in terms of responding to specific instances. The bombing of Tripoli, for example, provided a perfect
opportunity to raise a "pole of opposition." The overwhelming tide in the media,
public opinion, and official opinion was that this bombing was really the most
wonderful thing since sliced bread. And coming out in public against that bombing, for whatever reason, was creating an opposition that was sufficient to really
raise some thought on a lot of people's part, and provoke some action. Things got
really ugly on this campus, with right-wingers attacking us. It taught a lot of people
a lot of stuff.

Even if there's only two or three of you, you can be a strong vibrant group.
We've been down to three people in this organization. In Florida, eight students
came to a PSN meeting that I went to there, all from a Baptist school, 99.9% white;
you couldn't ask for a more conservative school. These students stick to a middle
road; they are real aware of what's happening in Central America, but they focus
on congressional work. And they've built sympathy on a campus that saw them as
oddballs at first. So we stress that. By keeping lists, by doing low-level education,
by adapting to the opportunities that you have, by stressing local complicity and
the ability to effect things that you're directly involved in.

For example, a good first campaign would be protesting CIA recruitment on
your campus; it's the ideal first campaign. A lot of small schools are involved in issues around access. You can look at racist attacks on campus, minority recruitment
programs. Those are things that take a little development. We don't stress material
aid campaigns to Central America; that's a fine thing to do if you're an organized
group, but it doesn't attract or bring new people in, nor do solidarity campaigns or

congressional actions. Focusing on Congress is really a dead step to involving undergraduates because there's no sense of a possibility to influence. It ends up being a letter-writing campaign. It doesn't involve people; it doesn't educate people. Sitting at a table is the most exciting thing you do. The type of stuff we do—leafleting extensively for weeks and doing educational events that culminate in candlelight marches or rallies—all involves new people. Part of it is just aimed at changing people's opinions, not really thinking that we're going to have a great influence on national policy, although that's certainly not divorced from it. If you look at students in history, you'll see that they allied with other social sectors, have had an effect on foreign policy."[13]

Elizabeth "Sibby" Burpee, University of Colorado and USSA, on changes: "I've seen a move to the left, even though people are saying campuses are getting more conservative. On this campus, students played a large part as voters and workers in electing the Democratic representative for this district, the Democratic senator and the Democratic governor. Also, in the increased support for the CIA issue, I've seen a move to the left. I think student activism is increasing. Students recognize the need to have a structure to follow in order to change the relations of power, to get concrete improvements in people's lives. You need to have a real plan, as opposed to being haphazard about it. For example, the CIA campaign has been going on for two years and it's been very organized—in terms of keeping it going, and having it build instead of starting over each time. With divestment, people didn't have a real structured plan and they failed. With the tuition issue, it's been real important for us to get on committees—to act like we're playing the game, get on the committees, and then not play what they want us to play."[14]

Rick Harbaugh, creator of the Divestment Disk, on how computer use will affect organizing strategies for progressive students: "If you look at strategies on the right, they have a very centralized system of using computers. They have mass mailings through systems which do a very good job of it. They've benefited enormously from having that capability whereas the left has not. I think the strength of the left has always been its grassroots nature. It's always had zillions more volunteers. Previous computer technology has always allowed the right to make up for that with these centralized mainframe computers and their mass mailings, for the purpose of getting money, and not necessarily for community-type things. But for national issues they were able to organize just as well by virtue of that computer technology. Now the technology has shifted. It's now in the field where the left can assert itself and take advantage of it. It's kind of interesting to look at the whole mainframe\micro technology shift in the computer world, and at the differences between right-wing and left-wing strategies for organizing. I think it is best suited for the kind of organizing that left groups do."[15]

Stephanie Weiner, **Bob Cutter** and **Joe Iosbaker**, students at the University of Illinois Circle Campus in Chicago, and PSN members on strategies and tactics at an urban commuter campus:

JI: First of all, we always have stuff in the middle of the day. Second of all—it took me a long time to learn this—you have to be more authoritarian. You have to bring people something they can do, preferably something they can do on their own, like, can you type this up for me, please? You've gotta have fewer meetings and do them faster. Fifty minutes—a class period. That core group is more important than ever. Those few people who will be in touch with everyone, and have all the information, so that they can rattle it off, over and over, when they see people. It just puts a huge strain on the whole organization. Then that core group has to be better at dealing with people, when they get mad about something. They don't have a meeting to air their views. That core group's just more important. There's no easy way, unfortunately. If you're more directed, and take who you have, and do your thing, and do it yourself if you have to. In PSN, we're very process oriented, but here, it's practically impossible to be process oriented.

BC: It's a constant process of, when you meet someone, trying to figure out what they can do. Some students will give you money—they have money, but they don't have any time. It's very hard to build this ongoing organization that can have its own kind of culture and friendships. You have to be more satisfied with a nice big punchy event. Then you keep in touch with people, and then maybe you can put together another nice big event.

SW: Also, we have been aided by the PSN resources. We've had concrete conferences to psych people. In terms of other activist exposure, and speakers and strategies, we don't have to be the leaders to infuse them with the ideas. We can rely on the Iowa conference of PSN, the steering committee for cross-fertilization, the mass mobilization to Washington, caravaning to nearby schools. So in that sense, the PSN, or at least that form of breaking the isolation, has really helped us to get resources we never would have been able to. It can be done. Slow and steady work. Every day standing by that table. Slow and steady. Someone will come by and sign. It can happen. We won divestment. It was partial divestment, but it was won through confrontation.[16]

    Lamoin Werlein-Jaen, Madison PSN, on the reasons for the success of their CIA protest: "First, during our campaign prior to the demonstration, the media had been focusing a great deal of attention on recent CIA crimes in Central America—the 'Contra Manual' and the mining of Nicaraguan harbors. Second, we organized a five-month campaign of agitation and education, encompassing all levels of activism and using all avenues of expression around the issue. And finally, the news from other campuses—Boulder, Brown and Tufts—and the conscious militancy of some organizers also helped to fuel the fire."[17]

    Ricardo Velasquez, a student at the University of California at Berkeley, and a member of the United People of Color, and the National Chicano Students Association (MECHA) on nationalism in third world groups: Internally, there was a tremendous rift among those who wanted nationalistic, selective membership, and those who didn't. MECHA had its origins in the late sixties, and early seventies, the brown berets, people who fought the system, people who wanted to develop a student sort of thing, much like SNCC in black areas. Part of this was rooted in the notion that these are occupied territories, laying waste what was Mexican territory in the 1860s, that the treaty of Guadelupe-Hidalgo had a lot of provisions that the United States has never quite met. So they acknowledge that our nation is still here, at least in a symbolic way, and that the consciousness of chicanos is linked. So people wanting to address those issues on a community level beget MECHA. At the beginning they had tremendous cultural linkages to chicanos only, to a nationalistic bent only. Even at the beginning, non-chicanos were involved. I feel very comfortable working with these issues, because they affect all latinos. So today, whether or not it was supposed to be a nationalistic movement, nationalistic steps ultimately fail to make steps toward larger human issues. It's missing the point. In general, in terms of student activism, I do believe this is going somewhere, and with any luck, any good combination of media and strong students who replenish the ones who graduate, this could go on for a long, long time."[18]

Leonard Weinglass, attorney for the defendants in the CIA on Trial Project in Northampton on campus activists in the courtroom: "Today, you have a lot going for you that you didn't have 20 years ago. The combined effects of the Vietnam War, Watergate, give you an opportunity in the courtroom to portray the CIA in terms that are credible to mainstream juries. Fifteen years ago, if you were to say anything against the CIA or the FBI, people would just reject it out of hand. Now there is a great climate of distrust, fear, apprehension, that makes a defense, like the defense we used in Massachusetts, plausible and ultimately credible.

In Iowa, 23 students went on trial around CIA recruitment—same charges, either blocking or occupying a building. They did not have lawyers. They did not call the expert witnesses we did. They argued *pro se* [on their own behalf] to the jury, cited our case, and were all acquitted. It's gotten no attention.

With the necessity defense you're essentially asking a jury to condone lawlessness. And they throw all kinds of roadblocks in your way. The law itself is difficult. You have to prove there's a nexus between your action and abating the harm. You have to prove there's no other reasonable alternative. Very, very difficult to make out the case for necessity. But we made that breakthrough, and it got a lot of publicity. And I'm very hopeful, after the Iowa result, that people will be successful in arguing this defense in these kinds of cases.

The University of Massachusetts cleverly cloaked its position in the First Amendment. They would like to have argued that, if you preclude the exercise of First Amendment rights by the CIA, that will lead to the preclusion of other groups coming onto campus. And do you maintain the campus as an open system, or closed. It's a very interesting cloak of cover, the First Amendment, that they employed."[19]

Roger Morey, CIA on Trial Project defendant, and student member of the UMass Radical Student Union, on meeting process: "One problem with process in a multi-issue constituency is the length of time it takes to get a consensus decision on one issue. Essentially, if you want to be in both a black organization and the Radical Student Union, you might not have time for classwork. Consensus decision-making is very good for a lot of different things—one of the best is for deciding what the group is, what it's doing when it starts out. I think it's very high quality decision-making for people that are interested in what's going on. With four people, you can usually come to a good decision. But the greater the number of people you have, the harder it is to arrive at a consensus decision. And the more diversity you have in the group, the harder it is. I would go to votes on most issues. The biggest problem you have is to decide when you're going to divide your group. If you sub-divide the group, you'd have more decisions on consensus right now. The other question is conformity. There's much greater pressure to conform under consensus. They'll say we can't go on unless you agree, and you say, I'll never agree to that. I've been forced to conform so much in this society, with the government, that I don't agree with. Why should I come to another meeting and be forced to conform again. At least when I vote, I can remain true to my ideals. It's not that I wouldn't support the majority vote, but I don't think I need to be badgered to change my mind, because I'm not going to. You can have tyranny by the minority. And there are other considerations about consensus—what happens when you have a facilitator who is out of control? This can be a big problem, especially when there are not procedures set up for training facilitators."[20]

Nick Komar, defendant in the CIA on Trial Project, UMass student, and founder of Biological Scientists for Social Responsibility, on meeting and organiza-tional process: "I think people should stop going to meetings—meetings should be held less often, and people should have working subcommittees. They have to be given independence to a certain extent. People should only meet with other mem-bers of their subcommittees to get things done, and then they should meet in a big-ger meeting, maybe once a month, or if it's a current issue maybe every two weeks. But having a general meeting once a week for any organization is a mistake. Those meetings usually last in excess of two and a half hours, and they're very draining, very tense. A lot of power struggles—not overt power struggles, but covert power struggles. But no one wants to admit it—which creates a lot of tension. I just think it's a drain on the movement. At our meetings, we usually call the chair the facilitator. I'm not sure what the difference is. The facilitator usually has the power to inter-rupt if things aren't going smoothly, to say, okay, we're going to use a different method. And everyone respects that. When the facilitator seems to be always call-ing on the same people, things start to break down. We use consensus decision-making, which doesn't work for us very well. I think the main problem is that people aren't very well-educated in how to use consensus decision-making or how to be an effective facilitator. If those things could be worked out, everything would run much more smoothly. At a Boston Area Network on Central America conference, a professional expert on consensus brought out that the only way you can use con-sensus decision-making effectively is if you have a fairly small group, and there's group trust. People really have to trust each other. I think that might be one fault of our organization. It's small, but people don't trust each other very well. In a group like CASA [Central America Solidarity Committee], which does long-term organiz-ing, there is much more trust than in a group like SCROC [Stop CIA Recruitment Or-ganizing Committee] where people feel, "We've got to do this NOW!" It's not a long-term organization.

One problem is, once the process of getting to know each other is underway, it's harder for new people to come in. At the SCROC group, one person blocked consensus decision-making for a long time, and brought out whether we should use consensus in the future. He had a point, but he didn't realize that the real problem in SCROC was poor facilitation. For example, we had a meeting for three, three-and-a-half hours, and everyone sort of blamed him for making the meeting run long, because he was blocking. I think he did it to show people how it didn't work. But the reason the whole meeting didn't work was because the facilitator never knew how to move beyond the problem, never called for an actual consensus vote. That was a big mistake. I raised my hand and said, what you have to do now is call for a vote. She said, thanks for your opinion. The meeting was perceived as a flop. One thing that came out of it was that we decided to have workshops on facilitation and consensus decision-making. But the problem has to do with a lack of trust. I think, for me, it's because I don't fit the image. If you have someone who, during the whole movement, was basically an activist rather than an organizer, he would be one of the people out in the forefront of the actions, he'd get his picture in the paper a lot. And people would respect him, they'd accept him right away in their group. I'm much more of an organizer. People don't recognize the work that organizers do. They don't see it. I had to fight for people to listen to me. It was a pain in the ass. I think you have to have a certain image for people to think you're worth listening to."[21]

Winston Willis, Columbia University, on subtle racism on campus: "It's incredibly hard to explain. For instance, imagine there's a white student checking ID's. Eight students file in ahead of you, they're white and you're black. And you notice that, to all the other students, he or she is either saying hello or ignoring them, and that once you come, it's 'ID please.' Often times, when black students come in as freshmen, after they're asked their names and where they're from, the next question often is 'what are your SAT scores?' A person in the admissions office told me many black and latino students leave this place very bitter. Your fellow white students and faculty will seldom if ever accord you an inherent respect you know you deserve."[22]

Elissa McBride, DSA Youth Section organizer, on racism: "Part of it is being very attentive to issues of racism in this country, and always linking the issue of apartheid to issues of racism in the US—not saying they're the same, but that we need to deal with both, not simply to export the problem. Also, making a concerted effort to address the issue of racism on a personal level, and in terms of government programs which harm people of color, and poor people, and women, etc. Also, I'm getting to read a lot of writings back from 20 years ago when the black community was saying what we needed to be doing in order to address issues of racism. In terms of bringing in more students of color to DSA, I'm not sure if I would be able to do that. I haven't thought of myself as a recruiter, but I am particularly wary of thinking that I might be able to do that because I come from a very white background, and a very white college (Carleton). I will need help in learning what issues are important to students of color."[23]

Pedro Noguera, former president of Associated Students at the University of California at Berkeley, on the effectiveness of confrontational tactics, and the role of students of color in student activism: "Students of color, in my experience at Brown and Berkeley, have been willing to engage in militant protest when the protest is organized, and the objectives and the plan are laid out clearly beforehand. People are not willing to go into something where they are not sure what is going to happen, where spontaneous acts may endanger those present. For example, when I was at Brown, we took over the financial aid office, which was a pretty militant protest. And that action included third world students. At Berkeley, we took over, or did a sit-in at Sproul Hall, which was also somewhat militant. We didn't fight the police. We didn't resist arrest. I've been to many campuses and seen what's going on, and I think Berkeley is more advanced in terms of the political debate than most campuses. I see the same splits in many places, but not the same dialogues and debates with a clear recognition of what's happening. At Berkeley, there's both myself and Ronnie Stephenson. Ronnie was a Black Panther starting in 1967, was underground for several years and came back as a student. I had similar ties in New York City when I was growing up. Our perspective on social change is certainly not conservative, and we have a sense of what went wrong with those earlier experiences. Because we know personally people whose lives were ruined, who are in jail now, who are dead now, who have since sold out, and we do not wish to repeat the past. So we are very much influenced by history, and seek to develop a movement that matches what's necessary for the conditions in the eighties.

I think that many of the militant white students are influenced by another current of thought. Basically, they're influenced by a kind of punk philosophy, and basically anarchistic. As many of them will tell you, the issues are less important than the actions, and just generally expressing their outrage and disgust with authoritarianism. And so whether the issue is Central America, divestment, whatever it is, their tactics are almost always the same. They say we're conservative. That we're scared. And we've had to struggle with that quite a bit. We've had to pull out our credentials, over and over, to prove that we're not conservative, that we're not scared. I've been beaten by the police when I was growing up, as a teenager—not for political reasons, but for walking home late at night with a radio that they didn't think was mine. So my attitude toward the police is different from theirs. Many of them grew up with the police as the guy you go to when you can't get your baseball out of a tree, or the friend on the corner. So we're coming from a different place. I think also we're coming from a different place socially and economically, many of us. I have a family, but if I get kicked out of school for my political activity, I am on my own. That's it. Many of them have support from their parents. If they grow out of this stage, and I think it is a stage for some of them, they can go back to the comfort and security of their parents. They can go to another school, start over. For us, and not just some of the older ones who have families, but even for the young ones, whose parents didn't go to college, or who worked their way through. Their parents, even though they struggled, and participated in protests, are telling their kids, look, you get your education first. Because if you don't have that, you don't have anything. You're just going to be a victim. And that's real. That's not bullshit. I can't tell these people, these young black students, don't worry if you get kicked out of school, what we're doing is more important. I want them to graduate. I want to keep them in this movement after they graduate.The struggle we're involved in goes way beyond the campus. It's a struggle that we want to win, and win these people who are getting their educations, to a movement, for life.

The campus doesn't have a multi-racial organization, and that really is a hindrance. We recognize that. The last two years a black was running for president of student government. I got in, but I don't think there'll be another one for years to come. White students generally will not vote for a black person. We need to have a multi-racial coalition to do anything. Part of it is on white students, to see that the issues they perceive as special interest concerns are much broader than that. They really are issues that are at the heart of what kind of country we live in, what kind of society we're going to have, and whether or not we're going to have any kind of equality and justice in the future. But part of it is on third world students, especially the more enlightened ones, to realize that the struggle against the war in Central America is definitely not a white issue. And the struggle against homelessness is definitely not a white issue. And even though we may not be affected by those problems directly, we have to have a position on them, and we have to participate in those struggles. And we have to engage those white students who want to work with us on the issues of tactics and strategy and organization-building. It's going to be a difficult and painful process, as it has been at Berkeley. You're trying to forge bonds where there is a lot of mistrust. I'm optimistic about the potential for that happening."[24]

Jonathan Klein, Rutgers University, National Student Convention committee, on the future of activism: "We've already seen, since the antiapartheid protests that rocked campuses nationwide in 1985, a growing sophistication on the part of student activists, in terms of both tactics and analysis. Over the next few years, this sophistication will undoubtedly deepen as radical students develop a structured national organization that unites the disparate threads of our nascent movement. The sooner this happens, the better we'll be able to help save our society."[25]

Barbara Ransby, United Coalition Against Racism, University of Michigan at Ann Arbor, on the direction of political activism on campuses today: "I'm always an optimist. People say you're on the brink of tremendous change, but you also see right wing forces coalescing at an alarming rate. In a situation where there's a lot of anger, a lot of frustration, fewer crumbs being thrown out to people in need, increased competition for slots among middle-class students, increased repression on a number of levels, increased class polarization. All those conditions make us more receptive to both left and right politics. I have to hope that people will be pushed to the left, and develop an analysis that sees the need to combat some of the fundamental injustices in our society in a very aggressive way, that people will start to form political organizations and coalesce with other organizations, define platforms, and march, and emerge into something we can call a movement. And I see an increased number of students being willing to get involved."[26]

The ideas of the next wave of college students may include support for new issues to the campus political scene, such as Palestinian rights, mandatory drug testing, and equal rights for the physically handicapped. Every issue, every movement, every cause, has experienced an increase in college student interest in the past three years. On university campuses, first-year students are taking the lead, joining groups, assuming positions of responsibility.

The End of the Beginning

When 27 students from around the country met in the unheated Hampshire College Student meeting hall known as the Red Barn the first weekend in 1987, they signalled the end of the beginning of a new stage in student political activism. Called together initially to plan support for the CIA on Trial project, they quickly moved to the lengthy list of concerns that had been surfacing on their 19 different campuses. They also began to discuss better links with one another.

Suggestions for a national student convention met with mixed reactions; the group most dedicated to the idea was from Rutgers. Within weeks, they had outlined a preliminary plan, printed brochures with their own money, and stated their willingness to host such an event.

In the following months, word spread. Other agenda-planning sessions took form, at Rutgers, MIT, and elsewhere with the intention of creating an event to serve the needs of independent activist students. The host group resisted advice that they involve existing national organizations, either from fear that they might be swallowed up, from a miscalculated belief that doing so would predispose the event to a particular conclusion, or from a naive arrogance that they did not need their help.

Publicity about the National Student Convention, to be held at Rutgers February 5-7, 1988 appeared in the National Student News Service, the National Student Action Center newsletter, the *Nation,* and in announcements on MTV. Three Rutgers students travelled by car to campuses from New York to California to generate interest. Organizers were caught off-guard when their projections that 200 activists would attend missed the mark so widely—nearly 700 showed up, most of them not preregistered, causing a logistical nightmare. But despite the chaos of food shortages, limited sleeping space, room changes, and security problems, the event rolled on, much of it relocated to the large Livingston Gym. The agenda proved far more problematic than the environment.

Students generally represented three different positions: 1) affiliated with existing national organizations, either student groups or sectarian political groups, with their own views on the idea of a new national organization starting up; 2) dedicatedly not affiliated, independent, focused on local and regional actions, and unwilling to be categorized by labels and ideologies of the past; 3) those in the middle—the largest number by far—who were not yet affiliated, but who believed in the need to act politically, and who came to deliberate, investigate, question, and possibly leave with a new vehicle to execute their beliefs. As the weekend wore on, the positions of the two smaller groups overtook the less focused intentions of the students in the middle.

Organizers had prepared extensive guidelines on process, solicited and copies proposed statements of unity and constitutions, called for workshops to be presented by volunteers, and envisioned a complicated but somewhat orderly event. Within hours of its official start, an open mike session had turned into a forum for those dissatisfied with the organizing efforts, or those opposed to the idea of a new national formation. Overwhelmed by the nearly unending influx of people, the hosts had little time to deal with these developments.

Through the next two days, between workshops, a garden of caucuses grew up, each addressing needs and concerns of groups there to do some work, make some progress. Third world students, in particular, but also gay, lesbian, and bisexual students, challenged the legitimacy of any new organization created by those present, since they believed their constituencies were underrepresented. By Saturday night, their positions were widely known, and their position widely discussed. By Sunday afternoon, plans to forge a constitution or a new organization had been abandoned and activists had dedicated themselves to working regionally, building more representational groups, contacting their constituencies and seeking others, with an eye toward another national student convention in the future.

Scenes throughout the weekend reflected how diverse and raw this group really was. Students from schools with histories of widespread student political activity, such as Kim Tows from Berkeley, could launch a caucus with little effort. Students from schools used to addressing their world issues, such as Dolores Mozone from Hunter College, carried their concerns into all parts of the convention.

Students like Rick Gustafson from Simon's Rock College in Massachusetts rode it out, sorting out the events as best they could. "It was one of the most incredible experiences I've had in my life," he commented, adding that "the fact that the two caucuses—the students of color, and the gay, lesbian, and bisexual student—broke off gave the message that all these people have to work together." To him, the idea "that these issues were brought up at all was the most important thing."

More significant than the specifics of the discussions was the spirit of the event: 700 people turned out, in the middle of winter, spending their own money, missing classes, losing sleep.

That most were not affiliated with existing national organizations proved equally significant. It indicates how independent a large segments of the student activist population is, and how fluid its future. Representatives from sectarian political organizations found little interest in their solicitations. In fact, when someone trying to take over the microphone was identified as being from the Progressive Labor Party, students ushered him off the platform. How the leadership of the existing student nationals address these students and their issues may determine how broad and legitimate the role of the organizations will be in coming years. Certainly, the drive to organize other student conventions, and the commitment from independent students like Christine Kelly from Rutgers to bring together these students, can only grow.

The increased political power and influence of college students rests partly in the resolution of an this question: should a national progressive students organization be formed? Two very different attitudes emerge. One calls for a student movement that unites all progressive students, interrelates the issues, combines the constituencies, pools resources whenever possible, and presents a weighty, serious force in American life. The California Alliance of Progressive Student Activists provides a model for this type of development. The drive to organize students as a free-standing constituency in the country takes on added impetus in the areas where students are affected most, such as financial aid for higher education. And the growing involvement of graduate students brings in those who have already developed skills, and who feel more at ease dealing with administrators as equals. A second view sees students organized to be a force within existing causes. Those who see this as the direction hope to make concrete changes in specific areas and believe that students want to contribute to those changes as part of larger movements.

These two positions are not mutually exclusive, and indeed, there are enough progressive students to fill both camps. And there are those who resist any attempt at confederation or consolidation.

The minimum step will be to create a system of information-sharing. During the next decade, students will have to cope with a rapidly-changing world, one in which their place and their future cannot be predicted. They have tasted the satisfaction of seeing their efforts rewarded, their actions prove consequential. Now, they are growing more determined, ready to organize actions that will institute the progressive policies they believe in, and equally ready to forge an identity, a new identity out of these issues and these times, for themselves and for their generation, and to make their voices heard—new voices.

CHAPTER FOURTEEN

A Sampling of Events

Political activity on college campuses takes many forms, and occurs at schools of every size and type, in every location. Here is a sampling from among the hundreds of events which took place between January 1986 and April 1987.

January 1986

- After 12 students attack the three shanties constructed on the campus of Dartmouth in December 1985 approximately 300 students occupy the school's main administration building in support of the pro-divestment students. The 12 students involved in the attack are subsequently suspended.

- Members of the Progressive Student Alliance at the University of Pennsylvania conduct a week-long series of anti-CIA events—including speeches by a former agent, a documentary film, and a campus rally—to discourage students from considering jobs with the CIA.

- Black students at the University of Tennessee stage a march protesting a Law School newsletter article claiming that most blacks would not be admitted were it not for affirmative action.

- United Campuses to Prevent Nuclear War launches a petition drive on 82 campuses to end SDI research.

- Reacting to protests, the University of Nevada, Reno student government agrees to recognize a Gay Student Union as an official campus organization.
- On the campus of Sonoma State University in California, students construct a "graveyard" of 311 white crosses bearing the names of civilians killed in El Salvador. Armed student "soldiers" stage "abductions" of three instructors and use the exercise to tell students about the activities of El Salvador's death squads.

February 1986

- About 200 students at Smith College take over the school's administration building after trustees announce they had decided not to divest.
- University of Wisconsin students hang 20 effigies on campus, to symbolize the victims of CIA crimes, with signs protesting CIA recruitment.
- Students at the University of Wisconsin Law School protesting FBI discrimination against gays and lesbians, charge the school with violating its policy against discrimination on the basis of sexual preference, and demand that the interviews not be conducted on campus.
- Three residence halls and the student government at Michigan State University vote to support a ban on the sale of Coca-Cola as an anti-apartheid protest.

March 1986

- At Cornell students react to a board of trustees vote against divestment by erecting 800 red-stained wooden crosses to symbolize the deaths that have occurred in South Africa.
- The Asian-American Student Association at the University of Oklahoma organizes a formal delegation to campaign for the establishment of an Asian Student Services Office.
- Students at Chico State University in California vote to urge faculty not to accept Star Wars research funds.
- University of Michigan students sit in at the office of Congressman Carl Pursell to focus attention on his continuing support of contra aid. All 118 are arrested.
- Ending the arms race is the theme of a coffee house night at the Rochester Institute of Technology.
- Students across the nation conduct a Fast for Peace in Nicaragua, joining students in Great Britain, Canada, Ireland, Greece, West Germany and Norway in raising more than $15,000 for solidarity efforts. Campuses participating include Catholic University in Washington, DC, the College of William and Mary, Cor-

nell, Rutgers, Sonoma State, and the Universities of Colorado at Boulder and at Denver, Minnesota in the Twin Cities, and New Hampshire.

April 1986

- An arsonist throws a Molotov cocktail at the shanty constructed on the campus of the University of Utah.

- Students join with other groups in filing a petition with a Philadelphia court seeking to void actions taken by University of Pennsylvania trustees which delay completion of divestment for at least 18 months.

- Students at Arizona State University in Tempe picket against CIA recruitment.

- Students at the University of Texas picket a party at the Phi Kappa Alpha fraternity pointing out that the only blacks at the party are porters, and calling the fraternity system racist.

- Five black students at the University of Virginia's anti-apartheid shantytown are assaulted while they are asleep.

- Students at Howard University organize a boycott of advertisers on radio station WWDC in Washington, DC after a disc jockey "jokes" about the killing of Martin Luther King, Jr.

- Students at 70 colleges and universities in 16 cities raise more than $30,000 in the annual Hunger Clean-up, sponsored by the National Student Campaign Against Hunger.

- Two Ohio campuses, Firelands and Cleveland State College, participate in "Unifying Ohio for Peace Week" including a concert and speakers.

- At Pennsylvania State University shanties are pelted with paint-filled light bulbs, damaging books and sleeping bags of those staying at the site.

- About 500 students from 32 states converge on Washington, DC to lobby Congress; many join a "leaky umbrella" parade, carrying broken umbrellas to symbolize the flaws of Star Wars.

- A "Take Back the Night" march at Cornell University is interrupted at least twice as cars drive into the crowd; one man is arrested for harassment.

- Discrimination against gays and lesbians is one of the reasons students at the University of California at Berkeley protest against the presence of recruiters for military subcontractors McDonnell-Douglas, General Dynamics, and General Electric.

- Campus religious organizations at the University of Southern Mississippi organize to counter the gatherings of campus evangelist Jim Gilles, a member of a group called The Destroyers. At one session, Gilles tells the crowd "To kill a queer is not murder." Christian music concerts are sponsored by the Baptist Student Union to attract students away from the Gilles events.

- At California State University at Hayward, students organize a petition drive to block the university's proposed plan to lease the vacant student union building to a bookstore; students want the space used for a day-care center.

- The University of California at Los Angeles hosts a conference of students interested in the sanctuary movement.

- Tensions between black and Jewish students heat up following a speech by Kwame Toure (Stokely Carmichael) at the College Park campus of the University of Maryland. Proclaiming that "the only good Zionist is a dead Zionist," Toure's remarks provoke a series of racial incidents and death threats. Jewish Student Union president Jacob Blumenthal calls pamphlets distributed by Toure, "Old and scary anti-Semitic tactics—the kind the Nazis used."

May 1986

- Western Michigan University Peace Week includes a performance by Pete Seeger.

- Students at Stanford University's Columbia House declare their cooperative residence a sanctuary, take in their first Central American refugee and begin to collect food and clothing for other refugees.

- Two members of the University of Nebraska's Gay and Lesbian Association sue the campus newspaper for refusing ads that refer to a person's sexual orientation and lose when the judge rules the *Daily Nebraskan's* "editorial discretion would inescapably be intruded upon."

- Wearing T-shirts that caution "No Violence," lesbian and gay students manage to keep tempers under control following a speech by anti-gay activist Paul Cameron at the Amherst campus of the University of Massachusettts.

June 1986

- Stanford University president Donald Kennedy announces that the school has agreed to include sexual orientation in its official statement on nondiscrimination.

- More than 2000 students at the University of California, Santa Barbara sign petitions calling for the chancellor's resignation, stating, "He runs the school like a business, but doesn't deal with the consumer—the students." Later, student government approves a resolution calling on the chancellor to institute an affirmative action admissions policy for gay, lesbian and bisexual students.

- Students at the New York Chiropractic College boycott classes for three days to call attention to claims that members of the school's board of trustees are using their positions to advance personal business interests; state authorities agree to meet with the trustees to investigate the charges.

- Claiming that she devoted time to her students instead of finishing her doctoral thesis within the prescribed period, students at the University of Massachusetts circulate petitions calling on the academic department to reconsider firing a faculty member whose work they admire.

August 1986

- To commemorate the 41st anniversary of Hiroshima, students at Marshall University sponsor a die-in.

- Northwestern University withdraws from a State Department-sponsored anti-terrorist training program in response to student allegations that some of the trainees are members of the Salvadoran National Guard, who have been implicated in human-rights abuses and murder.

September 1986

- Students at Temple University in Philadelphia protesting the presence of recruiters on campus join a suit against US Army recruitment, brought by the city of Philadelphia under the city's Fair Practices Act, which calls for the banning of recruiters. A Federal Appeals Court rejects the argument, stating that federal law takes precedence over state and local laws which interfere with federal activities.

- Stanford University students launch a massive voter registration drive and public education campaign, to help defeat a Lyndon LaRouche-sponsored statewide initiative which would prevent AIDS victims from attending school.

- About 500 University of Texas students stage a "study-in" outside the doors of the school's main library, to protest plans to reduce library hours.

October 1986

- "Give Peace a Dance" events are held at UCAM chapters on 17 campuses in 13 states to raise money for programs to reverse the arms race.

- Representatives from the statewide University of California Student Association appear before the state legislature, offering legislation to study the impact of planned cuts in the wages paid to student workers.

- Students at the University of Colorado organize a "Dial-a-Regent" campaign to protest a tuition hike and target state legislators for the next round of calls.

- At the University of Missouri in Columbia, 17 students who have been camping out at a shantytown erected on campus are arrested. The structure is torn down.

- Students at Bowdoin College in Maine stage a die-in at a CIA recruitment session to symbolize the death of victims from CIA intervention in other countries. One-third of the student body sign a petition condemning the agency's activities.

- More than 200 University of Iowa students picket to protest CIA recruitment; four chain themselves to the administration building and are arrested.

- Launching a citizens' arrest campaign, students from the University of Vermont successfully force CIA recruiters to move their interviews off campus.

- Approximately 1000 students demonstrate against CIA recruitment at the University of Minnesota in Minneapolis; the university seals off the building and students who try to push their way in are sprayed with mace by police. Later, riot police with attack dogs are called to the scene but protestors still refuse to leave for the rest of the day.

- Students from the University of California Santa Cruz participate in a sit-in at Lawrence Livermore Lab, the proposed site of new SDI research; 40 are arrested and 20 spend three nights in jail.

- At Reed College in Portland, Oregon students stop at 35 separate locations where sexual assaults or harassment have taken place, in a march sponsored by the women's center; at a "Speak-Out" victims relate their personal experiences.

- Students distribute a letter at the University of North Carolina Student Senate meeting demanding cancellation of "Lambda," the newsletter of the Carolina Gay and Lesbian Association. The letter charges the gay and lesbian group with wasting funds. CGLA retaliates with information that two-thirds of the paper's revenues come from ads.

- One out of six students at Iowa's Grinnell College march in a candlelight procession to mourn victims of the contras in Nicaragua.

- Armbands are worn by more than 300 students at the Chapel Hill campus of the University of North Carolina. Each armband bears the name of a victim of the contras.

- University of Arizona students sit in at the Tucson office of Representative Jim Kolbe, protesting his support for contra aid.

November 1986

- In East Lansing, students build shanties to urge the Michigan State University Foundation, a fund-raising entity, to divest its $500,000 in South Africa stocks.

- Adirondack Community College students organize a panel discussion to question the role of arms development in the United States.

- Prospective students touring Wesleyan College are interrupted by six students who tell them about sexual harassment incidents at the school. The Student Judicial Board files charges against the students, three of whom are then put on disciplinary probation.

- A Lesbian Alliance bulletin board at Mount Holyoke College in Massachusetts is vandalized. Following a campus-wide education campaign on homophobia, a banner bearing a "ban lesbians" symbol is anonymously hung from the college's Skinner Hall.

- Two thousand University of Arizona students jam the main facility to register their outrage at the cutback of library closing time from 2 a.m. to midnight.

December 1986

- Students at James Madison University in Harrisonburg, Virginia hold a benefit dance to raise funds for disarmament.

- One hundred and fifty Brandeis University students occupy the library for an all-night "study-in," protesting the school's failure to divest; days later, other students occupy an office in the main administration building. Twenty-five students are arrested and charged with trespassing.

- The Coalition for a Free Southern Africa from Johns Hopkins pickets the Maryland National Bank; after a meeting bank officials agree to divest holdings in South Africa, and to make low-interest loans available to low-income community people.

- A student group at Ohio State called "Winter Comfort for the Cold" gathers clothing for the homeless, and distributes it to homeless people living near the campus, and in nearby shelters.

- When Southern Utah State College announces plans to abolish its four-year biology degree program, on the grounds it duplicates those of other state schools, students help organize a response that also involves local ranchers and farmers: they drive tractors across the center of campus to get the administration to reconsider.

- Students from the University of Connecticut and Eastern Connecticut State University stage a coordinated four-day fast to draw attention to opposition to US aid to the contras.

January 1987

- Rutgers University students offer support for striking American Federation of State, County and Municipal Employees; classes at the New Brunswick, New Jersey campus are cancelled for nine days.

- About 20 male and female students at the University of Iowa ignore administration rulings to halt a birth control program offering free condoms.

- Students at East Stroudsburg (Pennsylvania) University begin work on a student and faculty referendum on the comprehensive test ban treaty.

- Students at William and Mary College in Virginia opposed to the editorial position of a conservative newspaper start a campaign to persuade local businesses not to advertise.

- After a campus radio station program disc jockey at the University of Michigan makes racist jokes on the air, 30 students protest, leading to the firing of the show's host. Later, following more racist incidents, hundreds of students stage additional protests, and the United Coalition Against Racism outlines its demands for action.

February 1987

- University of Wisconsin students picket the site where research would increase milk production in cows by as much as 40%, and drive small dairy farmers out of business.

- In Virginia, Mary Washington College students hold a vigil and collect 300 signatures on a petition calling for a comprehensive test ban treaty.

- A Peace Awareness Week features the film "War Without Winners" on the campus of Clarke College in Dubuque, Iowa.

- Calling it an illegal search, the captain of the Stanford University diving team refuses to submit to a drug test, which is required for NCAA competition. A California Supreme Court ruling allows her to compete.

- After a two-month boycott of all administration-sponsored events, conducted by student government at Alabama State University, the school agrees to include a student seat on the university's board of trustees.

- Forty high school students at Berkeley High School conduct a one-day fast to raise money for Nicaragua.

- Cal-PIRG students at the University of California, Santa Cruz conduct a food drive and donate proceeds to the Santa Cruz Emergency Food Bank.

- In a coordinated effort by the National Student Action Center, students on 42 campuses recruit more than 1300 participants in the Second Annual Student Fast for Peace in Nicaragua. More than $40,000 is raised for humanitarian relief. The Washington, DC area action, involving students from American University, Catholic University, Georgetown University, George Washington University and the University of Maryland, is held at the Vietnam Veterans Memorial.

March 1987

- Three hundred Penn State University students march through the school's administration building to push for full divestment, and to demand that their president resign from the board of Carnegie Mellon Bank. Students succeed in convincing several local businesses to close their accounts in the bank, because of its ties to South Africa.

- The Pennsylvania State Department of Human Rights charges Pittsburgh Baptist College with discrimination for requiring black students to provide letters of permission from their parents if they wish to date someone who is not black.

- Black students at Vanderbilt University wear white armbands to signify "the death of Vanderbilt's commitment to minorities."

- More than 100 college students from throughout the New York metropolitan area attend a seminar on the Coors boycott, sponsored by Frontlash's New York regional office.

- Editors from two student newspapers in the California State University 19-campus system challenge a system-wide regulation banning political endorsements by campus papers and win in US District Court.

- A coalition of about 200 Harvard students—from DSA, South Africa Solidarity Committee, Gay and Lesbian Alliance and Committee on Central America—join to demonstrate against a speech on campus by William Coors.

April 1987

- The George Mason University Student Coalition Against Apartheid and Racism conducts its second annual Rock Against Racism. Proceeds are used to start a Jimmie Lee Jackson Freedom Fund, named for a student civil rights activist killed in 1965 by Alabama police, to help organizations fight racism.

- Hourly teach-in lectures on the nuclear arms issues highlight a series of events, including a rally, a march, and several speakers at the University of New Hampshire.

- Ocean County College, New Jersey students organize two lectures on nuclear arms issues.

- The University of Chicago's Gay and Lesbian Law Students Association conducts a day-long symposium on sexual orientation and the law following weeks of anonymous harassment, in which gay students receive death threats on the phone and in the mail, and letters are written to their parents, employers and landlords charging them with being AIDS carriers.

- Protesting their school's opposition to collective bargaining in a wage dispute, graduate students at SUNY, Stony Brook stage a two-day work stoppage, closing down most job-related activities and leaving many undergraduate classes without instructors.

- Citibank branches, because of the bank's ties to South Africa, are the sites of protests by college students from Hamilton College (Syracuse), Medgar Evers College (Brooklyn), and a coalition of students from several Chicago colleges.

- The DC Student Coalition Against Apartheid and Racism—including students from Johns Hopkins, Georgetown, George Washington, George Mason and American University and the University of the District of Columbia—targets 15 branches of Sovran Bank because of its ties to South Africa's Standard Bank.

- Following a brawl involving black and white students, hundreds march through the campus and nearby neighborhoods, including Harlem, to oppose institutional racism at Columbia.

- Rutgers University students join other protesters at an action opposing Johnson & Johnson's dealing with South Africa.

1. National Organizations

American Committee on Africa (ACOA)

Oldest of the organizations involved in campus political activism, ACOA was founded in 1953 to support African people in their struggle for independence. Its call for divestment predated by two decades the organizing that swept American campuses in the mid-1980s. Once the message spread through university communities, ACOA served as a prime source of information, providing background on the history and politics of South Africa and the region, as well as data on corporate and institutional investment ties. ACOA is also in touch with speakers, including opposition leaders from southern Africa, and is linked with the United Nations Centre Against Apartheid.

ACOA operates from offices on lower Broadway in New York City, with a small but growing staff. Its relationship to campuses is strictly advisory and informational, but its Student Anti-Apartheid Newsletter attempts to foster coordinated actions and its "Action News" offers background and current news on southern Africa. Each spring it calls for Spring Weeks of National Anti-Apartheid Action, from mid-March through early April. Activities include demonstrations at offices of banks and corporations financially tied to South Africa, and assistance in monitoring the financial operations of universities to prevent "sham divestments."

In 1985, groups working on Central America activities began to link with ACOA to present a joint campaign against the CIA's intervention in both regions. As campus divestment spreads, ACOA has attempted to refocus students' energies to a wider concern with the whole of southern Africa. Some of this work proceeds through ACOA's affiliation with the Call to Conscience Network,[1] which concentrates on the problems in that region and includes a number of groups, among them the USSA. At other schools, students have chosen to concentrate on domestic racism. Leaders who got their training coordinating divestment campaigns have turned their attention to the problems of blacks and other people of color in this country.

Committee in Solidarity with the People of El Salvador (CISPES)

Formed in 1980, CISPES seeks to end US intervention in Central America, and to educate the public about this country's policies toward that region.[2] The CISPES network, run from Washington headquarters and regional offices in Boston, San Francisco, Mobile, New York City, Los Angeles and Chicago, includes some 200 campus chapters. At some universities, independent organizations are affiliated with CISPES. Chapters are under no obligation to support national campaigns, but can design their own actions; these have included rallies and demonstrations, protesting the presence of CIA recruiters on campus, inviting refugees to speak and raising money for material aid.

CISPES, using staff people devoted to campus activities, also advises students about sending telegrams to Salvadoran government and military figures to protest threats, harassment and attacks against El Salvadoran students, some of whom have been killed. It has been a leader in putting student work brigades together. Its printed materials, including its newspaper *Alert!*, cover all political activity related to Central America. Its high visibility has led to a series of office break-ins and telephone disruptions documented by the Center for Constitutional Rights; in February 1987, former FBI informant Frank Varelli told a House Judiciary subcommittee about a three-year effort by the FBI to break CISPES.[3] More recent revelations in January 1988 indicate government surveillance of 50,000 US citizens involved in Central America solidarity work.

Democratic Socialists of America—Youth Section

Democratic socialism, according to DSA, means "full worker and community control of all economic decision-making."[4] Its youth section extends DSA's goals. Author Michael Harrington, a DSA founder and one of its two co-chairs, believes the youth section is unique in left politics. "The unusual thing about the DSA Youth Section is that if you look at the history of socialist youth movements in the United States, the youth were always rebelling against the adults. The extraordinary thing about this youth section is that that hasn't happened. There has been remarkably amicable relations for eleven, twelve years. I think it shows that our relationship has really been a cooperative one."[5]

DSA Youth Section has chapters at about 40 colleges. DSA students convene twice a year—in February in New York, in August in the midwest—to conduct workshops, training sessions and to chart the organization's next year. Jeremy Karpatkin, Youth Section director from 1983 to 1985, says, "DSA tries to radicalize students that might not ordinarily be radicalized. It tries to make them aware of the major political institutions that affect their lives. DSA is concerned that students become connected to off-campus movements, like the labor movement or environmental issues—a really important element is in the drive to create a broader coalition, not just students acting alone. We also try to educate them to get geared in for the long haul."[6]

Chapters can choose their priorities, but many concentrate on those selected during the summer conference; they are helped by background and resource materials prepared by the Youth Section staff. However, chapters will often initiate action on local issues such as material aid campaigns for Central America, Pro-choice actions, or rallies supporting the reduction of arms.

Foundation support, contributions, fund-raising events, and chapter dues are the primary sources of DSA support, which translates into salaries for the Youth Section staff, who share space with national DSA staff in New York, and into printed materials. These include a quarterly, "Days of Decision: Journal of the Youth Section of DSA" which carries position papers and information on the issues of concern; the "Activist" which appears occasionally and lists chapter actions and projects; and special publications which provide in-depth information about specific topics. Campus chapters must cover their own local costs.

Current Youth Section organizer, Elissa McBride, says the organization has been re-evaluating its methods. "We seem to be taking a closer look at the politics of how we do politics, issues of racism, sexism and classism within movements. Sometimes student movements become so concentrated on a particular goal that the process gets sacrificed for whatever goal people have in mind. People end up feeling bad about the whole experience. I'd like to think of ways to do politics that are maybe more creative."[7]

The perception that DSA covers many issues works as a strength and a weakness for college students. Still, the DSA Youth Section has grown in the last four years, and appears to attract students looking for structural answers to the social and political issues they care about.

National Student Action Center

This is the smallest, the newest and the hardest to categorize of all the national organizations. NSAC's most influential contribution is a quick-takes newsletter which highlights what's going on around the country, offers organizational tips and

information, and lists a calendar of upcoming student actions—no small task, given
the transience of student leaders and the changeability of their plans.

Founded in the fall of 1985 and officially opened for business the following
January, NSAC grew out of a series of programs for students orchestrated by the
PIRG network which developed a set of proposals for a national clearinghouse for
information. Backing comes from foundation grants. NSAC has managed to create
a presence in a relatively short time with limited resources. More than 1,400 activists
receive the newsletter free. With two staffpeople and interns, the Center also
provides in-person or on-the-phone advice on strategies for putting together new
groups, for carrying out actions and for building skills; it helped coordinate national Star Wars protests, hunger relief campaigns, and the April 25, 1987 march on
Washington. Its Student Fast for Peace in Nicaragua campaign grew from 15 schools
in 1986 to 42 schools in 1987, fund-raising jumped from $15,000 to $40,000, and
more than 1,300 students became involved.[8]

Maintaining and building a network of contacts takes up most of their time.
Director Kim Paulis travels about one week each month, and often spends three or
four hours on the phone every night. ("You can't reach most students until after
eleven o'clock.")[9] Staffer Dave West says they often start from scratch, calling the
student activity office and asking if there are any issue-oriented groups on campus.
"We send out mailings generically: 'Peace Group: State University.' We've gone to a
lot of conferences, and people are now starting to refer their friends."[10]

Dave sees some problems with long-term foundation support, and feels that
many in the progressive foundation community "don't understand the importance
of working with students."[11]

Most leaders of progressive organizations, he says, were active as students.
"The right wing knows that, and they're being sure to nurture their next generation.
They set them up with jobs in Washington through the Heritage Foundation and
groups like that. We're not in any way trying to hook people into jobs in government, or in any position to spend money in any way like the Heritage Foundation,
supported by places like Coors. But leaving students out in the lurch is short-
sighted."[12]

As issues-based organizations mature and formalize their places within the
student movement, some students may make an active push for greater coordination, and better exchanges of information. The Action Center may be positioned
correctly to fulfill that need. "I see the Action Center as a real flexible thing," Kim
concludes. "I used to get really traumatized when people would ask me, so what
are you going to be doing in five years? There's no way we can know."[13]

The Progressive Student Network (PSN)

The PSN was founded according to steering commitee member Bruce Nes-
tor, "right after the election of Reagan, in 1980,"[14] and invites the most comparisons
to earlier student political activism. Its midwest roots—it was born in Iowa City—

and its loose decentralized structure echo some of the early SDS days. But PSN charts a different course. With chapters on nearly 60 campuses, most in the midwest, PSN remains the model of decentralized political activity. Each chapter has a representative on the steering committee, which meets twice a year and administers the organization but does not make policy decisions. Low dues and minimal funding make it a close-to-the-bone operation.

Its tabloid newspaper, the *Progressive Student News,* supplies updates on chapter news, and includes developments in other organizations and movements, also. A group officially becomes a PSN chapter by paying a $20 affiliation fee.   Bruce says the Iowa City office maintains membership lists, "but in terms of organization around any specific issues, or any particular conference, it's usually switched around between campuses."[15] There is no paid staff.

Meetings, most in the midwest, have drawn students from Louisiana, California, Florida and Pennsylvania. Bruce says, "With people from other regions we emphasize that we'd love to correspond with them, publish stuff about their struggles in the newsletter, hopefully have some meetings with them, but that their primary work should be in regional development.

"We have groups—say, from the University of North Dakota—which are primarily feminist; on the west coast, there's a MECHA group; multi-issue groups in the midwest, groups in Miami do more contra work, Louisiana does environmental work—they cosponsored a demonstration with the Oil and Chemical and Atomic Workers."[16]

PSN's ad hoc administration arrangements attract a wide range of students, and in fact enable quick responses to local problems. Bruce concludes, "By and large, we are composed of multi-issue progressive student organizations, people who have come together not as a coalition but people in an organization that really seek to connect issues and to build the student movement, to recruit people to a perspective which really analyzes what's necessary to create social change in this country."

United Campuses to Prevent Nuclear War

UCAM, founded in 1982, is proud of its distinction as the only North American network of students, faculty and staff working on the major issues connected with the arms race. UCAM promotes education and debate on campus, lobbies for arms control measures, facilitates the introduction of courses on the arms race, opposes the Star Wars program, organizes US-Soviet university exchange visits and educates students for leadership roles.[17]

UCAM, operating out of offices in Washington, DC, with staff and interns, has more than 80 chapters on campuses in the United States and Canada and contacts on more than 300 campuses. An elected steering committee, and a paid staff administer the organization; chapters choose the degree to which they want to participate in nationally-coordinated events. Its annual Lobby Day is described in the War Machine chapter.

Its student/faculty mix provides UCAM with a distinct advantage in creating and promoting a petition drive urging scientists and engineers on college campuses to refuse projects connected to Star Wars research. UCAM has working relationships with both student and non-campus nationals concerned with issues of war and peace.

Funding comes from private foundations, individuals and from the chapters. A well-researched, informative monthly newsletter titled "Network News" presents current data on arms-related subjects, as well as news from chapters and other like-minded groups.

United States Student Association

Student governments on college and university campuses are no longer simply concerned with allocating funds for the spring dance. Over the last year, a visitor could have heard student government at Wellesley drafting a letter calling for the resignation of a trustee accused of making racist remarks or Carleton College representatives debating whether to continue funding the campus gay and lesbian students' organization; at Berkeley, endorsement of an ethnic studies required course could be on the agenda. And everywhere, you might hear discussions on whether to sponsor fasts to raise money for Central America material aid campaigns. The USSA has as its constituency the members of student governments that have voted to affiliate with USSA, a commitment which involves paying dues and sending representatives to annual meetings. USSA, "dedicated to the principle of equal access for all students, regardless of race, sex, income or physical ability,"[18] lobbies in Washington on behalf of students. It operates out of a few small offices in Washington with a handful of paid staff and a sprinkling of volunteers and student interns.

USSA traces its beginnings to 1947, and is now the country's largest and oldest national student membership organization, with affiliations on more than 400 campuses. Its principal activities are two conferences, one in Washington, DC each winter, the other at a different campus each summer, where the organization charts goals and strategies for the coming year. Both sessions include dozens of workshops, speakers and training sessions. USSA also sponsors political leadership training weekends called Grassroots Organizing Workshops (GROW), designed and taught by the Midwest Academy. While many of the workshops deal with nuts-and-bolts topics ("Improving Your Student Government," "Trends in Enrollment and Student Employment on Campus") there are others with a decidedly political message; "Organizing Against Racism and Sexism on Your Campus," and "Student Control of Fees" draw capacity crowds. In its structure and direction, USSA borrows heavily from the model of state student associations, particularly the New York State Association of Student Unions. The board includes 42 members—two from each of 13 geographic regions, three elected at-large by board members, two each from caucuses representing community colleges, the third world and women; one from the gay/lesbian/bisexual caucus, one disabled student, one veteran and one nontraditional. The board meets five times a year. According to director Tom Swann, "Our affirmative action policy is really bringing in a lot of diversity. It gives a chance to weak groups, and educates the other groups."[19]

With its strong base of support through member dues, and with the help of foundations, USSA regularly publishes excellent materials on the state of federal student financial assistance. Its long-term objective is to facilitate the creation of state student associations in every state, and eventually forge a true union of American college and university students. This formation, similar to those in many other countries, would guarantee a permanent, political voice to express the needs and demands of American students of all ages, backgrounds and beliefs.

The National Student Campaign Against Hunger

Formed in 1981 from a coalition of 25 state PIRGs, this organization, headquartered in Boston, sponsors or cosponsors five principal events each year for students.[20] On World Food Day, students conduct fund-raising and education campaigns. The Hungerthon Contest encourages creative approaches to hunger problems; the Hunger Clean-Up program matches student volunteers with community service activities, and raises money for hunger relief. An annual Food Stamp Survey and a Call for Action petition drive complete the list.

The Campus Outreach Opportunity League (COOL)

This Washington-based group sponsors annual conferences to train student volunteers in community organizing, aimed at community service projects. Delegates are usually representatives of independent campus organizations. The group also holds regional conferences, and coordinates information on volunteer activism among college students nationally.

Other Organizations

Other organizations serve particular constituencies, or have an influence in one region of the country. These include the Asian Pacific Students Union, the East Coast Asian Students Union and the Northeast Lesbian and Gay Students Union. One not-quite-national, the National Chicano Student Association, now in its ninth year, is slowly consolidating its position, and launching chapters in the Midwest and

East, away from its original areas of strength, the West and Southwest. The group's concerns are discussed in the Racism chapter.

Five other organizations often participate in college-oriented political activities, although they may have little presence on campuses. The Young Socialists, the Socialist Workers Party, the Spartacist League, the Revolutionary Communist Youth Brigade and No Business as Usual frequently can be found distributing literature and handouts at rallies called by other groups on university campuses. These groups occasionally have small chapters at some schools, and from time to time, generate an event of their own.

The National Third World Student Coalition does offer a newsletter, legislative updates and other resources to students of color, but it is not truly independent, since it functions as an affiliate of the USSA.

Campus Green, a volunteer action group operating out of Durham, NC, has has a number of campus chaptors administering local environmental actions.

Resources

THE NATIONAL ORGANIZATIONS

American Committee on Africa (ACOA), 198 Broadway, New York City, NY 10038

Committee in Solidarity with the People of El Salvador (CISPES), P.O. Box 50139, Washington, DC 20004

Democratic Socialists of America (DSA) Youth Section, 15 Dutch Street, Suite 500, New York City, NY 10038

National Chicano Students Association (MECHA), Campus Box 207, UMC Room 182, Boulder, CO 80309

National Student Action Center, P.O. Box 15599, Washington, DC 20003-0599

National Student Convention, 69 Welton Street, New Brunswick, NJ 08801

The Progressive Student Network (PSN), P.O. Box 1027, Iowa City, IA 52244

United Campuses to Prevent Nuclear War (UCAM), 220 I Street, NE, Suite 130, Washington, DC 20002

United States Student Association (USSA), 1012 14th Street, NW, Suite 403, Washington, DC 20005

National Gay & Lesbian Student Task Force, c/o National Gay & Lesbian Task Force, 1517 U Street, NW, Washington, DC 20009

SOUTHERN AFRICA

ACOA (see above)

TransAfrica, 545 8th Street SE, Washington, DC 20003

Interfaith Center for Corporate Responsibility, 475 Riverside Drive, Room 566, New York City, NY 10027

The Divestment Disk, c/o Byteing Back Software, Box 221, STF, Philadelphia, PA 19104

CENTRAL AMERICA

CISPES (see above)

National Network in Solidarity with the People of Guatemala (NISGUA), 1314 14th Street, NW, Washington, DC 20005

Nicaragua Network, 2025 I St., NW, Washington, DC 20006

Technica, 2727 College Avenue, Berkeley, CA 94705

Pledge of Resistance, P.O. Box 53411, Washington, DC 20009

THE WAR MACHINE

UCAM (see above)

American Friends Service Committee, 1501 Cherry Street, Philadelphia, PA 19102

Central Committee for Conscientious Objectors (CCCO), 2208 South Street, Philadelphia, PA 19146

Fellowship of Reconciliation, Box 271, Nyack, NY 10960

War Resisters League, 339 Lafayette St., New York, NY 10012

Witness for Peace, 198 Broadway, New York City, NY 10038

RACISM

MECHA (see above)

D.C. Student Coalition Against Apartheid and Racism (DC SCAR), P.O. Box 18291, Washington, DC 20036

East Coast Asian Student Union (ECASU), c/o BU Asian Student Union, GSU Student Union, 775 Commonwealth Avenue, Boston, MA 02215

Asian Pacific Student Union, c/o Asian Student Union, Eshleman Hall, Room 505, Berkeley, CA 94704

General Union of Palestine Students, P.O. Box 2302, Astoria, NY 11102

American-Arab Anti-Discrimination Committee, 1731 Connecticut Avenue, NW, Washington, DC 20009

November 29th Committee for Palestine, P.O. Box 27462, San Francisco, CA 94127

THE ECONOMY AND THE GENERAL WELFARE

USSA (see above)

DSA (see above)

Bread for the World, 802 Rhode Island Avenue, NE, Washington, DC 20018

Campus Green, 126 Few Federation, PO Box 10072, Duke Station, Durham, NC 27706

Campus Outreach Opportunity League (COOL), 810 18th Street, NW, Suite 705, Washington, DC 20006

Dwight Hall, Yale University, 404-A Yale Station, New Haven, CT 06520

Earth First!, POB 5871, Tucson, AZ 85703

Frontlash, 815 16th Street, NW, Washington, DC 20006

The Green Movement, P.O. Box 30208, Kansas City, MO 64112

National Student Campaign Against Hunger, 29 Temple Place Boston, MA 02111

Oxfam America, 115 Broadway, Boston, MA 02116

United Farm Workers of America, La Paz, CA 93570

GAY, LESBIAN AND BISEXUAL RIGHTS

National Gay and Lesbian Task Force, 1517 U Street, NW, Washington, DC 20009

Northeast Lesbian and Gay Student Union, c/o National Gay & Lesbian Task Force, 1517 U Street, NW, Washington, DC 20009

Boston Intercollegiate Lesbian and Gay Alliance (BILGA), Box 8426, Boston, MA 02114

Texas Gay and Lesbian Student Organization Coalition, Box 275, UNB-Austin, TX 78712

University of California Lesbian and Gay Intercampus Network, 1740 Walnut Street, #E, Berkeley, CA 94709

Western States Lesbian/Gay Students United, 500 Landfair Avenue, Los Angeles, CA 90024

WOMEN'S ISSUES

National Organization for Women (NOW), 1401 New York Avenue, NW, Washington, DC 20005

Men Stopping Rape, Box 305, 306 North Brooks Street, Madison, WI 53715

STUDENT EMPOWERMENT

USSA (see above)

MECHA (see above)

PSN (see above)

Student Association of the State University of New York (SASU), 41 State Street, Albany, NY 12207

California Alliance of Progressive Student Activists (CAPSA), P.O. Box 6788, Stanford, CA 94309

OTHER SOURCES

International Union of Students, 17th November Street, 110 01 Prague 01, Czechoslovakia

Greeks for Peace, c/o Matt Greene, University of Michigan, 820 Oxford, Ann Arbor, MI 48104

INFORMATION SOURCES

College Press Service, 2505 West Second Avenue, Suite Seven, Denver, CO 80219-1630

Movement Support Network, 666 Broadway, New York City, NY 10012

National On-Campus Reports, 2718 Dryden Drive, Madison, WI 53704

National Lawyers Guild, 55 Avenue of the Americas, New York, NY 10013

National Student News Service, Box 3161, Boston, MA 02101

Network of the Alternative Student Press, c/o the *Gadfly,* Billings Student Center—Box 130, University of Vermont, Burlington, VT 05405

PeaceNet, 1918 Bonita, Berkeley, CA 94704

Radio Free New England, c/o WGDR Goddard College, Plainfield, VT 05667

Student Press Law Center, 800 18th St. NW, suite 300, Washington, DC 20006

2. Survey

To provide a better idea of what politically-active students were thinking about a range of subjects, I drew up a survey of questions with the assistance of Columbia professor Dr. Richard Christie. Together with Columbia student Tom Judson and a few other students, the surveys were distributed at the 1987 spring conferences of the Democratic Socialists of America Youth Section, the Northeast Lesbian and Gay Student Union and the United States Student Association. I do not suggest that this exercise was in any way scientific, or exactly representational of the views of progressive student activists around the country. But the combination of these three constituencies from 113 different schools did offer an opportunity to gather comments from a national cross-section of students who identified themselves as activists on their campuses. The results of the informal survey are printed here.

Question	DSA	NELGSU	USSA
(Figures represent percent of respondents who answered "yes.")			
School has women's center	83	73	61
School has black student's center	87	90	74
School has Asian student's union	59	50	54
School has ROTC on campus	48	50	54

	DSA	NELGSU	USSA
School has gay student's organization	x	92	65
School has sanctuary movement	20	10	18
There is a boycott on campus now	27	10	20
Since September 1986, there have been student actions on my campus to protest these issues:			
Anti-apartheid	82	87	59
Central America	71	68	50
CIA recruitment	39	45	25
Military recruitment	21	29	8
Hunger/Homelessness	29	66	35
Environment	19	24	25
Discrimination against bisexuals, gays, lesbians	38	68	28
Students' role in decision-making	34	55	42
Campus war research	20	11	14
College employee labor conditions	17	21	19
Economy/student loans	12	11	35
Reproductive rights and women's issues	49	45	28
Drug testing	10	8	12
Faculty tenure	19	29	12
Racism	47	45	30
Computers used in organizing and political work	53	47	66
I, or someone I know, has been to Central America	74	58	56
Visit resulted in helping organize students	83	46	53
Tried to learn about '60s student activism	85	70	73
Tried to learn about '30s student activism	35	8	15
We've worked with other activist campus groups to organize coordinated actions	79	45	79
School has published rules governing student protest	66	53	36
If yes, the rules are enforced	81	73	56
If yes, the students are punished	59	56	*
If yes, protest in last two years	95	80	*
If yes, police were called in	43	37	*
If yes, the protests were videotaped	50	46	37
If yes, administrators met with students	73	*	71
Student judiciary at school	56	63	76
School has alternative left publication	40	42	32
Controversy over student life regulations, such as drinking on campus	73	68	74
I prefer working with a group with ties to a national organization	81	67	81

(* = question not included on that survey)

	DSA	NELGSU	USSA
The political climate on my campus is (1-reationary, 2-conservative, 3-moderate, 4-liberal, 5-radical)	3.0	2.6	2.9

	DSA	NELGSU	USSA
On a scale of 1 (low) to 5 (high)...			
Relevance of '60s activism to today	3.9	3.8	3.5
How politically aware (as opposed to apathetic) are students at your school?	2.4	2.2	2.0
How active were they when I first started school?	2.3	2.2	2.0
Effectiveness of student government as a voice for student concerns	2.1	2.7	3.8
How well student paper covers student political issues	3.0	3.0	2.9

My school has approved divestment of South Africa-related stocks (% of total respondents): fully-21.4%   partly-59.5%   not at all-19%

It is important to note that not all students responded to all questions. The average student from all three groups who reponded to the survey was a junior. DSA students responding ranged from first-year students to second-year graduate students, from age 18 to 30, average age 20.8. NELGSU students responding ranged from first-year students to seniors, from age 17 to 33, average age 21.6. USSA students responding ranged from first-year students to fourth-year graduate students, from age 18 to 42, average age 21.6. DSA respondents were 62.4% male, 37.6% female (59-34); NELGSU respondents were 78.6% male, 21.4% female (33-9); USSA respondents were 59.9% male, 40.5% female (94-64). Seven did not indicate gender.

Other characteristics of students who responded (in percentages):

Married	2	0	3
Single	95	90	89
Divorced	1	2	1
Living together	2	8	7
Asian	3	1	3
Black	2	7	11
Native American	1	2	1
Hispanic/Chicano/Latino	0	2	5
White	94	88	80
Urban College	39	49	37
Rural College	26	27	21
Suburban College	35	24	42
Public School	39	27	88
Private School	61	73	12
Non-denominational	89	89	77
Religiously-affiliated	11	11	23
Bisexual	6	7	2
Gay/Lesbian	10	88	3
Heterosexual	84	5	95

Colleges and universities respondents came from: American University (DC), Amherst (MA), Barnard (NY), Bloomsburg (PA), Boston U. (MA), Bowaoin (ME), Bryn Mawr (PA), Bucknell (PA), Central Connecticut U, (CT), Chapel Hill (NC), Chicago State (IL), Cleveland State (OH), Colby (ME), Columbia (NY), Connecticut U. (CT), Cornell (NY), Dartmouth (NH), Dickinson (PA), East Carolina U. (NC), Eastern Michigan (MI), Erie C.C. (PA), Fairfield U. (CT), Fordham (NY), Framingham (MA), Franklin & Marshall (PA), George Washington U. (DC), Graceland (IA), Hamilton (NY), Hartwick (NY), Harvard (MA), Hartford College for Women (CT), Holyoke C.C. (MA), Hunter (NY), Iowa State (IA), Los Angeles Chiropractic (CA), Lehigh (PA), Manhattan College (NY), Marquette (WI), Mesa (CO), Miami U. of Ohio (OH), Michigan (MI), Millersville (PA), MIT (MA), Mohawk Valley C.C. (NY), Monterey Peninsula (CA), Montgomery (MD), Mt. Holyoke (MA), Nassau C.C. (NY), Northeastern (MA), Oberlin (OH), Ohio U. (OH), Oregon U. (OR), Penn State (PA), Portland C.C. (OR), Princeton (NJ), Prince George's C.C. (MD), Rensselaer (NY), Rutgers (NJ), San Francisco State (CA), Sarah Lawrence (NY), Shoreline C.C. (WA), Southeastern Massachusetts U. (MA), Southeastern Connecticut State (CT), Southern Methodist U. (TX), Stockton State (NJ), SUNY Albany, Binghamton, Morrisville, Oneonta, Plattsburg, Purchase, Rutland, Stony Brook (NY), Swarthmore (PA), Teacher's College (NY), Temple (PA), Trinity (CT), Tufts (MA), U. of Bridgeport (CT), U. of California, Berkeley (CA), U. of Cincinnati (OH), U. of Dayton (OH), U. of Hartford (CT), U. of Illinois (IL), U. of Iowa (IA), U. of Lowell (MA), U. of Maine (ME), U. of Michigan (MI), U. of Missouri, St. Louis (MO), U. of Northern Iowa (IA), U. of Oregon (OR), U. of Pennsylvania (PA), U. of Pittsburgh (PA), U. of Rhode Island (RI), U. of Southern Maine (ME), U. of Texas (TX), U. of Vermont (VT), U. of Wisconsin, Eau Claire, Madison, Milwaukee, Parkside, Stevens Point (WI), Western Michigan U. (MI), Williams (MA), Yale (CT) and York (PA).

Notes

Chapter One: Assessing the Situation

1. Many college housing officials now employ devices such as the "Myers-Briggs Type Indicator," a system of identifying preferences, among freshpersons to soften the possibility of incompatibility with new roommates. "Self-Selection Patterns of College Roommates as Indenified by the Myers-Briggs Type Indicator", W. Scott Anchors and John Hale, Jr., Journal of College and University Student Housing, Sept., '86

2. "School Enrollment—Social and Economic Characteristics of Students: October 1984 (Advance Report)—U.S. Department of Commerce, Bureau of the Census, November 1985" indicates that, from 1967 to 1984, black enrollment at least doubled, while white enrollment rose by one-third. Enrollment of women rose from 43 percent of the college population in 1972 to 51 percent in 1980. Approximately 36 percent were 25 years old or older in 1984, compared to 28 percent in 1972. The "Minorities in Higher Education—Fourth Annual Status Report" from the American Council on Education states that enrollment in higher education institutions grew from 8.6 million in 1970 to 12.5 million in 1983. Full-time enrollment grew by 25 percent, while part-time enrollment (students who may also have a job or a family at the same time they enrolled), increased 88 percent with projections that by 1993, this segment will comprise 8 percent of the college population. From 1976 to 1982, total minority enrollment increased from 15.4 percent to 16.6 percent. Blacks suffered a decline, from 9.4 percent to 8.9 percent, while hispanics increased from 3.5 to 4.2 percent, Asian-Pacific student from 1.8 percent to 2.8 percent, and native Americans remained constant at .7 percent.

3. USA Today, "It's a matter of course to seek choice," Tony Vellela, May 1, 1986.

4. The New York Times, "How Tuition Costs Are Set: An Education in Itself," 5/14/87, p. B13.

5. "No Ivory Tower: McCarthyism and the Universities," Ellen W. Schrecker, Oxford University Presss, New York, 1986, pp. 16-18.

6. *Ibid.* p. 28.

7. "The Movement: A History of the American New Left, 1959-1972," Irwin Unger, Harper and Row, New York, 1974, pp. 66-67.

8. "Eyes on the Prize: American Civil Rights Years" television documentary series; Episode "Ain't Scared of Your Jails: 1960-1961," Orlando Bagwell, producer; Henry Hampton, executive producer, Blackside, Inc., 1986.

9. "Letter to the New Left," C. Wright Mills, *New Left Review,* Sept.-Oct. 1960, p. 19.

10. University of Wisconsin, Stevens Point Pointer, Feb. 26, 1987, "Kent State massacre survivor shares views," Keith Uhlig.

11. *The New York Times,* "Seoul Police Act Forcefully To Block Start of a Protest," Claude Haberman, 4/20/87, p. A3.

12. *The New York Times,* "Students Protest Again in Beijing" Edward A. Gargan, 6/15/87.

13. *The New York Times,* "Students in Spain, Protesting College Plan, Shut Most Schools," 12/18/86, Edward Schumacher; "Clashes in Paris Worst Since 1968" Richard Bernstein; "At a Mexican University, Plans For Change Stir Protest" William Stockton, 12/8/86.

14. Interview with Dave Edquist, 3/14/87.

15. *Ibid.*

Chapter Two: Examining the Strategies

1. Interview with Rick Harbaugh, 2/7/87.

2. Informal survey of student activists, details in Appendix.

3. *UCSA Spectrum,* Winter, 1987, p. 4.

4. *Ibid.*

5. PeaceNet flyer, 2/87.

6. Interview with Rick Harbaugh, 2/7/87.

7. Interview with Stephanie Weiner, 3/8/87.

8. Informal survey of student activists, details in Appendix.

9. *The New York Times,* April 6, 1987, p. B-5.

10. Interview with Howard Zinn, 4/10/87.

11. Informal survey of student activists, details in Appendix.

Chapter Three: The Issue: Divestment

1. American Committee on Africa report, "Divestment Action on South Africa by US Colleges and Universities," 12/12/86.

2. United Nations Centre Against Apartheid, Notes and Documents, New York City, September 1986.

3. *Ibid.*

4. *Ibid.*

5. *Ibid.*

6. *Ibid.*

7. "South Africa Protesters Target Three Big Banks," *Banking Week for Financial Services Executives,* Philip T. Sudo, 4/13/87.

8. "Maryland National severs relations with three banks in South Africa," leaflet published by Johns Hopkins University Coalition for a Free South Africa, 1987.

9. "End Trade Financing to South Africa! End Rescheduling of the South African Foreign Debt!" leaflet published by the Interfaith Center for Corporate Responsibility, 1987.

10. *Student Anti-Apartheid Newsletter,* American Committee on Africa, New York City, Dec./Jan. (#1/87).

11. *Ibid.*

12. The Sullivan Principles are a voluntary code of conduct for US firms doing business in South Africa, calling for non-segregation in the workplace. They were drafted by Rev. Leon Sullivan in 1976, but repudiated by him as ineffective in the mid-eighties.

13. Interview with Michael Barr, 6/6/87.

14. *Ibid.*

Chapter Four: Central America

1. *Under the Big Stick,* Karl Berman, South End Press, Boston, 1986.

2. *Central American Education Fund Newsletter,* July 1986, (CAEF, 1151 Mass. Ave., Cambridge, MA 02138).

3. Interview with Mark Rudd, 4/2/87.

4. Interview with Doug Calvin, 2/2/87.

5. Interview with Carolyn Helmke, 3/9/87.

6. *Ibid.*

7. Interview with Dean Baker, 3/6/87.

8. *Ibid.*

9. Movement Support Network, "Harassment Update" Eighth Edition, revised May, 1987, Center for Constitutional Rights, New York City.

Chapter Five: The CIA

1. *The New York Times,* 2/16/66.

2. *The Boston Globe,* 10/23/84.

3. *The Boston Globe,* 11/26/84.

4. "Something Happenin' Here: the Student Movement in Madison: Spring, 1985 to Spring, 1986," Lamoin Werlein-Jaen, PSN, University of Wisconsin, Madison, 1986.

Chapter Six: The War Machine

1. An incomplete list of these groups, in no particular order, includes the Council on Economic Priorities, the Star Wars Education Project, the World Policy Institute, the Union of Concerned Scientists, the Institute for Peace and International Security, Women's Alliance for Nuclear Disarmament, the Progressive Foundation's Nuke Watch, National Mobilization for Survival,

the American Friends Service Committee, the War Resisters League, Educators for Social Responsibility, Women's International League for Peace and Freedom, and the Center for War, Peace and the News Media.

2. *UCAM Network News,* May, 1986.

3. *UCAM Network News,* Dec., 1986.

4. Interview with Erica Etelson, 5/14/87.

5. *New York DSA Monthly Newsletter,* May, 1987.

Chapter Seven: Racism

1. Clay Carson, "In Struggle," Harvard University Press, 1981, pp. 234-5.

2. Interview with Sonia Pena, 12/18/86.

3. Interview with Michael Berry, 2/27/87.

4. Report on University of Massachusetts Investigation, February 5, 1987, *The Report of Frederick A. Hurst.*

5. Interview with Matthew Countryman, 12/10/86.

6. *Ibid.*

7. *Ibid.*

8. Interview with Pedro Noguera, 2/28/87.

9. Interview with Donald Gallegos, 12/17/86.

10. Interview with Sonia Pena, 12/18/86.

11. Interview with Hilary Shadroui, 3/31/87.

12. *Ibid.*

13. Interview with Tarek, 3/13/87.

14. Interview with Peter Premarajah Granarajah, 3/15/87.

15. Interview with Winston Willis, 5/8/87.

16. *Ibid.*

17. *The Washington Times,* "Blacks avoid school success as 'White Act,'" Carrie Dowling, 3/13/87, p. 1.

Chapter Eight: The Economy and the General Welfare

1. *USSA Organizing Manual,* Spring, 1987.

2. "Paying for College: Trends in Student Financial Aid at Independent Colleges and Universities," J. Thrift and C. Toppe, 1985, National Institute of Independent Colleges and Universities, Washington, DC.

3. *The National Boycott Newsletter,* Vol. 1, No. 3, Fall, '85.

4. Interview with Arturo Rodriguez, 5/13/87.

5. *Ibid.*

6. Worldwatch Institute, "Earth's Future Habitability Threatened," 2/14/87.

7. "The Forest for the Trees," Kirkpatrick Sale, *Mother Jones,* 11/86.

8. Interview with David Lakin, 12/5/87.

9. Interview with David Lawrence, 4/4/87.

10. "More Students Finding Time to Give the Needy a Hand" Thomas J. Meyer, *Chronicle of Higher Education,* 2/27/85.

11. Interview with Bill Hoogterp, 4/4/87.

12. Interview with Janet Ng, 4/18/87.

Chapter Nine: Women's Issues

1. Interview with Mimi Adler, 4/20/87.

2. Interview with Stephanie Berger, 3/7/87.

3. "Stealing the Stage," Susan Benesch, *Broadway Magazine,* Columbia University, 3/18/86.

4. "Planning a Project on Reproductive Rights" Lisa Laufer, Days of Decision, DSA, Fall, 1986, p. 4.

5. "Reproductive Rights," PSN, University of Wisconsin, Madison, 1986.

6. Interview with Sarah Buttenweiser, 3/7/87.

7. "The Year of Living Dangerously," *Newsweek,* April, 1987.

8. "Stop UW's Protection of Sexual Harassers," PSN, University of Wisconsin, Madison, 1986.

9. "Women's Groups Say Campus Progress is Stalling Out," Susan Skorupa, College Press Service, Oct. 27, 1986.

Chapter Ten: Gay, Lesbian and Bisexual Rights

1. "Familiar Faces, Hidden Lives: The Story of Homosexual Men in America Today," Howard Brown, MD., Harcourt, New York, 1976, p. 20.

2. *The New York Times,* "Columbia Charters Homosexual Group," Murray Schumach, May 3, 1967, p. 1.

3. "Out of the Closets: The Sociology of Homosexual Liberation," Laud Humphreys, Prentice, New York, 1972, p. 8.

4. "Hostile Eyes," Peggy Bendet, *Campus Voice Magazine,* Aug./Sept. '86; National Gay Task Force report, 1987.

5. *Op. cit., The New York Times,* Schumach.

6. *Op. cit.,* Brown, p. 200.

7. Interview with Paula Ettelbrick, 12/4/87.

8. Bowers, Attorney General of *Georgia v. Hardwick et. al.,* Supreme Court of the US, No. 85-140, 6/30/86.

9. *Ibid.*

10. Interview with Tim O'Connor, 6/28/87.

11. Interview with Matthew Alexander, 3/10/87.

12. Interview with Darryl Brown, 3/28/87.

13. Interview with Mary Kay Kaster, 3/14/87.

14. Interview with Matthew Alexander, 3/10/87.

15. Interview with Erwin Keller, 3/11/87.

16. Interview with Carolyn Breen, 2/21/87.

17. Interview with Ricardo Velasquez, 2/27/87.

Chapter Eleven: Student Empowerment

1. *Tinker v. Des Moines* Independent Community School District (393 US 503, 89 S. Ct. 733, 1969).

2. "Protestors meet with UT official," Stephanie Scott, *The Daily Texan,* 10/27/86.

3. Interview with Chris Cabaldan, 3/15/87.

4. Interview with Jack Lester, 4/7/87.

5. *Op. cit.,* Tinker.

6. *Shamloo v. Mississippi State Board of Trustees, etc.* (620 F. 2d 516. US Court of Appeals, Fifth Circuit, 1980).

7. *State v. Ybarra,* Oregon App. (550 P. 2d. 763, Court of Appeals of Oregon, 1976).

8. *National On-Campus Report,* 1/19/87.

9. Interview with Jack Lester, 4/7/87.

10. *State v. Schmid,* (423 A. 2d. 615-1980).

11. *Commonwealth v. Bohmer,* (372 N.E. 2d 1381. Supreme Judicial Court of Massachusetts, Middlesex, 1978).

12. *Abramowitz v. the Trustees of Boston University,* Superior Court Civil Action No. 82680, May, 1986).

13. *National On-Campus Report,* 1/19/87.

14. *Healy v. James,* 408 US 169, 1972.

15. Interview with Mark Schulte, 4/4/87.

16. *Dixon v. Alabama State Board of Education,* 294 F 2d. 150 (Fifth Circuit, 1961) cert. denied, 368 US 960 (1961).

17. *Esteban v. Central Missouri State College,* 277 F. Supp. 649 (W.D. Mo. 1967).

18, *Tedeschi v. Wagner College,* 427 N.Y.S. 2d. 760, Court of Appeals of New York, 1980.

19. "Rally Held Without Arrests," Martha Ashe, Paula Blesener, Brian Edwards, *The Daily Texan,* 11/2/86.

20. *Ibid.*

21. *Ibid.*

22. Interview with Elena Manitzas, 4/9/87.

Chapter Twelve: The Role of the Media

1. "Exposing Media Myths: TV Doesn't Affect You As Much As You Think" Joanmarie Kalter, *TV Guide,* May 30, 1987.

2. *Ibid.*

3. *Ibid.*

4. "Hundreds Arrested at CIA In Protest on Foreign Policy" Bernard Weintraub, *The New York Times,* 4/28/87 p. A-18.

5. "Marchers in Washington Condemn Reagan policies," Sheila Dresser and Rafael Alvarez, *The Washington Post,* 4/28/87, p. 1.

6. *Op. cit., The New York Times.*

7. "College Playing Larger Role in Guiding Lives of Students" Edward B. Fiske, *The New York Times,* 2/22/87, p. A1.

8. "4 Boston Students Win in Test on Free Speech," *The New York Times,* 12/4/86, p. A-18.

9. "5 Arrested at Brandeis in Investment Protest" *The New York Times,* 12/11/86.

10. "College Republicans Declare North a Hero" *The New York Times,* 12/11/86.

11. "Carter defends anti-CIA protest," *Philadelphia Inquirer,* 4/14/87, p. 3-A.

12. "Amy Carter's Trial Starts," *New York Newsday,* 4/7/87, p. 4.

13. "Carter wants focus on CIA during her trial," *Boston Globe,* 4/8/87, p. 25.

14. "Campus Race Incident Disquiets U. of Michigan," Isabel Wilkerson, *The New York Times,* 3/9/78, p. A-12.

15. *Op. cit., TV Guide.*

16. "Television and the Troubled Campus," Neil Hickey, Triangle Publications, 1971, p. 14.

17. Tapes gathered through the services of Vanderbilt Television News Archive, Vanderbilt University Library, Nashville, TN.

18. "CBS Evening News," Oct. 9, 1969.

19. "CBS Evening News," Oct. 15, 1969.

20. "CBS Evening News," Sept. 26, 1984.

21. "NBC Nightly News," Sept. 26, 1984.

22. "NBC Nightly News," April 8, 1985.

23. "NBC Nightly News," April 16, 1986.

24. "CBS Evening News," April 24, 1986.

25. "CBS Evening News," April 26, 1986.

26. "CBS Evening News," Feb. 9, 1986.

27. "NBC Nightly News," April 3, 1986.

28. "CBS Evening News," April 3, 1986.

29. "CBS Evening News," April 4, 1986.

30. "CBS Weekend News," April 5, 1986.

31. "CBS Evening News," April 19, 1986.

32. "NBC Nightly News," Nov. 15, 1986.

33. "NBC Nightly News," Nov. 29, 1986.

34. "ABC World News Tonight," Nov. 17, 1986.

35. "NBC Nightly News," Nov. 17, 1986.

36. "NBC Nightly News," April 14, 1987.

37. Cable News Network, April 16, 1987.

38. Cable News Network, April 17, 1987.

39. Cable News Network, April 25, 1987.

40. "News 4 New York," April 25, 1987.

41. "CBS Weekend News," April 25, 1987.

42. Cable News Network, April 27, 1987.

43. Informal survey of student activists, details in Appendix.

44. *National On-Campus Report,* Oct. 6, 1986.

45. *Directory of College Student Press in America,* sixth edition, Oxbridge Communications, Inc., 1986, p. vii.

46. *National On-Campus Report,* May, 18, 1987.

47. Interview with Mark Giaimo, 3/9/87.

48. Interview with Purvette Bryant, 3/16/87.

49. *National On-Campus Report,* 3/2/87.

50. *National On-Campus Report,* 4/20/87.

51. "The Press and Student Activism," Allan Freedman, Columbia University, May, 1987.

52. Interview with Jack Steinberg, 1/8/87.

53. Interview with Rick White, 6/15/87.

54. Informal survey of student activists, details in Appendix.

55. Intercollegiate Broadcasting System, Vails Gate, NY flyer, 1987.

56. Interview with Michael Deacon, 3/16/87.

57. *The Whole World is Watching,* Todd Gitlin University of California Press, 1980, p. 193.

58. Interview with Ricardo Velasquez, 2/27/87.

59. Interview with Mark Caldiera, 5/25/87.

60. Interview with Roger Morey, 4/10/87.

Chapter Thirteen: The Outlook

1. *Hazelwood School District v. Kuhlmeier,* No. 86-836 *New York Times,* January 14, 1988.

2. *The Insight,* Barnstable High School, Barnstable, MA, 11/26/86.

3. *The Echo Times,* College of Marine, Kentfield, CA, 12/11/86.

4. *The Hawkeye,* Alta High School, Sandy, Utah, 10/3/86.

5. *The Circle Voice,* Groton School, Groton, MA, 12/18/86.

6. *The Bengal's Purr,* Lewiston High School, Lewiston, IN, 10/24/86.

7. *The Garfield Messenger,* Garfield High School, Seattle, WA, 6/20/86.

8. "Detroit Students gets close look at Nicaragua," Steven Donziger, *Detroit Free Press,* 8/27/85, p. A-3.

9. "Nicaraguans impress 4 Ithaca teens," Steven Donziger, *Syracuse Herald American,* 8/25/85, p. B-1.

10. Interview with Doug Calvin, 5/2/87.

11. Interview with Ethan Felson, 3/29/87.

12. Interview with Kim Paulis, 4/27/87.

13. Interview with Bruce Nestor, 5/22/87.

14. Interview with Elizabeth Burpee, 12/16/86.

15. Interview with Rick Harbaugh, 2/7/87.

16. Interview with Stephanie Weiner, Joe Iosbacker and Bob Cutter, 3/8/87.

17. Interview with Lamoin Werlwin-Jaen, 3/9/87.

18. Interview with Ricardo Velasquez, 2/27/87.

19. Interview with Leonard Weinglass, 5/17/87.

20. Interview with Roger Morey, 4/10/87.

21. Interview with Nick Komar, 4/11/87.

22. Interview with Winston Willis, 5/8/87.

23. Interview with Elissa McBride, 6/1/87.

24. Interview with Pedro Noguera, 2/28/87.

25. Interview with Jonathan Klein, 7/18/87.

26. Interview with Barbara Ransby, 3/6/87.

Appendix

1. "A Call to Conscience, A Challenge to US Foreign Policy in Southern Africa," leaflet from American Friends Service Committee, Des Moines, IA, 1986.

2. Interview with Doug Calvin, 1/25/87.

3. *The Washington Post*, "Hill Told of FBI Drives on Foreign Policy Critics," Eric Pianin, 2/21/87, p. A8.

4. "Which Way America? - The Political Perspective of the Youth Section of the Democratic Socialists of America," 1985, p. 5.

5. Interview with Michael Harrington, 7/30/86.

6. Interview with Jeremy Karpatkin, 7/30/86.

7. Interview with Elissa McBride, 6/1/87.

8. Student Action, National Student Action Center, April, 1987.

9. Interview with Kim Paulis, 4/27/87.

10. Interview with Dave West, 4/26/87.

11. *Ibid.*

12. *Ibid.*

13. Interview with Kim Paulis, 4/27/87.

14. Interview with Bruce Nestor, 5/22/87.

15. *Ibid.*

16. *Ibid.*

17. "The Arms Race will continue until enough informed citizens decide it must stop. Where better to begin than on our campuses," UCAM pamphlet, 1986.

18. Membership Booklet, 1987, USSA.

19. Interview with Tom Swann, 12/20/86.

20. Membership flyer, Public Interest Research Group, Boston, 1986.

Index

Abramowitz, Yosef, 191, 207
Adamson, John, 106-111
Adirondack Community College, 73, 245
af Klinteberg, Kirsten, 175-178
African National Congres, 19, 24, 25, 37, 89
AGEUS (General Association of Salvadoran University Students), 42
Alabama State College, 192
Alabama State University, 246
Alexander, Matthew, 166, 167
Allain, Jay, 69
Alta High School, 226
American Committee on Africa (ACOA), 7, 20-23, 25, 33-37, 129, 202, 224, 249, 250
American University, 247, 248, 262
Amherst, University of Massachusetts at, 41, 62, 67, 69, 86, 130, 140, 168, 231, 232, 242, 243, 262
Anderson, Peter, 128-131
Ann Arbor, University of Michigan at, 43, 44, 74, 75, 81, 82, 89, 90, 93, 94-103, 149, 167, 168, 188, 213-215, 235, 240, 246, 262
Aquinas College, 138
Arizona State University, 241
Arizona, University of, 244, 245
Armstrong, Danny, 25
Asian Pacific Students Union, 8, 90, 113, 255
Association of Arab-American University Graduates, 89
Atlanta University, 21
Atwell, John, 142, 143
Ault, Phil, 170-175
Avonworth High School, 226

Barbiarz, Chris, 129
Baker, Dean, 44
Baker, Ella, 83
Barnard College, 150, 261
Barr, Michael, 37, 38
Barrett, Joy, 50-52
Berea College, 21
Berger, Stephanie, 150

Berkeley, University of California at, 8, 9, 33, 40, 57, 58, 63, 73, 86, 87, 94, 103-106, 116, 149, 162, 189, 208, 212, 216, 230, 233, 237, 241, 262
Berry, Michael, 14
Besansine, Jeanne, 81, 82
Black Panthers, 10, 85
Block, Sarah, 138
Bloomsburg State University, 262
Boston Intercollegiate Lesbian and Gay Alliance, 165
Boston University, 16, 30-33, 68, 86, 108, 109, 138, 191, 207, 262
Boulder, University of Colorado at, 50-52, 61, 63-65, 86, 89, 90, 129, 137, 149, 157, 158, 193, 194-198, 209, 229, 241, 243
Bowdoin College, 244, 262
Boyle, Francis, 68
Brandeis University, 245
Bread for the World, 138
Breen, Carolyn, 168
Breiseth, Kristin, 153
Bridgeport, University of, 262
Bronx Community College, 140
Brower, David, 136
Brown, Darryl, 166
Brown, Lester, 136
Brown University, 60, 61, 169
Bryant, Purvette, 210, 211
Bryn Mawr, 261
Bucknell University, 261
Buffalo City College, 195
Buffalo State College, 138
Buffalo, University of, 195
Bunker Hill Community College, 138
Burpee, Elizabeth, 129, 229
Buthelezi, Gatcha, 30
Butler, Angela, 83
Buttenweiser, Sarah, 150

Cabaldan, Chris, 58, 189
Caldiera, Mark, 69, 128, 217